TAX HAVEN ROADMAP

RICHARD CZERLAU

Published in 1998 by Uphill Publishing Ltd.
190 Attwell Drive, Suite 400, Toronto, Canada M9W 6H8

First printing: June 1995
Second Printing: January 1998

Czerlau, Richard
Tax Haven Roadmap

ISBN 1-896912-07-9. 2nd revised edition, 1998
(ISBN 0-9698432-2-4. 1st edition, 1995)

1. Tax Havens. I. Title
K4464.5.C94 1997 343.04 C98-930008-0

Editor: Uphill Publishing Ltd.
Cover Artwork: Steven Nease
Printed in Canada

I am very fortunate that many of my family and friends took the time to help me develop this book. I am especially grateful to my wonderful wife Monique, whose help and encouragement brought this second edition to a successful completion.

Richard Czerlau

DISCLAIMER

The information contained in this book has been developed using various research data. Such information is believed to be accurate and reliable at the time it was written. While every precaution has been taken in the preparation of this book, it must be understood that this information is very technical in nature and sometimes laws, rules, and regulations change quickly.

The author and publisher specifically disclaim any liability, loss or risk, personal or otherwise, incurred directly or indirectly as a consequence of the use and application of any of the information contained in this book. In no event will the author, editor, publisher, or any distributor of this book be liable to the purchaser for any amount greater than the purchase price of this book.

This publication is sold with the understanding that neither the author nor the publisher is engaged in rendering legal, accounting, tax, or other professional assistance or advice. If legal, accounting, tax, or other professional assistance or advice is required, you should seek the services of a competent professional with the required qualifications.

This book is being provided for your reading enjoyment and information purposes only. While some countries may consider these techniques perfectly legal, there may be some that do not. A competent professional can guide you correctly.

TABLE OF CONTENTS

PREFACE

Something for you to think about. Government officials will have you believe that our debt and defecit situation is improving. Unfortunately, that's not necessarily true. To illustrate, I'd like to tell you the story about the 500lb man.

The 500lb man was told by his doctors that he was dangerously overweight. So he agreed to a weight loss program, and set a target of losing 100lbs. The year went on, and everyone monitored his progress. At the end of the year, everyone celebrated his huge success. Why were they celebrating? Because at the end of the year, the 500lb man lost 100lbs. Now can anyone tell me how much the man weighed at the end of the year? The man only weighed 600lbs! So how can I say that he lost 100lbs? Because without the diet, he would have weighed 700!

Wouldn't you say this is something like how our government presents their debt reduction figures?

INTRODUCTION

The Offshore Trilogy

There are three major advantages to offshore financial planning, something that I call the Offshore Trilogy:

- tax minimization;
- asset protection; and
- estate planning.

Through proper offshore financial planning, those who live in high-tax, high-litigaion countries can take advantage of financial tools that help ensure privacy, minimize taxes, avoid probate and inheritance taxes, and protect important assets from lawsuits and creditors. Using specialized offshore financial planning techniques, often through the use of offshore company and trust structures, both individuals and companies can legally obtain the benefits provided by the Offshore Trilogy.

By investing through a properly set up offshore structure, you can reduce, defer, or eliminate taxes on your investments. I have found over the years that this is the number one reason why individuals and companies domiciled in high-tax countries are exploring the offshore option. Lately, however, I've noticed that the asset protection benefits are becoming more and more important to those who are accumulating assets, especially for those who are directors of companies, business owners, and medical professionals. Estate planning is something that is often ignored until it is too late. Yet those who take advantage of offshore planning techniques find that a properly set up offshore structure easily accommodates their estate and succession planning concerns, allowing a tax free (and problem free) transfer of wealth to the next generation.

This book is designed to give you the foresight to use the financial resources of the world to protect your assets close to home. *Tax Haven Roadmap* is dedicated to the protection, preservation, and expansion of assets and income, and the ownership of personal private property from which those assets are produced.

CHAPTER 1

TAX HAVENS AND THEIR APPLICATIONS

How did tax havens originate?

The twentieth century has seen income tax rates spiral higher and higher with seemingly no end in sight. The United States, founded in 1776 because of a tax revolt, functioned for nearly 137 of its first 220 years without any form of income tax. An income tax was briefly imposed during the Civil War, however, it remained in effect for only a few years.

Drastic change came in 1913, when the United States government passed a law making income tax on individuals legal. Opponents to this form of taxation feared that once the state was given power to levy income taxes, the tendency would be to continually raise taxes. At the time, the mere suggestion of a country imposing a maximum 20% rate of income tax was considered at the time "outrageous" by the advocates of such a temporary measure. Unfortunately, today a nation with a 20% rate of tax would probably be classified as a tax haven jurisdiction.

It isn't simply the ever increasing tax rates that have lead to outrage among individuals, but the fact that governments, in their constant search for new ways to generate revenue, have increased the scope of their taxation to encompass nearly every event of daily life. Today, making a gift is often seen as a taxable event, and to die is the ultimate "financial sacrifice," since estate taxes can be as high as 60% in some jurisdictions.

Supporters of tax systems that impose higher tax rates on those who earn higher incomes often argue that taxation is required to change the distribution of wealth within society. However, many individuals prefer to make their own decisions on who gets what portion of their hard earned money. Fortunately, an entire industry has developed for the sole purpose of assisting highly taxed individuals and businesses to legally avoid confiscatory taxes.

What is a tax haven?

The most compelling reason for the existence of tax havens is directly related to the fact that not every country in the world has the same need to levy taxes at punitive rates. As long as differences exist in either the types of taxes, or the rates charged, taxpayers will constantly seek to carry out their activities in jurisdictions which impose the least financial burden.

The importance of tax havens has increased dramatically within the past few decades and there seems to be no end in sight. Even the once popular misconception that tax havens existed for only the extremely wealthy has noticeably diminished. As tax havens become more commonplace, the need to understand their policies, requirements, economics, and laws also increases. Not every individual may be able to benefit from the utilization of a more friendly tax jurisdiction, but everyone should have the opportunity to make an informed decision.

Implicit in the everyday meaning of the word "haven" is a place where one is protected from something. A tax haven is traditionally viewed as a place of shelter, particularly from high income taxes and currency controls. In general, a tax haven is a jurisdiction that possesses one or more of the following characteristics:

1. either no tax or low tax is imposed;
2. a high level of bank and commercial secrecy is maintained;
3. banking and similar financial activities are significant to the country's economy;
4. modern transportation and communication facilities are available;
5. there is a lack of currency controls on foreign deposits of foreign currency; and
6. the jurisdiction is engaged in self-promotion as a tax haven or offshore financial centre.

No tax or low tax.

The term "tax haven" describes the concept of an absence of tax, or a lower rate of tax, as compared to the tax imposed by the country in which an individual or corporation resides. There are numerous ways that a country can achieve distinction as a tax haven. However, it is generally agreed by tax specialists that the following five main tax categories exist:

1. Countries in which there is no direct taxation at all. There is no income tax, profit tax, capital gains tax, wealth tax, or estate tax. The following jurisdictions are commonly included in this category:
    - Anguilla
    - Bahamas
    - Bermuda
    - Cayman Islands
    - Cook Islands
    - Nauru
    - Turks & Caicos
2. Countries in which direct taxation is imposed at relatively low levels. The following jurisdictions are commonly included in this category:
    - Barbados
    - Channel Islands
    - Luxembourg
    - Switzerland
3. Countries that apply the territorial concept, where only domestic-source income is taxed, and foreign-source income is excluded from the tax base. The following jurisdictions are commonly included in this category:
    - Antigua and Barbuda
    - Austria
    - Belize
    - British Virgin Islands
    - Gibraltar

- Hong Kong
- Isle of Man
- Liechtenstein
- Malta
- Monaco
- Panama
- St.Kitts & Nevis

4. Countries that have tax treaties with high taxing jurisdictions permitting their use as a tax haven. The following jurisdictions are commonly included in this category:
    - Austria
    - Barbados
    - Luxembourg
    - Malta
    - Switzerland
5. Countries that offer special tax privileges with respect to particular activities. A number of jurisdictions fall within the parameters of this category.

Bank and commercial secrecy.

In all countries there exists some form of commercial confidentiality, such as certain professional relationships (for instance, lawyers have what is known as client/attorney confidentiality, which prohibits a lawyer from disclosing information obtained from a client). The tax haven jurisdictions referred to in *Tax Haven Roadmap* also provide some level of secrecy to persons transacting business, particularly with banks. This secrepcy has originated either in Common Law or through the implementation of specific secrecy legislation.

Secrecy is of such importance to the effectiveness of a tax haven that certain countries have gone so far as to enact laws making it a criminal offense to reveal any information that is protected under such secrecy legislation. For example, bank secrecy in Switzerland is governed by the 1934 Swiss Federal Law Relating to Banks and Savings Institutions, as amended in 1970, and provides for imprisonment of up to six months or a fine of up to SFr50,000, as a penalty for anyone who discloses such bank secrets or attempts to induce someone else to do so. Despite such legislation, some bank secrecy laws are not nearly as effective as tax planners are led to believe. There always exists a possibility that details of any particular financial transaction may be disclosed.

Despite such secrecy legislation, there often exist tax treaties between tax-haven countries and high taxing countries, allowing for double-taxation relief, including in certain cases the sharing of information. This exchange of information, however, generally does not grant foreign tax authorities the right to arbitrarily request information in cases that are not related to the relief of double taxation. For example, the tax treaty between Switzerland and the United States provides for the exchange of information in double-taxation cases, and this does not breach the right to bank secrecy enshrined in the Swiss Federal Constitution.

Relative importance of the financial sector.

Both the banking and financial sectors tend to be of greater importance when considering the economy of a tax haven in comparison to the economies of non tax haven countries. In fact, in many tax haven countries, the banking industry is responsible for over 40% of the country's revenues. The banking industry has a significant effect on the economy of a tax haven by producing revenues in the form of fees and modest stamp duties on certain financial transactions, such as transferring funds. For this reason, most tax havens follow the policy of encouraging offshore business. The most common way for a tax haven to achieve such a policy of encouragement is by distinguishing between resident and non-resident accounts. By providing incentives for non-resident accounts, tax haven jurisdictions draw increasing volumes of offshore banking business. Some common incentives include:

- allowing non-resident accounts to be free of foreign exchange and other currency controls;
- eliminating reserve requirements on non-resident accounts; and
- the reduction or elimination of tax on non-resident accounts.

Modern transportation and communications.

To be effective as a tax haven, strong communication facilities are required. If reliable and cost-effective communications are unavailable, individuals lose confidence in utilizing the tax haven, reducing its inherent attractiveness. Most tax haven countries have excellent transportation and communication facilities, including good telecommunication and telex services. Recent advances in computer modem technology and data communication links have also been an aid to communication.

Lack of currency controls on foreign deposits.

It is essential that individuals and corporations making use of tax havens are free to move money in and out of the country at will. Most major tax havens either impose no form of exchange controls, or they operate with a dual currency system where non-residents, or companies formed by non-residents, are exempt from exchange control regulations. The exemption of foreign exchange control restrictions is often crucial in selecting a tax haven jurisdiction. The importance of the absence of exchange controls is clearly important when considering the operation of a captive insurance company, as it is imperative to have insurance premiums exempt from exchange control restrictions, making it easier to transfer this money out of the country.

Self-promotion as a tax haven.

It is quite common for tax havens to solicit financial business and to promote themselves as tax havens. Most tax havens are typically countries with few natural resources, heavily dependent upon the uncertainties of the tourist trade. For this reason, the banking and financial industry is seen as the only relatively stable source of revenue that, otherwise may be unattainable. Tax haven countries view this self-promotion as a necessity, often advertising the advantages they offer through seminars, articles in the press, and advertisements.

What are tax havens used for?

When considering the use of a tax haven, one must remember that although tax havens may have the potential to attract illegal activity, they should not be condemned for this reason alone. Such a generalization would in essence be a condemnation of international tax planning, which has long been regarded not only as a privilege, but as a right. Mr. Justice Sutherland, speaking for the United States Supreme Court, clearly expressed this view in the following quote:

> "*The legal right of a taxpayer to decrease the amount of what otherwise would be his taxes, or altogether avoid them, by means which the law permits, cannot be doubted.*" - Gregory vs. Helvering, 293 U.S. 454 (1935).

The utilization of tax havens is clearly only limited by the imagination of individuals, companies, and their respective tax planners. Tax havens openly acknowledge the needs of individuals to safeguard their assets, and to place limits on the high tax burden they are exposed to in their current country of residence. If all countries recognized these needs, or at the very least considered them, the utilization of tax havens would probably diminish over time. However, until these needs are recognized, tax havens will continue to play an ever increasing role in all facets of tax planning.

Why utilize a tax haven?

The following list provides many of the most common reasons why individuals and corporations utilize tax havens. Most tax havens have been organized to permit the following objectives to be easily achieved:

1. **Taxes on Income** - To eliminate the reporting and paying of income tax on earnings, interest, dividends, and investments.
2. **Taxes on Capital gains** - To protect against high capital gains taxes and reporting requirements.
3. **Taxes on Estates** - To prevent inheritance taxes, estate taxes, executor's fees, and probate fees.
4. **Asset Protection** - To protect assets from creditors, malpractice claims, judgements, liens, and bankruptcy, and to deter the initiation of civil litigation.

5. **Divorce and Separation** - To prevent the erosion of assets as a result of divorce or separation.
6. **Safekeeping** - To prevent any individual or government agency from locating your private documents.
7. **Public Record** - To prevent any knowledge of your assets or affairs from becoming public.
8. **Investment** - To protect the privacy of your involvement with investment houses, brokers, and securities markets.
9. **Share Holdings** - To protect the privacy of corporate ownership from becoming known to any individual or government.
10. **Cash** - To prevent any person or government from gaining access to your hard currency.
11. **Management** - To centralize the holding of securities, real estate and various other assets, which may be held and managed in several jurisdictions around the world.
12. **Active Business** - To earn tax free income through the operation of an active business. Examples include advertising, consulting, factoring, leasing, and trading.
13. **Intellectual Property** - To earn tax free income generated by the licensing of trade marks, patents, royalties, software licenses, and other rights from an offshore company.
14. **Travel** - Use offshore funds and automatic teller machines to gain immediate access to hard currency anywhere in the world.

CHAPTER 2

CONFISCATORY TAXES AND THEIR IMPACT

Look to the past to learn about the future.

History does repeat. Much can be learned by studying the fall of the Roman Empire. Three successive Roman emperors, Caligula, Claudius, and Nero the Fiddler, squandered their government's reserves to pay for opulent private villas, grandiose monuments and temples, armies of civil servants, lavish ceremonial feasts, and bribes to the Praetorian Guard to ensure their loyalty. Predictably, their reserves ran low, and these foolish emperors raised taxes, expropriated the assets of wealthy citizens, and expanded the money supply by re-minting coins using less gold and silver. Roman commerce was destroyed by high taxes. Once proud Roman cities were reduced to ruin because of the lack of investment in infrastructure. Citizens became impoverished, plagued with riot and civil strife. History clearly shows that the foolish government policies of the Roman empire led to its bankruptcy and inevitable collapse.

History has shown that in countries where the government provides a minimum standard of living for its citizens, a certain amount of taxation is required to ensure that the costs of providing this standard are spread fairly among the entire population. However, once implemented, tax systems often take on a life of their own. Rather than utilizing the tax revenue to assist in providing essential services, governments often begin to see taxpayers as a never ending source of revenue.

"*It must be nice to belong to some legislative body and just pick money out of the air.*" - Will Rogers

Projects get planned and implemented without immediate financing. Governments borrow and increase debt, with the only way out being to raise revenues by increasing taxation. Most of the high tax countries in the world have now reached the "tax wall." Citizens are at a point where increased taxation will not be tolerated. Individuals now, more than ever, must arrange their affairs to reduce their tax liabilities.

Courts have been asked to rule on whether people can plan their business and personal affairs so as to pay the minimum amount of tax possible. Decisions have been reached over the years agreeing with the statement that arranging one's affairs to pay as little tax as possible is entirely acceptable.

> "*Anyone may so arrange his affairs that his taxes to be as low as possible; he is not bound to choose that pattern which will best pay the Treasury; there is not even a patriotic duty to increase one's taxes.*" - Federal Judge Learned Hand, Gregory vs. Helvering, 69 F.2d 809, 1935.

> "*Every man is entitled, if he can, to order his affairs so that the tax attaching under the appropriate Acts is less than it otherwise would be. If he succeeds in ordering them so as to secure this result, then, however unappreciative the Commissioners of Inland Revenue or his fellow taxpayers may be of his ingenuity, he cannot be compelled to pay an increased tax.*" - Lord Tomlin, Inland Revenue vs. Duke of Westminster, 1936.

The decline of many great civilizations in history has been due to extreme levels of taxation. In fact, the United States was founded in 1776 because a significant number of early colonists revolted against unreasonable taxation.

Wealthy citizens of high tax countries have been using offshore centres to protect their assets.

Wealthy Europeans have been transferring assets to tax havens since the French Revolution. Today, citizens of the Persian Gulf countries are also protecting their assets from ruthless dictators and other financial enemies.

Not surprisingly, increasing numbers of Americans are giving up their citizenship to avoid estate taxes that in some cases can exceed 60%. However, because of the Health Insurance Portability Act of 1996, the rules have changed. If an American citizen wishes to renounce their U.S. citizenship, the renunciation may be deemed tax-motivated if certain tests are met, having a net worth above $500,000 being one of them. For a period of 10 years following expatriation, U.S. sourced income and income connected with U.S. trade or business may be caught under the new IRS rules, effectively making this income taxable to the ex-patriate.

Uncle Sam's power even extends beyond the border, requiring foreigners to pay estate taxes on assets such as property or business interests held within the United States. The Foreign Investment in Real Property Tax Act of 1980 requires foreigners to pay a capital gains tax when they sell U.S. real estate. Can you imagine what would happen to the U.S. markets if all foreign holdings were taxed in a similar manner to real estate?

Are higher taxes the result of government debt, or is government debt the result of high taxes?

In 1980 the U.S. national debt reached one trillion dollars. By 1990, the national debt had increased to over four trillion dollars. Throughout this period, we witnessed an increase in tax rates rise to cover the rising debt payments. Following are actual United States Government debt figures over the last 50 years (in trillions of dollars).

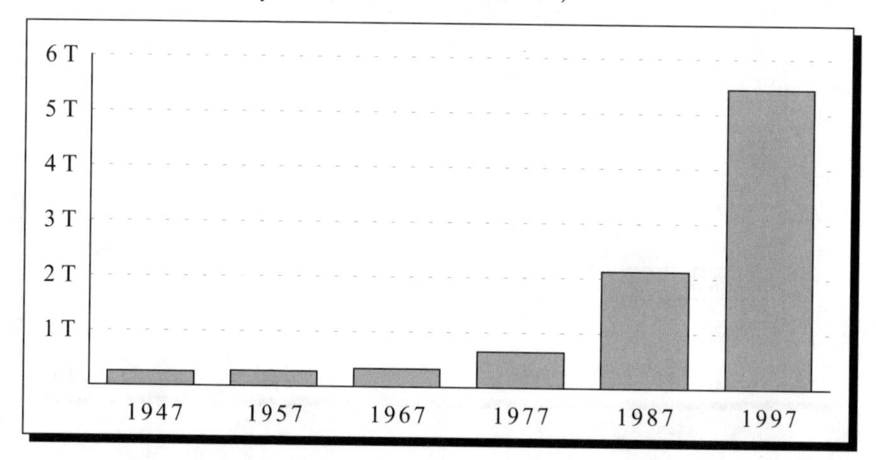

In Canada, the picture is not any brighter. As at March 31, 1995, the Government of Canada reported total liabilities of $583 billion, of which

$438 billion was borrowed on the financial markets, representing 73 percent of Gross Domestic Product. In both the United States and Canada, the deficit figures (receipts less outlays) are equally as disturbing, although it is encouraging to note that the numbers have been gradually improving since 1992.

Annual United States deficit.

Figures shown are in billions of dollars.

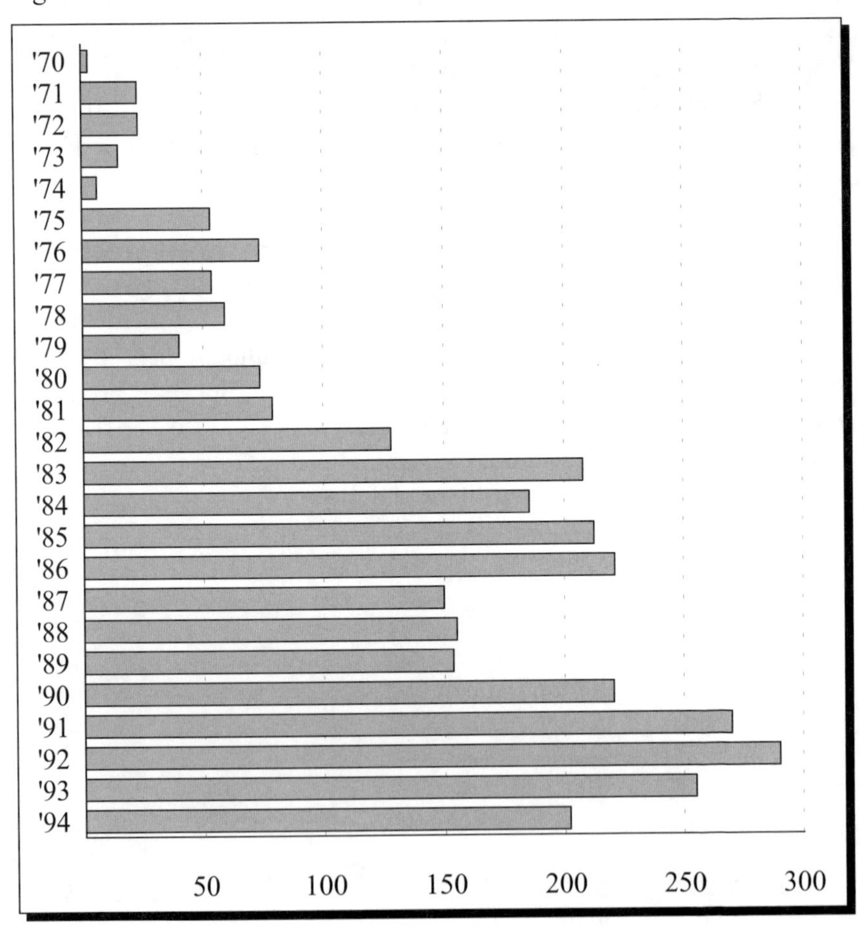

Personal tax rates around the world.

The high rate of income tax paid by citizens of the major industrialized nations negatively influence the potential that they could otherwise attain. The following table shows rates of income, capital gains, and dividend taxes for 1995:

	Income Tax	Capital gains Tax	Dividend Tax
Belgium	60.5%	n/a	n/a
Britain	40%	40%	33%
Canada (Ontario)	53%	39%	39%
France	56.8%	19% to 56.8%	56.8%
Germany	57%	n/a	53%
Italy	51% to 67%	25%	51% to 67%
Japan	65%	65%	35%
Switzerland	49.5%	n/a	n/a
United States	39.6%	39.6%	39.6%

An encouraging trend is the gradual reduction in certain types of taxes in different parts of the world. For example, the income tax rate in Ontario, Canada was 53.19% in 1995, and is slated to be reduced over the next few years to below 50%. Not a huge reduction, but at least a step in the right direction.

The use of offshore tax havens.

The result of properly structuring your affairs offshore is illustrated by the following example. The base investment is $100,000 earning 10% annually. When invested in a no-tax environment (top line), the investment grows to $1,744,940 after 30 years. In a fully-taxed environment, subject to a 45% tax rate, the investment is only able to grow to $498,395 (bottom line). The impact of the tax over 30 years in an incredible $1.25 million!

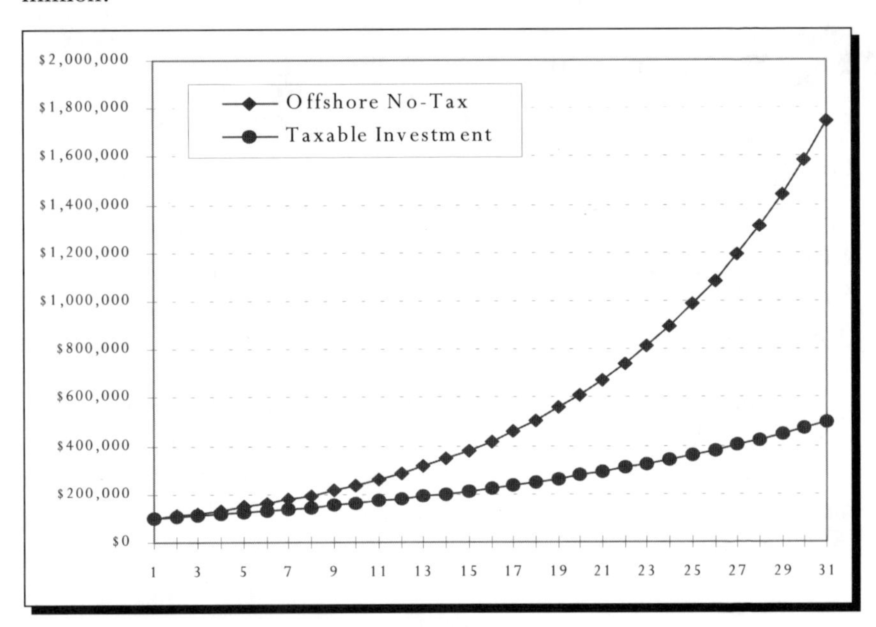

Something to note in this example is the compounding effect of taxes. Look at the difference between the taxed investment, and the non-taxed investment. Note that the difference between the two, growth lost due to taxes, actually increases at a compounded rate.

No wonder we're seeing an increase in offshore investing.

CHAPTER 3

PRIVACY AND CONFIDENTIALITY

Why are privacy and confidentiality important?

Recent headlines: A retired postal worker in West Virginia who bought a cabin downstream from an old coal mine is now in federal penitentiary because he refused to pay an environmental cleanup bill for over a million dollars, a result of the coal mine's operations long before he purchased the cabin. Ontario's highest court has ruled three corporate directors to personally pay Cdn$491,082 to former employees. The New Hampshire Supreme Court has allowed a liability suit for wrongful death to proceed against the Ford Motor Company because an 18-year-old girl died while speeding in a Ford car. A burglar collects from the owner of a mansion after falling on the property.

Who needs asset protection? The answer is obvious, anyone who owns assets. If you have debt-free assets, you are the prime target of frivolous lawsuits. As a successful individual, you may find yourself as a defendant of one of over 20 million civil lawsuits filed every year. Many of these lawsuits, although frivolous, result in judgements that can reduce a substantial net worth to virtually nothing. By properly structuring the ownership of your assets, a potential plaintiff may be dissuaded from commencing costly litigation.

George Orwell's *1984* - closer than you think.

The blame for the loss of privacy is not completely due to our governments. In fact, it can be said that business has equally to blame for the gradual erosion of personal privacy. Think about it... many events in our daily lives expose our personal information to those who have no right to see it.

Seemingly innocent actions, such as applying for a loan, sending in a credit card application, purchasing insurance, taking out a membership at a video rental store, or simply filling out the warranty card that came with your new VCR, can all result in having your personal information entered into some database, available for all to see with a simple cross-reference of your Social Security or Social Insurance number.

Thanks to modern computer technologies and Artificial Intelligence applications, there are now databases that monitor these actions and store them for future use. Many of these uses are commercial. And many are part of the government's ongoing data acquisition operations.

"Big Brother" is watching you.

The United States government has recently established the Financial Crimes Enforcement Network (FinCEN) in Arlington, Virginia. FinCEN has access to all bank records, credit records, insurance and medical records, criminal records, driving records, census data, and other personal records on the majority of the U.S. population. This information is also available for much of the population residing in the G7 countries, and in most of the developed countries worldwide. In fact, former Russian President Boris Yeltsin turned to FinCEN for help in recovering funds stolen by former Russian officials.

FinCEN acts as a global database for the IRS (Internal Revenue Service), FBI (Federal Bureau of Investigation), CIA (Central Intelligence Agency), DEA (Drug Enforcement Agency), ATF (Bureau of Alcohol, Tobacco, and Firearms), and other U.S. government agencies.

FinCEN also works with Revenue Canada, the RCMP, Inland Revenue, InterPol, and other agencies world-wide. Peter Djinis, a Treasury official aware of FinCEN's operation, said in a 1994 interview, "*It's the first ever government-wide, multi-source intelligence and analytical network brought together under one roof to combat financial crimes.*"

FinCEN has access to the most private of information. For instance, FinCEN performs a real-time analysis of all electronic currency movements into and out of the United States by utilizing data supplied by the National Security Agency. Currently, FinCEN is working on computerizing all land transfer and real estate records in the U.S. Now you can be monitored 24-hours-a-day, thanks to the U.S. government.

Wiretaps on the rise.

The use of electronic surveillance for national security and criminal investigations increased substantially in 1996, according to statistics released by the Department of Justice. Court orders for national security wiretaps and bugs approved under the Foreign Intelligence Surveillance Act (FISA) increased at the greatest rate, rising over 20 percent, from 697 orders in 1995 to 839 orders in 1996. Such orders are approved by the Foreign Intelligence Surveillance Court, a secretive panel of nine judges appointed by the Chief Justice of the United States. No FISA applications were denied in 1996 – in fact, the FISA court has never denied a request for a surveillance order in its 20-year existence.

Court orders for electronic surveillance by state and federal agencies for criminal purposes also increased, in this case 9% between 1995 and 1996. However, for the first time in eight years, a court denied a surveillance application. Extensions of surveillance orders increased from 834 to 887. In all, interceptions were in effect for a total of 43,635 days in 1996. The vast majority of interceptions continued to occur in drug-related cases: 71.4% of them for drug investigations; 9.9% for gambling; 9.1% for racketeering; 3.5% for homicide and assault and a few each for bribery, kidnapping, larceny, theft, and loan sharking.

Approximately 2.2 million(!) conversations were monitored in 1996, with a total of 1.7 million of them deemed "not incriminating" by prosecutors. Each operation resulted in the monitoring of an average of 1,969 conversations, of which 21.4% were deemed "incriminating."

Not only in North America.

German tax authorities are upset with Luxembourg banks that refuse to provide confidential banking information on German nationals. Germany has been retaliating against the Luxembourg banking community by raiding the homes (an illegal action) of Luxembourg bank employees who live in Germany. Investigators have seized documents in the hope that information on German customers would be contained in the documents. The aggressive move is based on the Luxembourg banking communities unwillingness to assist with German tax office information requests. As a precaution, Luxembourg bank employees living in Germany are forbidden from working on confidential documents at home. Let's hope that they continue to maintain the high level of secrecy that has helped make Luxembourg one of the world's premier banking countries.

Assets are the target.

In the mid 1980's, Congress gave law enforcement agencies the power to confiscate assets of anyone involved in drug trafficking. The intent was to prevent criminals from profiting from their illegal activities. Beginning in the late 1980's law enforcement agencies began to keep the confiscated assets, and have continued to abuse these powers.

In a further attack on its citizens, the US government has been given increased powers to confiscate property, as a result of a five to four ruling by the US Supreme Court. As a result of this ruling, a Michigan woman had her car confiscated because her husband had sex with a prostitute in it! Effectively, what this ruling does is allows police to seize items that are owned innocent people - a move that has been called "blatantly unfair" by three of the Supreme Court Justices. Chief Justice William Rehnquist noted that "...a long and unbroken line of cases holds that an owner's interest in property may be forfeited by reason of the use to which the property is put, even though the owner did not know that it was being put to such a use." So how's that for the land of the free? Here's the kicker: one of the justices against the ruling, Justice John Paul Stevens, stated "...for centuries, prostitutes have been plying their trade on other people's property" going on to say that recently governments have taken to confiscating private property as though it were where "...a single transaction with a prostitute has been consummated. The logic of the court's analysis would permit the states to exercise virtually unbridled power to confiscate vast amounts of property."

So is this how the US government is going to pay down the debt? Will they find any reason to confiscate property from innocent citizens, and then sell it on the open market? Can Canada be that far behind?

Maintaining privacy and confidentiality is the first step in lowering your profile in the eyes of those who may place a claim on your assets. As commercial databases, credit rating agencies, and government monitoring becomes increasingly widespread, it will become increasingly important to take steps that will ensure your privacy and confidentiality. You never know what will happen years from now as a result of actions you take today. For example:

- Ontario, Canada's highest court has ruled three corporate directors to personally pay Cdn$491,082 to former employees. The directors resigned from XYZ Manufacturing Inc. (name intentionally changed) on September 23, 1988, days before the factory closed. The resignations caused the bank to withhold funds, resulting in the company's inability to pay wages and termination pay. The court ruled the directors failed to prove they had no knowledge of the events that led to the company's failure (they resigned to protect themselves from the fallout). This precedent setting ruling should prompt other corporate directors to shift their personal assets to properly structured offshore corporations and trusts.
- In 1994, Bob Jones (name intentionally changed), a man who became a quadriplegic in an accident that broke his neck, was awarded $5 million dollars in damages. His lawyer said that while Jones had consumed six alcoholic drinks, he completed three successful dives (diving eight feet from a rooftop into a 3-foot deep pool) before his ill-fated plunge. The court found the homeowners 40% responsible, requiring them to pay $2 million dollars in damages. Even though the homeowners tried to stop Jones from jumping from the roof, the court stated that "*it was stupid and dangerous and (he) shouldn't have done it, but the homeowners should have used force to stop him from doing something reckless.*"
- A charter airline based in Nevada flew a customer to an airport in California. The FBI was waiting for them, arresting the customer, who was carrying $2 million cash. The cash, along with the airplane, were confiscated by the FBI. Eventually, the customer was

released without being charged for any crime. However, the airplane was not released, forcing the charter airline out of business.

- Police in Florida are randomly stopping vehicles (they look for vehicles with hanging air fresheners, the theory being that the air fresheners are used to mask the smell of drugs). If they discover more than $1,000 in cash, the money is immediately confiscated. There is no due process because the police take the position that the money was acquired illegally.

Of course, we should also expect that the tax collectors will also have an interest in our assets that are out in the open. In a recent report from the General Accounting Office, it was revealed that the IRS had been severely abusing its powers. The report stated "...(the) IRS does not effectively monitor employee activity, accurately record browsing violations, consistently punish offenders, or widely publicize reports of incidents detected and penalties imposed." According to IRS officials testifying before a Senate committee, the IRS had investigated over 4,500 incidents of "browsing" since 1993. These investigations resulted in the firing, resignation, or retirement of 285 employees.

In a recent *Newsweek* article, it was revealed that "...'Problem resolution' caseworkers assigned to look into complaints actually fall under the authority of the managers they're supposed to be looking at." No wonder most Americans are afraid of an audit, even though fewer than 2 percent of U.S. tax returns are ever audited. Of course, even though this represents a small percentage of tax returns, we find that collections through audits are increasing at a steady rate. For example, using liens, levys, seizures, and other measures, collections have increased from $23.5 billion in 1994 to $29.8 billion in 1996. And as the following example illustrates, some of the collection measures in the past have not been ethical or legal:

Daniel Smith (name intentionally changed), a Miami lawyer, had served as general counsel to a newspaper that ran a 1973 exposé of an illegal IRS spying operation. The newspaper had found that the IRS was engaged in spying on the sexual habits of important local officials, and had reported it on the pages of the newspaper. Because Mr. Smith refused IRS agents' demands to name the sources used for the exposé, they built up an investigation into his personal financial affairs, fabricating evidence that led to him being unfairly indicted on tax evasion charges. In 1987, Mr. Smith was forced to serve a four month sentence in a minimum security prison at Elgin Air Force base after he was indicted for tax evasion in 1982. Smith struck back, and eventually was awarded an out-of-court settlement in the amount of US$500,000, because the U.S. Court of Appeals found that he had been framed by his own accountant, after the accountant was forced by the IRS to lie under oath.

The solution? A properly set up offshore structure will not only legally prevent your assets from becoming part of any public record, it will also help to maintain your privacy and confidentiality when dealing with those who may feel that they have some sort of claim to those assets. And let's face it, it's pretty hard to take something away, if you don't even know it's there.

CHAPTER 4

THE WORLD OF OFFSHORE

Global tax planning brings with it a whole host of new concepts and procedures that are not readily apparent to individuals operating in a traditional taxing jurisdiction. What follows is a brief listing of certain concepts, procedures, and protocols that anyone considering utilizing a tax haven must understand.

When selecting and utilizing a tax haven, or implementing global tax planning strategies, individuals require certain preliminary information. The following list, although not exhaustive, provides a good review of some of the major concepts, such as:

- Global Investing.
- Private Accounts.
- Transferring Funds.
- Mail Forwarding.
- Secret Safekeeping.
- Computer Privacy.
- Personal Privacy.
- Counter-Intelligence.
- Information Sources.

GLOBAL INVESTING

The benefits of global investing.

Investing offshore gives you the "launching pad" to obtain direct access to many international investments not available in North America. Take mutual funds, for example. Most international firms such as Templeton, GT Global, and Fidelity, have offshore registered versions of their funds that seem to provide better returns than their North American counterparts. In other cases, funds from firms such Guinness Flight, Atlantis, Standard Private Trust, and KB Lux, are not even available to North American investors. However, by using an offshore company/trust structure, through an offshore investment firm, you can gain access to these previously unavailable funds.

Some of these funds can offer truly extraordinary returns. For instance, at the time of writing, the average rate of return on a five year Certificate of Deposit was 6%. Fully taxable. Yet offshore, funds such as the Atlantis Yield Plus Fund from Blue Chip Capital offer a 10.25% guaranteed rate of return over five years, tax-free. Which would you choose for the fixed income part of your portfolio?

Much of the investment planning process requires an evaluation of the investor's profile. When seeking out an offshore investment firm, you should be looking for a level of service equal to or better than what you would expect from a domestic firm. On the operations side, important considerations include ease of communications, consistent reporting with semi-annual statements at the very least, and efficient money transfer capabilities. Recommended investment products should follow a plan that is actively managed to reflect the dynamic global investment environment at all times.

When looking at growth markets, we once again find opportunities when investing internationally through offshore structures. Many economies are growing more rapidly than the world's established economies. Investing globally provides an opportunity to invest in higher growth regions of the world, with a greater range of investment opportunities, while reducing risk through diversification of assets over various countries.

Top Performing Markets.

12 months to March 31, 1996, percentage growth:

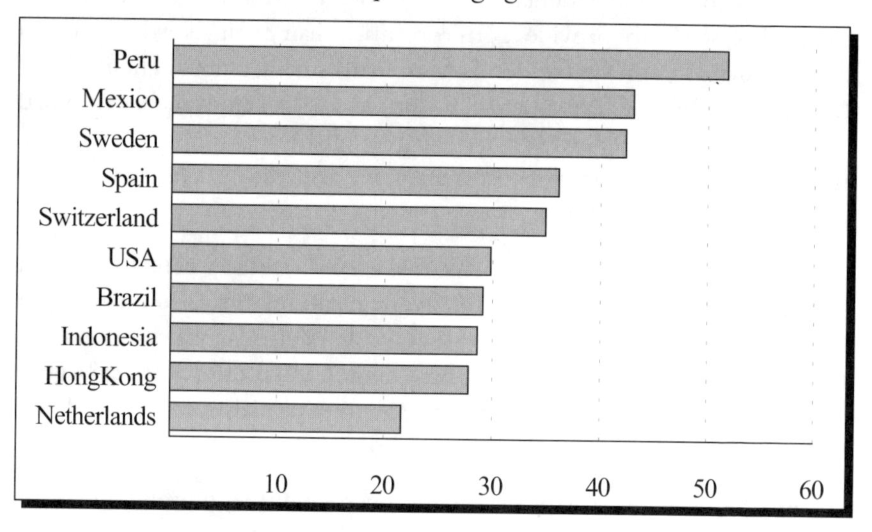

Offshore financial services.

In addition to virtually every mutual fund in the world, offshore investment firms also offer specialized products such as:

1. **Private Asset Management** - Managers structure segregated portfolios based on specific mandates, often diversified across the three asset classes, as well as across various investment styles and geography within each asset class.
2. **Non-Discretionary Asset Management** - For sophisticated investors who prefer to direct the management of their own portfolios, through a full range of global securities, derivative and fixed income trading services, and foreign currencies.

3. **Multi-Currency Deposits** - Fixed term deposits are available in a variety of currencies, ranging from overnight deposits to fixed maturities ranging from one week to five years.
4. **Foreign Exchange Services** - Because offshore investing often involves a change of currency, a more competitive range of foreign exchange options are offered.
5. **Insurance-Based Investment Options** - In many cases innovative international insurance programs provide solutions for succession planning and estate preservation simply not available domestically. For those requiring a fixed income, an annuity can be set up to flow a steady stream of guaranteed monthly payments.
6. **Margin Accounts** - Although very rare, some offshore investment firms do offer facilities allowing funds to be borrowed for the purchase of securities.

North American global investing contacts:

Blue Chip Capital Management Limited
c/o 1701 Woodward Drive, Suite 114
Ottawa, ON, Canada, K2C 0P7
toll free 888-265-6661, fax 613-226-1074

- *Services Offered:* investment advisor, mutual fund manager, private banking, global investing information, deposit backed MC/Visa

---

Blue Chip Capital Management Limited
c/o 1575 Military Road
Niagara Falls, NY, USA, 14304-4706
toll free 888-265-6661, fax 800-560-0645

- *Services Offered:* investment advisor, mutual fund manager, private banking, global investing information, deposit backed MC/Visa

---

Chemical Bank Private Banking
270 Park Avenue, 46th Floor
New York, NY, USA, 10017-2070
tel. 212-270-3359, fax 212-687-0967

- *Services Offered:* investment advisor, private banking, retail banking, loans and credit, safekeeping services

---

Global Mutual Fund Investor
14 West Mt. Vernon Place
Baltimore, MD, USA, 21201
tel. 410-783-8440, fax 410-783-8438

- *Services Offered:* global investing information, Global Mutual Fund Investor newsletter.

International Research
16 Daybreak Road, PO.Box 2323
Cleveland, GA, USA, 30528
tel. 706-865-6602, fax 706-865-2988

- *Services Offered:* global investing information, Investment Trust Report.

Smith Barney Inc.
311 Park Place Boulevard, Suite 100
Clearwater, FL, USA, 34609-6498
tel. 813-799-5700, fax 813-791-7092, toll free 800-237-5232

- *Services Offered:* investment advisor, deposit backed MC/Visa

---

Swiss Bank Corporation (Canada)
207 Queen's Quay West, Suite 780, PO.Box 103
Toronto, ON, Canada, M5J 1A7
tel. 416-203-2180, fax 416-203-4384

- *Services Offered:* investment advisor, private banking

Union Bank of Switzerland
299 Park Avenue
New York, NY, USA, 10171-0026
tel. 212-715-3000, fax 212-715-3946, telex, MCI 620317 UBS UW

- *Services Offered:* investment advisor, private banking, retail banking, loans and credit, safekeeping services

PRIVATE ACCOUNTS

The concept of a numbered, or "private" account began before World War II when financial institutions in Switzerland created the accounts to keep the financial assets of fleeing German Jews secret and confidential, a practice that continues to this day. Austria even permits bank accounts to be opened without a name, requiring only a code number or word to make transactions.

Private accounts can be used as part of a safe wealth building strategy, allowing you to invest the cash portion of your portfolio in foreign currencies. Private accounts also provide an extra level of protection against anyone seeking to seize your assets. A creditor is required to file a court action and get a judgement in the jurisdiction where you hold the account, a very expensive action for the creditor to undertake. This allows you time to fight the court action, or simply move the funds to another jurisdiction.

Individuals often cite the lack of FDIC (Federal Deposit Insurance Corporation) or CDIC (Canadian Deposit Insurance Corporation) account insurance as a concern with respect to such accounts. However, most offshore banks are either insured by independent insurance companies, or are self insured, maintaining a liquidity factor of 1:1, meaning that there is $1 for every $1 held in public deposits. If you are at all concerned with the liquidity factor of 1:1, consider that most U.S. financial institutions have less than 10 cents cash for every $1 on deposit.

Even with such good reserve ratios, when dealing with an offshore financial institution it is wise to inspect a copy of the bank's annual financial report before making any deposits. Be sure the report you receive is an audited annual report, stating the names of the financial institution's principals. While you're at it, maybe now would be a good time to look at the financial statements of your local United States or Canadian bank.

A private account is easily opened.

Most offshore banks will require a reference letter from your current financial institution. This is a result of the "know your customer rules" that banks are required to follow, as a preventative measure to protect against money laundering.

Sample letter of reference.

Your Bank's Letterhead

Date

To whom it may concern,

We wish to advise that Mr.______________ has been a satisfactory client of this Bank in excess of 3 years. He has various deposit and borrowing accounts with us, all being maintained as agreed.

We trust that the above information is satisfactory for your purposes, and if you should have any questions or require any additional information, do not hesitate to contact the undersigned.

Yours very truly,

Account Manager

Some banks will require a personal meeting to set up a banking relationship, while many others offer the option of opening the account by mail or courier. Once the banking relationship is established, you can conduct business by mail, telephone, fax, or telex.

Advantages and benefits of private accounts:

1. **Anonymity** - A numbered account opened in a tax haven jurisdiction with legislated bank secrecy laws ensures that the assets held in the account will remain private, and the ownership of the account will not be disclosed to outside parties.
2. **Security** - The secrecy aspect of a numbered account will help deter frivolous lawsuits. This will help protect you from liens, bankruptcy, foreclosures, liability, and malpractice claims, as well as protection from divorce and alimony payments.
3. **Additional Protection** - A numbered account combined with a certificate of deposit in the name of an offshore corporation adds an additional layer of "protection" to your secrecy and privacy. This ensures that your personal name will never appear on any bank records, adding an additional stumbling block between you and the IRS, Revenue Canada, or Inland Revenue.
4. **Higher Earnings** - Many offshore financial institutions located in low-tax countries pay slightly higher interest than financial institutions located in high tax jurisdictions. This is because offshore banks pay lower income, property, and payroll taxes. Taxes are one of the highest non-recoverable costs of doing business in punitive-tax countries such as the U.S. and Canada. Banks operating in low-tax jurisdictions, not burdened by those non-recoverable tax costs, can offer depositors a much higher return. However, some banks in tax haven jurisdictions pay little or no interest, so shop around.

TRANSFERRING FUNDS

It is important to reduce the paper trail when transferring funds to and from your offshore bank. When you send a personal or business check to be invested, you are leaving a very clear paper trail that can be easily audited by the IRS, Revenue Canada, or Inland Revenue. Although the transfer of funds may be perfectly legal, you may want to avoid having to explain your actions to the IRS or Revenue Canada, or anyone else for that matter.

In the United States, specific legislation (P.L. 91-508; 31 USC 5316) requires the filing of a Currency Transaction Report (CTR) that details a transaction of "currency" or certain "monetary instruments" in an amount exceeding US$10,000. Financial institutions must also file a CTR, or IRS form 4789, if a transaction under US$10,000 is considered suspicious. The IRS uses an extensive list to determine whether a transaction is to be considered suspicious. It is important to know the exact definition of Currency and Monetary Instruments:

> **Currency** - ...the coin and currency of the U.S. or any other country, which includes U.S. silver certificates, U.S. notes and Federal Reserve notes, but does not include bank checks or other negotiable instruments not customarily accepted as money.
>
> **Monetary Instruments** - ...the coin and currency of the U.S. or any other country, including travellers checks, money orders, investment securities in bearer form or otherwise if such title thereto passes upon delivery, and negotiable instruments (except warehouse receipts or bills of lading) in bearer form or otherwise if such title thereto passes upon delivery. The term Monetary Instruments includes bank checks, travellers checks, and money orders which are signed, but on which the name of the payee has been omitted, but does not include bank checks, travellers checks or money orders made payable to the order of a named person which has not been endorsed or which bear restrictive endorsements.

Based on the exceptions, if a bank draft, bank check, travellers check or international money order is made payable to an offshore entity such as a corporation, there is no requirement to report such transactions in the United States.

In Canada, Bill C-9 of 1993 reduced reporting requirements to Cdn$1,000 for the purchase of postal money orders and travellers checks. Identification in the form of a driver's license, passport, or credit card is now required to purchase international money orders and travellers checks. Under the law, frequent transactions in excess of Cdn$1,000 are enough to spark an investigation.

Options for transferring funds.

To transfer funds to your offshore account, and to make use of the funds at a later date, you may wish to consider one of the following options:

1. **Bank Draft** - If you purchase a bank draft (or bank check, travellers check or international money order) payable to an offshore corporation, there is no requirement to report this transaction. Despite this, it is still possible that an overzealous or misinformed bank officer may report such a transaction. Therefore, it may be wise to purchase bank drafts in denominations of less than US$3,000. The reason for recommending US$3,000 instead of US$10,000 is a result of the *Comprehensive Money Laundering Prevention Act* of 1986. The Act established guidelines that in some cases reduce bank reporting requirements to US$3,000, including the purchase of money orders, travellers checks, and cashier's checks. Under the law, frequent transactions in excess of US$3,000 may be enough to spark an investigation.
2. **Bank Wire Transfer** - While this method is a fast and efficient means of transferring funds back and forth from your offshore account, it leaves an easily identifiable paper trail if you use your name on the wire transfer. There are many offshore banks that allow you to wire transfer money anonymously with a code name, which is an acceptable means of transferring funds, as long as the sending bank does not ask for the sender's identification.

3. **Personal or Company Checks** - Do not send money to your offshore account with personal or company checks. Every check you write or deposit is scanned, entered into a document retrieval system, and retained by your financial institution. The information is then readily available to the IRS, Revenue Canada, or Inland Revenue.
4. **Personal or Company Check "Recycling"** - To prevent any type of trace on your incoming checks, endorse them over to your creditors to make payments. You may also use a check cashing service to cash your checks, although most charge a small fee. Do not cash checks at any bank where you hold an account. The checks are scanned by a document retrieval system and linked to your account, providing an easy paper trail for investigators.
5. **Private Credit Cards** - Many offshore banks offer a private credit card (Visa, MasterCard, or American Express) backed by deposit, and commonly referred to as "debit cards." Because the card is backed by deposit, you are not required to supply credit information or personal information such as your Social Security Number or Drivers License. The credit card limit is set by the amount of money you have on deposit. You can have the private credit card issued in your own name, or in the name of your offshore company, adding to the privacy and secrecy of the card. Funds can be withdrawn from your account simply by using the card for purchases, or by cash advance from any financial institution that honors the card. You can purchase goods wherever your card (Visa, MasterCard, or American Express) is honored. You can also go to any Automatic Teller Machine (ATM) in the world and withdraw funds from your account. Because these transactions are processed offshore, your secrecy, privacy, and confidentiality are guaranteed by the issuing bank's secrecy laws.
6. **Money Market Accounts** - A legal way of getting around both the reporting requirements and the Money Laundering Control Act is to transfer funds from a Money Market Account with check writing privileges. The process involves writing a check from your personal account to the money market account, and then using a money market check to send the money to your offshore bank.

Once the transaction is complete, the money market account may be closed to avoid the issue of structuring under the *Money Laundering Control Act*. Although this creates a minimal paper trail, it is a paper trail that is difficult to uncover.

7. **International Postal Money Orders** - Believe it or not, this is still a very good method. Shop around for the best price, trying postal outlets, packaging and postage services, banks, and trust companies. Be sure not to purchase money orders from a bank where you have an account, because the institution may file money order records with your account records. For additional security, use an alias name for purchasing postal money orders. This privacy step has no effect on the transfer of funds. Be sure to retain your copy of the international money order if a trace is required. It is possible to send a maximum of $1,000 without any easily identifiable paper trail. To send an amount greater than $1,000, you may wish to use multiple money orders.
8. **The Western Union** - A safe form of transferring funds if you use a code word or name. Simply pay for the Western Union money transfer, stating the name or company it is to be made payable to, and the address of the receiving agent. The fee for a Western Union money transfer is usually 3% to 5%, depending on amount. There is also a fee to have it delivered to your offshore agent.
9. **Travelers Checks** - It is possible to purchase travellers checks in denominations of up to $1,000 each. By spreading your purchases of travellers checks among several financial institutions, and keeping the total amount purchased less than US$3,000 or Cdn$1,000, you can transfer a virtually unlimited amount of funds without any of the financial institutions reporting currency transactions. Travelers checks are an efficient means of transferring large amounts of money without creating an easily traceable paper trail.
10. **Gold Legal Tender** - The US government requires the reporting of any amount over US$10,000 on form 4790 when it is being taken out of the country, withdrawn or deposited. Transactions of more than this sum in any form are reported to the IRS. One

exemption, however, is to use legal gold tender to transfer funds. A US$20 gold piece is still legal tender, therfore its official value is US$20. However, collectors and investors will pay about $500 for them. So by posessing up to five hundered $20 gold pieces you are still under the $10,000 reporting requirement but are actually carrying about $250,000 in liquid assets. Keep in mind that this applies only to gold that is legal tender and does not apply to gold bullion or gold bullion coins like the Krugerrand.

MAIL FORWARDING

Mail forwarding services fulfill a necessary need in providing secrecy, privacy, and confidentiality.

A mail forwarding service will forward mail for individuals and companies virtually anywhere in the world. Who uses mail forwarding services?

1. Individuals or companies who wish to eliminate a "paper trail" for offshore accounts and investments, securities trading, and ownership of foreign companies.
2. Individuals, investors, and shareholders who require an address in another city or country.
3. Foreign firms requiring an address in another city or country to pose as a branch office or local address.
4. Individuals who require an address other than their own due to separation or divorce, alimony, support payments, job transfers, or military service.
5. Individuals or companies that require a confidential storage safe deposit box or vault.
6. Individuals who wish to eliminate a "paper trail" to protect themselves from creditors, liability suits, malpractice claims, judgements, liens, and bankruptcy.
7. Individuals or companies wishing to keep the ownership and location of assets confidential.

When choosing a mail forwarding service, look for one that guarantees secrecy, privacy, and confidentiality. A mail forwarding service may receive inquiries from banks, trust companies, finance companies, insurance companies, the IRS, Revenue Canada, wives, husbands and friends to divulge your real address. Establish guarantees to ensure your address will not be given to anyone who telephones, writes, or visits the mail forwarding service.

Why be so concerned about your re-mailing services' integrity? Consider the following example. Suppose you have made a decision to keep your financial affairs totally secret, private, and confidential. You decide to use a mail forwarding service you feel you can trust. Two years later someone contacts your re-mailing service claiming to be your brother. He explains that your uncle has died and would like to get in touch with you. Your re-mailing service decides on "compassionate grounds" to provide the brother with your real address. Unfortunately, the person calling you is not your brother, it is an unauthorized person trying to gain a better understanding of your "private financial affairs." You are now back at square one trying to deal with disruptions to your secrecy, privacy, and confidentiality. This incident will cost you in both time and money, having to once again find a reliable re-mailing service. Please choose your re-mailing service carefully.

Consider this next example. In the late 1960's, the IRS began intercepting private mail from Switzerland. Even though bank statements were sent in plain envelopes, the IRS was able to penetrate this secrecy without unlawfully opening any of the mail. Most of the envelopes from Swiss banks used metered postage, instead of postage stamps. IRS agents copied the fronts of these envelopes to record the postal meter number and the addressee of the envelope. Agents then contacted the Swiss banks for information, recording the postal meter number on the reply envelopes. They then matched the envelopes to the Swiss postal meter numbers, compiling a list of possible tax evaders, who were then audited by the IRS.

Most mail forwarding services will also send mail for you from their location. This works by placing your correctly addressed mail in a larger envelope, and sending it to the mail forwarding service with instructions to mail it from their address. The postmark will be from the area that your mail forwarding service is located. This service may be a necessary part of your outgoing correspondence.

Sample "hold statements" letter.

A typical letter indicating that you wish to have all statements issued upon request reads as follows:

Your Company Letterhead

Date

Standard Private Trust Ltd.
Caribbean Place, Leeward Highway
Providenciales, Turks & Caicos Islands, BWI

re. statements - company checking account

Dear Sirs,

This letter is to confirm our instructions to only issue statements for (your company name) upon request. Periodically the company may give written instructions by a signatory on where the statements are to be posted, or they will be picked up by a signatory of the account.

Thank you for your assistance.

Yours faithfully,
(your company name)

per ___________ (director)

company seal

Private courier services.

Most mail forwarding services will offer private courier services that allow you to send and receive couriered material virtually anywhere in the world, while maintaining your secrecy, privacy, and confidentiality.

Private communication services.

Some mail forwarding services offer voice mail and paging services. For sensitive fax communications, they may also offer a confidential fax service.

Postal money orders and bank drafts.

You may require an international money order from your mail forwarding services' local post office. For larger amounts of money, you may require an international bank draft drawn on a bank in the area of your "phantom address." An international bank draft has the advantage of being available in any amount and in any currency. A few of the mail forwarding services can do this for you for a reasonable fee. Having your mail forwarding service prepare international postal money orders and international bank drafts offers you an opportunity to gain an extra degree of secrecy, privacy, and confidentiality.

Private printing services.

Some mail forwarding services also offer related printing services, such as business forms, business cards, letterhead and stationery. You may also wish to have personalized mailing labels printed for your "phantom address."

Mail forwarding services (in country order):

March & Partners Ltd.
PO.Box 2.222
Andorra La Vella, Andorra
tel. 376-837595, fax 376-835008

- *Services Offered:* company formation, law office, accounting services, corporate services, mail forwarding

---

Ausmail
GPO 2027
Brisbane, Australia, 4001
fax 617-384-88646

- *Services Offered:* mail forwarding

Sunnyland Business Centre
PO.Box GT2470, International Bazaar, Bay Street
Nassau, Bahamas
tel. 242-328-6322, fax 242-328-6326

- *Services Offered:* mail forwarding

Financial Engineering Consultants Inc.
PO.Box 959, Centro Colon Towers 1007
San Jose, Costa Rica
tel. 506-31-6575, fax 506-20-3470

- *Services Offered:* company formation, mail forwarding

BF Continental Services Ltd.
Eurolife Building
Gibraltar
tel. 350-51115, fax 350-51116

- *Services Offered:* company formation, corporate services, safekeeping services, mail forwarding

---

Form-A-Co (Gibraltar) Limited
PO.Box 563, 25 Turnbull's Lane
Gibraltar
tel. 350-79959, fax 350-79894

- *Services Offered:* company formation, corporate services, mail forwarding

---

A.E.V. Ltd.
Zaloska cesta 99
Ljubljana, Slovenia, 61000
tel. 386-61-443-242, fax 386-61-1403-105

- *Services Offered:* mail forwarding

Citibox
2 Old Brompton Road
South Kensington, UK, SW7
tel. 44-1715-848648, fax 44-1715-814445

- *Services Offered:* mail forwarding

David Lewis Associates
Waterlooville, UK, P08 9JL
tel. 44-1705-592255, fax 44-1705-591975

- *Services Offered:* mail forwarding

KBC
Chantry Bridge
Wakefield, UK
tel. 44-1924-200580, fax 44-1924-200581

- *Services Offered:* mail forwarding

Leyton Office Services
St. Georges House, 31A St. Georges Road, Leyton
London, UK, E1O 5RH
tel. 0181-556-2979, fax 0181-539-2862

- *Services Offered:* mail forwarding

Mrs. Messenger
4 Gurdon Road
Colchester, UK, C02 7PB
tel. 44-1206-575328, fax 44-1206-540039

- *Services Offered:* mail forwarding

The Leyton Office
UK
tel. 44-1815-562979, fax 44-1815-392862

- *Services Offered:* mail forwarding

CHQ Incorporated
1555 E. Flamingo Rd., Suite 240 Q
Las Vegas, NV, USA, 89119
tel. 702-796-5487, fax 702-732-0883

- *Services Offered:* company formation, mail forwarding

Delaware Registered Agents & Incorporators, Inc.
1220 Market Building
Wilmington, DE, USA, 19801
tel. 302-571-1117, fax 302-571-8115, toll free 800-346-1117

- *Services Offered:* company formation, corporate services, mail forwarding

---

Eagle Flight Financial Group
7127 E. Becker Lane
Scottsdale, AZ, USA, 85254
tel. 602-368-7229, fax 602-368-5568, toll free 888-690-7066

- *Services Offered:* travel services & information, mail forwarding, camouflage passports, security devices

---

Fast Forward
FL, USA
toll free 800-321-9950

- *Services Offered:* mail forwarding

Mail, Messages & More
NV, USA
toll free 800-722-7468

- *Services Offered:* mail forwarding

Outpost
WY, USA
toll free 800-331-4460

- *Services Offered:* mail forwarding

Private Postman
PO.Box 87210
San Diego, CA, USA, 92138

- *Services Offered:* mail forwarding

PS (Postal Services)
PO.Box 29656
San Antonio, TX, USA, 78229-0656

- *Services Offered:* mail forwarding

S&A Mail Forwarding
402 West Broadway, Suite 810
San Diego, CA, USA, 92101
tel. 619-238-8550, fax 619-696-3550

- *Services Offered:* mail forwarding

The Mail Post
2421 West Pratt Boulevard
Chicago, IL, USA, 60645
tel. 312-764-0100

- *Services Offered:* corporate services, mail forwarding

SECRET SAFEKEEPING

Many individuals find it important to have cash or other assets safely stored, yet available for easy access. Where you physically store your cash and assets is a significant consideration. If there is a major natural disaster, is it going to destroy the depository you use for your safekeeping? It may be worth having more than one safekeeping depository for that reason alone.

Some of the best safekeeping depositories are:

1. **Safe Deposit Boxes** - Renting a safe deposit box has certain limitations in protecting your assets and important documents. First, your access is limited by the bank's hours of operation. Second, and more importantly, government investigators have the authority to search and seize the contents of your safe deposit box. Third, bank employees may also have access to your safe deposit box. To protect yourself, your financial institution may offer insurance for the contents of the safe deposit box. Fourth, video surveillance systems and increased monitoring help protect the security of your safe deposit box, but they also reduce your privacy. Records are kept of your visits, and some banks require photos of renters. And finally, although the cost can be deducted as a business expense, you are providing a tip-off as to the location, and possibly the contents of the safe deposit box.
2. **Offshore Safe Deposit Boxes** - An advantage over a local safe deposit box is that government investigators do not have the authority to search and seize the contents of your safe deposit box, provided it is located in a country that offers bank secrecy. Of course, your access is limited by your ability to physically travel to the location of your offshore safe deposit box.
3. **Private Security Vaults** - It is possible to rent space in security vaults operated by privately run companies. If you decide on this option, be sure the vault provides extensive security measures, and access 24 hours a day. Standards are set by the National Association of Private Security Vaults. However, because these

companies are privately run, company stability and integrity should be the primary concerns.

4. **Home Safes** - Fireproof safes in your home are excellent for maintaining your secrecy, privacy and confidentiality. Keep the safe well hidden, and keep quiet about it. It is best to mount the safe in a concrete foundation to prevent it from being removed. A good idea is to have two safes, one that is extremely well hidden, and another "dummy safe" in an ordinary location. If, for any reason, someone was to gain access to your home, the dummy safe should contain fake papers and a small amount of cash, in order to convince the intruder that he's got the real thing.

What can you put in a safe deposit box? Documents relating to your offshore structure, banking documents, offshore investment certificates and other documents, stock certificates, bonds, wills, insurance policies, passports, jewelry, rare stamps and coins, and other items of a sentimental nature. In fact, about the only things you can't place in a safe deposit box are liquids or anything of an explosive or dangerous nature. When you rent a safe deposit box, you are usually supplied with two keys, which you should keep in separate, easily remembered places. If one key is lost, get a duplicate made as soon as possible, as the fees for having a locksmith create a new key will cost you more than the annual box rental.

Should you be concerned about insuring the contents of the safe deposit box? If there are valuables contained in the box, the answer is a definite "yes." One of the important features of a safe deposit box is confidenitality. The bank or private security vault is not supposed to know about the contents of your box. Because of this, it is up to you to determine whether the items in your box should be insured. It is suggested that you keep a separate inventory of the contents along with photocopies of documents and photographs or a video of the jewelery or other valuables in your box.

A common mistake is keeping assets in a domestic safe deposit box that has been rented in your own name. There are companies that for less than $100 can search all of the banking institutions in the country to find out if you are a safe deposit box customer. Of course, the IRS and Revenue Canada can easily do these searches as well. It's even easier for them to track down safe deposit boxes that you pay for with a personal check or credit card - they simply scan your cancelled checks and credit card statements. If you use a domestic safe deposit box, and you want to keep it secret, here's a few ideas you might want to take advantage of:

- pay with cash so there is nothing in your records relating to your safe deposit box;
- rent the box in the name of a corporation, or for added secrecy rent it in the name of an offshore corporation; and
- consider naming another person as signatory in addition to your self – in an emergency, that person would be able to get into the safe deposit box.

Secret safekeeping contacts:

Beekins Archival Service
619 W. 51st Street
New York, NY, USA, 10019
- *Services Offered:* safekeeping services

Czerlau & Associates Limited
1701 Woodward Drive, Suite 114
Ottawa, ON, Canada, K2C 0P7
tel. 800-226-5703, fax 613-226-1074
- *Services Offered:* corporate services, safekeeping services, telephone calling cards, mail forwarding, books or newsletters, data encryption, security devices, surveillance equipment

---

Czerlau & Associates Limited
Bahamas Financial Centre, 3rd Floor, Shirley & Charlotte Streets
Nassau, Bahamas
tel. 800-226-5703
- *Services Offered:* corporate services, safekeeping services, telephone calling cards, mail forwarding, books or newsletters, data encryption, security devices, surveillance equipment

---

Harris & Harris Barristers & Solicitors
190 Attwell Drive, Suite 400
Toronto, ON, Canada, M9W 6H8
tel. 416-798-2722, fax 416-798-2715
- *Services Offered:* company formation, trust formation, law office, corporate services, estate planning services, safekeeping services

Secretaries Limited
5th Floor, Wing On Centre, 111 Connaught Road
Central, Hong Kong
tel. 852-2544-2808, fax 852-2541-6840

- *Services Offered:* company formation, corporate services, safekeeping services

Standard Private Trust Ltd.
Caribbean Place, Leeward Highway
Providenciales, Turks and Caicos Islands, B.W.I.
tel. 809-946-4387, fax 809-946-4928

- *Services Offered:* investment advisor, mutual fund manager, company formation, trust formation, corporate services, deposit backed MC/Visa, safekeeping services

Wayne Budd Incorporated
RR#1, Box 63
Eldorado, ON, Canada, KOK 1Y0
tel. 613-473-4838, fax 613-473-4443, fax 613-473-4460

- *Services Offered:* safekeeping services, mail forwarding

COMPUTER PRIVACY

Computers have been an incredible aid to "Big Brother," providing agencies such as FinCEN the power necessary to do real-time monitoring of financial accounts. Computers have also given the individual concerned about secrecy, privacy and confidentiality the ability to "encrypt" personal and financial information, making a breach of security virtually impossible.

Computer data encryption.

The phenomenon of Public/Private-key encryption was first discovered by mathematicians Whitfield Diffie and Martin Hellmann in 1976. Public-key encryption is based on the principle that it is relatively easy for a computer to multiply two very large prime numbers, while it is virtually impossible to work backwards and derive the numbers from the sum without knowing either of the two numbers. Powerful personal computers are able to encrypt any message with the "Public-key," and decrypt the message with the "Private-key." The first commercial implementation of this technology was known as the RSA encryption technique. At the same time, similar development was taking place at the National Security Agency.

The RSA encryption technique was patented in the United States by RSA Data Security Inc (http://www.rsa.com). It is this company that licenses the technology for products such as Lotus Notes. RSA Data Security Inc. also markets a product called Ripem. An American underground programmer and computer privacy advocate, Philip Zimmerman, has developed an E-mail encryption program called PGP (Pretty Good Privacy) and has released it onto the Internet, making it available world-wide.

In August 1994, Philip Zimmerman was targeted in a federal criminal investigation to determine whether he violated a U.S. law prohibiting the export of encryption software. He has also run into trouble with RSA Data Security Inc., the owner of the patent on the mathematical algorithm used in PGP. In a 1994 interview, Zimmerman summed up the concept behind data encryption:

"Two hundred years ago, when they wrote the Constitution, they never thought it was necessary to put a special amendment in the Bill of Rights for the right to have a private conversation. You could just go behind the barn and talk. But today, you have copper wires and glass fibres carrying our conversations. So, do we want to sacrifice our privacy because of that? Our civil liberties are eroding because of the Information Age. Cryptography will bring them back."

Two companies involved in PGP distribution, ViaCrypt and Austin Codeworks, have received grand jury subpoenas to investigate potential export law violations. Encryption techniques are on the State Department's list of restricted technologies, along with military and space technologies. As mentioned above, even though it is supposedly restricted, PGP is available world-wide through the Internet. Information on PGP can be obtained at *http://pgp.com*.

Why are governments world-wide so concerned about data encryption technologies? Because RSA encryption technologies will soon make investigative techniques that are dependent on the surveillance of data communications virtually obsolete. Imagine being able to easily complete an anonymous (but verifiable) E-mail transaction with your offshore bank by using Public-key encryption. The Public-key encryption guarantees to both parties that they can correspond with complete secrecy and privacy, and that they can verify that it is the same party they dealt with before, rendering electronic financial transactions virtually impossible to monitor.

E-mail privacy.

E-mail is a technology that has become a standard form of business communication. When E-mail is used to transmit confidential information, it is no longer confidential. E-mail isn't really erased when you use your computer's delete function. First, experts can often recover old data, despite it being erased from a hard drive or computer network. Second, a copy of the message may still exist in the E-mail transmission log. Finally, copies often exist on backup tapes.

The lack of laws protecting the privacy of E-mail, combined with the easy access to E-mail files, makes this form of communication a mistake for people interested in secrecy, privacy, and confidentiality. Several examples of E-mail snooping have been documented:

- In one case, a U.S. firm called Drug Company (name intentionally changed) monitored discussions by female employees about setting up an E-mail conference for professional women, assuming that the discussions were being used to start a unionization drive.
- In another case, two former employees working for the American head office of a major Japanese auto maker launched a lawsuit against the auto maker, because they were fired when supervisors read their E-mail.
- Copies of E-mail messages between former national security advisor John Poindexter and Colonel Oliver North were ruled to be admissible evidence in the Iran-Contra court proceedings against Poindexter.
- During an investigation by the Los Angeles police force into the beating of motorist Rodney King, investigators were able to find more than 700 offensive slurs in the officers' E-mail, some of which were used by the commission in its findings.

Personal computer data encryption.

Some hackers have designed log-on programs that look exactly like the real log-on procedure. The crucial difference is that when your ID code and password is entered, the program fakes an error and returns you to the real log-on screen. Your password and other pertinent information is sent to a file that the hacker can retrieve. If this happens to you, check your computer for stray files. It is rumored that IRS agents have been using this procedure for obtaining information.

The Pentagon and the National Security Agency recently conducted "Information War Games" to test their new computer programming. They selected 12,000 major computer systems and in 87% of those they were able to break security in a way that enabled them to copy and alter files.

Several products are available to keep both your personal computer and your local area network secret, private, and confidential. When evaluating a data encryption product, you should look for the following features:

- access control requiring the entry of a user ID and password;
- audit trails to monitor and record attempted security violations and users logging on and off;
- virus protection to check the integrity of system files;
- keyboard lock feature to blank the screen and lock the keyboard when the system is unattended; and
- compatibility with network systems if required.

Internet sites devoted to computer privacy can be found at *http://www.upenn.edu/security-privacy/privacy.html* and *http://www.cias.net/sawicki/privacy.htm*. Internet Usenet newsgroups devoted to PGP and other computer security issues can be found at *alt.security.pgp*, *alt.security*, *alt.security.index*, *comp.risks*, and *comp.security.announce*.

Data encryption contacts:

Czerlau & Associates Limited
Bahamas Financial Centre, 3rd Floor, Shirley & Charlotte Streets
Nassau, Bahamas
tel. 800-226-5703, fax 242-356-0223

- *Services Offered:* corporate services, safekeeping services, telephone calling cards, mail forwarding, books or newsletters, data encryption, security devices, surveillance equipment

---

Fischer International Systems Corp.
4073 Mercantile Avenue
Naples, FL, USA, 33942
tel. 813-643-1500, fax 813-643-3772, toll free 800-237-4510

- *Services Offered:* data encryption, Watchdog PC Data Security Software, Watchdog Armor, and MailSafe, products based on the RSA Public Key Cryptosystem.

Scrambler Systems Corporation
13625 NE 126th Place, Suite 400
Kirkland, WA, USA, 98034
tel. 206-820-7117, fax 206-821-3961

- *Services Offered:* data encryption

Secure Computing Corporation
2675 Long Lake Road
Roseville, MN, USA, 55113
tel. 612-628-2700, fax 612-628-2701, toll free 800-692-5625

- *Services Offered:* data encryption, security devices

ViaCrypt
9033 North 24th Avenue, Suite 7
Phoenix, AZ, USA, 85021-2601
tel. 602-944-0773, fax 602-943-2601, net: viacrypt@acm.org

- *Services Offered:* data encryption

Virtual-Open Network Environment, Inc.
12300 Twinbrook Parkway
Rockville, MD, USA, 20852
toll free 800-881-7090, fax 602-943-2601, net: http://www.v-one.com

- *Services Offered:* data encryption

PERSONAL PRIVACY

The greatest violator of personal secrecy, privacy, and confidentiality in the United States is the United States government, and similarly in Canada, the Canadian government. The same is true in many other countries throughout the world. Even though governments claim that the breaches of privacy are necessary to uphold or enforce laws, you should still be concerned about your personal privacy.

Maintaining telephone privacy.

You may have noticed that your long-distance telephone bill details the date, time, duration, location, and telephone number of every long-distance call you make. In an IRS or Revenue Canada investigation, or in a lawsuit, these records can be easily obtained by investigators, revealing the location of your "secret" bank account.

So how do you contact your offshore bank without leaving a long-distance paper trail? The first, and simplest option is to use a pay phone. It may not be very convenient, but at least it works.

The second option is to use a pre-paid long distance telephone calling card. When using a pre-paid calling card, your card is automatically debited for the cost of the call. No records are added to your phone bill, keeping all of your telephone conversations secret and private. To use the card, you dial a local or toll-free number, input the number on your calling card, and input the long distance telephone number you wish to call. The card is debited for the cost of the call.

The third option is to use a callback service. How does this work? Callback involves the use of one call-in line for all your international telephone calls. When you want to phone somebody you dial the call-in line at no charge to you. Seconds later, the callback company's switch calls you back and you are connected to a world-wide network ready to dial away. The call you make will not be recorded on any local telephone bill.

If you have a personal situation that requires secrecy, don't forget about Caller Identification. Caller ID can capture your phone number, along with your name and address. Imagine calling a phone sex hotline, then being bombarded in the next few weeks with junk mail and phone calls from other hotlines. Now consider the fact that your government may believe that calling a sex line must mean that you lack moral values, and you are now a good target for a tax investigation. The technology is already available for this to happen.

For extreme situations where privacy is a must, some general tips are:

- use a pay phone (or callling card) for sensitive calls;
- rotate calls among several locations;
- do your calling from outside the neighborhood;
- send and receive sensitive faxes from third-party locations; and
- try to use code words.

Maintaining cellular privacy.

Cellular phones compromise your privacy by broadcasting your conversation on an open radio frequency that can be listened to by anyone. Cellular bills detail the date, time, duration, and telephone numbers of both incoming and outgoing calls. When using a cellular phone, follow these common-sense rules:

- never use a cellular phone for confidential conversations (either to receive calls or to make calls);
- never register a cellular phone in your own name – put it in the name of a corporation, or better yet, in the name of an offshore corporation; and
- use a digital cellular phone – at least they can't be monitored by a hobby store scanner.

Don't be fooled by the new "secure" digital cellular phones, as they can still be monitored by the telephone company. For example, the issuing of Canadian licenses for PCS mobile telephone networks was held up because of concerns that the new phones could not be monitored by law enforcement agencies. Apparently, the companies did not have the technical capability to open their telephone switches to the authorities. The ability to monitor these calls directly from the switches is now in place, allowing access to PCS phone conversations.

Maintaining fax privacy.

Fax transmissions work over ordinary telephone lines, and represent a security risk due to the simplicity of tapping into a fax line. Fax lines can be easily intercepted, producing a beautiful hard copy for persons intercepting your fax transmissions. Use codes if possible, and remove the fax header from your fax transmissions. Remember to delete any information identifying yourself as the sender or receiver.

One of the best ways of making your fax transmissions as secure as possible is to use a notebook computer for sending and receiving sensitive documents. You can transport your notebook computer anywhere there is a phone jack, plug it in, and use it as a secure fax device.

Credit card privacy.

Cut down or completely discontinue use of credit cards issued by banks that do not offer bank secrecy. Credit card statements provide a complete picture of your whereabouts and purchasing patterns. Any information available to a credit card company is available to the IRS, Revenue Canada, Inland Revenue, or other government agencies.

Eliminate the use of credit cards issued in your home country. Credit records give investigators an accurate picture of where you have been, and how much you have spent on what. How many times have you returned home from another country without declaring your purchases? Next time, you may not be so lucky. Customs officials inspect the credit card statements of citizens to determine if they have purchased goods and imported them into the country without paying import duties. An offshore credit card would eliminate this invasion of privacy.

Beware of the Mondex Express. Mondex is an electronic cash substitute that is made up of a card (similar to a credit card) and an electronic wallet. They are also known as stored-value cards, smartcards, and electronic wallets. To use Mondex, you must first transfer money from your bank account to your electronic wallet by using the Mondex card in an ATM or Mondex phone. To spend electronic cash, simply slide the card in a participating retailer's card reader (currently on trial in Guelph, ON and Swindon, UK). The electronic wallet acts as a personal ATM that can manage up to five accounts. If two individuals have Mondex wallets, they can transfer funds from one another by simply inserting the Mondex card in each other's electronic wallet and keying in the funds desired.

Unfortunately, this transaction is traceable by the authorities. The Mondex card keeps a 10-transaction rolling log. If you hook up with something other than another individual Mondex wallet, your transaction log can be read by the other party, which is then stored in an electronic database. Worse, if you use Mondex on-line, your past spending habits are now available to any snoop who knows where to look. In fact, Mondex (and similar) cards have the ability to store and track every aspect of your lifestyle, including all of your identification, your medical records, your government records, and anything else.

One way to make it more difficult for undesirables to access your private information is to use two Mondex wallets to make 20 card-to-card transactions, or 10 for each card, to wipe out the 10-transaction rolling log in each Mondex wallet. Then, when you purchase something with the Mondex, it will only transfer information on the previous 10 transactions with the other card, although it is only a matter of time before the Mondex wallets have a memory increase to allow them to store thousands of transactions.

There is one other breach of privacy incorporated in the Mondex card – the ability to track every purchase made to an individual bank account. Which means that if you wish to buy something, and keep it confidential, you're out of luck, because your Mondex card is linked to your bank account, the bank account is linked through your identification numbers to the tax department, and the tax department is linked to every other government agency. There is only one bright spot to all of this – the fact that financial institutions in jurisdictions with bank secrecy will also be able to issue Mondex cards. A "bank secrecy" Mondex card will keep its owner's financial transactions secret, private, and confidential, the way it should be.

Personal financial discretion.

Which investments have your social security number or other identification numbers attached? If your financial privacy is compromised by some of your current investments, consider new investments in "tax haven" countries.

Consider it a priority to establish a credit card from a country with bank secrecy laws. Have the statements either held at the bank for pickup, or sent to a re-mailing service in a country other than your country of residence. Conduct as much of your business in cash as possible.

Use a complicated single stroke signature if possible that is consistent, but unreadable. This allows for greater privacy on documents you may be required to sign.

Do not have your address printed on checks. There is no reason for anyone to know where you live. This is good advice to help reduce financial crime as well.

If you are well known in your community, or if you live in a small town, consider using a bank in another town. This will reduce the possibility of bank employees connecting you with your money.

Secure garbage disposal.

Use a paper shredder to prevent unauthorized individuals from gaining any personal information from your garbage. Burn your shreddings if possible. If your information is important enough, someone will take the time to piece it together.

Personal identification numbers.

Personal identification numbers are very powerful because they are unique, accurate, and widely used. Computer technology makes it possible to use your personal identification number to find and match your information from one database to another. This amounts to "data surveillance," which can pose a serious threat to your secrecy, privacy, and confidentiality.

Stores, financial institutions, and landlords may request your personal identification number to check your credit rating. If you refuse to provide your personal identification number, the organization may deny you the service. If asked for your personal identification number when not required by law, tell the person you prefer not to use your personal identification number and offer an alternate form of identification. Protect yourself from "data surveillance."

United States - Social Security Number - Protect your social security number very carefully. You are required to supply your social security number only to your employer, your bank, savings & loan company, trust company and stock broker when buying financial products or services that report your interest earnings to the government. No one else may demand it.

Canada - Social Insurance Number - Canada's *Privacy Act* sets out strict rules limiting other people's access to your personal information in federal data banks. The law does not prevent provinces or local governments from using your Social Insurance Number (SIN). However, all provinces (except Alberta and PEI) have privacy laws to protect personal information, including SINs, in government files.

Using camouflage passports.

A camouflage passport is a document identical to a legally issued passport, with your photo, personal information, and entry/exit stamps. The only difference between a camouflage passport and a real one is that the camouflage passport is issued from a country that has changed its name, such as British Honduras (now Belize). Why consider carrying an imitation passport? The following are two very good reasons:

- Have you ever checked into a foreign hotel, only to find that the passports of guests are kept in an unlocked drawer by the hotel staff? Any thief can grab the passport of his choice without too much trouble. You can protect yourself with a camouflage passport. The hotel staff certainly don't know the difference between a camouflage passport and a real one, allowing you to keep your legitimate passport with you at all times.
- Imagine yourself on an international flight that is hijacked by terrorists. The first thing the terrorists do is identify their expendable hostages, knowing that they will get an immediate response by threatening to kill an American, Israeli, or British citizen. You feel lucky that you have a camouflage passport, that identifies you as

being a tourist from some small nation that they have never heard of, potentially helping you avoid a nasty situation.

Many international travellers have found camouflage passports to be extremely valuable. An added bonus is that you can travel under cover, assuming an alternate identity once you arrive at your destination. It should be noted that, camouflage passports should never be used for crossing international borders.

Pre-paid calling card sources:

CallMart
FL, USA
tel. 407-455-1511, fax 407-455-1576

- *Services Offered:* telephone calling cards

City Telecom Inc.
1420 Kootenay Street
Vancouver, BC, Canada, V5K 4R1
tel. 604-298-6988, fax 604-298-8116

- *Services Offered:* telephone calling cards

Czerlau & Associates Limited
1701 Woodward Drive, Suite 114
Ottawa, ON, Canada, K2C 0P7
tel. 800-226-5703, fax 613-226-1074

- *Services Offered:* corporate services, safekeeping services, telephone calling cards, mail forwarding, books or newsletters, data encryption, security devices, surveillance equipment

---

Czerlau & Associates Limited
1575 Military Rd.
Niagara Falls, NY, USA, 14304-4706
toll free 800-226-5703, fax 242-356-0223

- *Services Offered:* corporate services, safekeeping services, telephone calling cards, mail forwarding, books or newsletters, data encryption, security devices, surveillance equipment

---

Executive TeleCard, Ltd.
8 Avenue C
Nanuet, NY, USA, 10954
tel. 914-627-2060

- *Services Offered:* telephone calling cards

Incomm / U.S. South Communications
3200 Professional Parkway, Unit 210
Atlanta, GA, USA, 30339
tel. 404-953-1520

- *Services Offered:* telephone calling cards

InterFON
PO.Box 2208, 805 North 10th Street
Fairfield, IA, USA, 52556
tel. 515-472-2044, fax 515-472-0605, fxbak, 515-472-5414

- *Services Offered:* telephone calling cards, Phone Drop international real-time call forwarding system and world-wide prepaid calling cards.

K.Telecom
850 N. Kings Road, Suite 305
West Hollywood, CA, USA, 90069
tel. 213-651-3358, fax 213-651-0240

- *Services Offered:* telephone calling cards

KallBack
417 Second Avenue West
Seattle, WA, USA, 98119
tel. 206-286-5280, fax 206-282-6666, toll free 800-959-KALL

- *Services Offered:* telephone calling cards

PrimeCALL
1520 Eastlake Ave. East, Suite 205
Seattle, WA, USA, 98102
tel. 206-328-0123, fax 206-328-7580, toll free 800-698-1232

- *Services Offered:* telephone calling cards

Telesave / Discount Long Distance
4892 Kodiak Avenue
Santa Barbara, CA, USA, 93111-2831
toll free 800-872-1355, fax 805-683-4792

- *Services Offered:* telephone calling cards, 17.5 Calling Card.

USA Global Link International Headquarters
50 North Third Street
Fairfield, IA, USA, 52556
tel. 515-472-1550, fax 515-472-1620

- *Services Offered:* telephone calling cards

Camouflage passport sources:

Eagle Flight Financial Group
7127 E. Becker Lane
Scottsdale, AZ, USA, 85254
tel. 602-368-7229, fax 602-368-5568, toll free 888-690-7066

- *Services Offered:* travel services & information, mail forwarding, camouflage passports, security devices

Maritime International S.A.
PO.Box 2296, 43C Redcliffe Street
St.John's, Antigua, W.I.
tel. 809-462-2718, fax 809-461-2024

- *Services Offered:* camouflage passports

Paladin Press
PO.Box 1307
Boulder, CO, USA, 80306
tel. 303-443-7250, fax 303-442-8741, toll free 800-872-4993

- *Services Offered:* camouflage passports, books or newsletters

Privacy Reports Inc.
26A Peel Street, Ground Floor
Central, Hong Kong
fax 852-2850-5502

- *Services Offered:* camouflage passports, books or newsletters

Scope International Ltd.
Forestside House, Rowlands Castle
Hants, UK, P09 6EE
tel. 44-1705-631751, fax 44-1705-631322

- *Services Offered:* mail forwarding, camouflage passports, books or newsletters, Mouse Monitor, Passport Report, Tax Exile Report, Tax Haven Report, Banking in Silence.

Sources for travel products and services:

Canadian Society for International Health
170 Laurier Avenue West, Suite 902
Ottawa, ON, Canada, K1P 5V5
tel. 613-230-2654, fax 613-230-8401

- *Services Offered:* travel services & information

Caribbean Tourist Association
20 East 46th Street
New York, NY, USA, 10170
tel. 212-682-0435

- *Services Offered:* travel services & information

Channel Islands Tourist Board
Taurus House, 512 Duplex Ave.
Toronto, ON, Canada, M4R 2E3
tel. 416-485-8724, fax 416-267-7600

- *Services Offered:* travel services & information

Georgetown University School of Medicine
Washington, DC, USA, 20007
tel. 202-687-8672

- *Services Offered:* travel services & information

International Association Medical Assistance to Travellers
40 Regal Road
Guelph, ON, Canada, N1K 1B5
tel. 519-836-0102, fax 519-836-3412

- *Services Offered:* travel services & information

International Travel Health Guide
351 Pleasant Street, Suite 312
Northhampton, MA, USA, 01060
tel. 413-584-0381, fax 413-584-6656, toll free 800-872-8633

- *Services Offered:* travel services & information

Johns Hopkins University
Hampton House, Room 113, 624 N. Broadway
Baltimore, MD, USA, 21205
tel. 410-955-8931

- *Services Offered:* travel services & information, Offers complete range of vaccines, specialization in tropical diseases.

Magellan's
PO.Box 5485
Santa Barbara, CA, USA, 93150-5485
toll free 800-962-4943, fax 805-568-5406

- *Services Offered:* travel services & information, Travel Essentials Catalog.

U.S. Center for Disease Control
GA, USA
tel. 404-332-4559, tel. 404-332-4565

- *Services Offered:* travel services & information

University Hospital Travel Immunization Service
339 Windermere Road, 3rd Floor
London, ON, Canada, N6A 5A5
tel. 519-663-3395, fax 519-663-3743

- *Services Offered:* travel services & information, Travel advice and immunization services.

BUPA International Lifeline
BUPA Centre, 141 Connaught Road West
Hong Kong
tel. 852-5548-1618, fax 852-5548-1848

- *Services Offered:* expat health insurance

BUPA International Lifeline - Head Office
Provident House, Essex Street
London, UK, WC2R 3AX
tel. 44-1713-535212, fax 44-1718-361385

- *Services Offered:* expat health insurance

CLA-Colin Luke & Associates
Barnett Building, Thomas Russell Way, PO.Box 144
Grand Cayman, Cayman Islands, B.W.I.
tel. 345-949-2721, fax 345-949-6000

- *Services Offered:* expat health insurance

ExpaCare Insurance Services
Dukes Court, Duke Street
Woking, Surrey, UK, GU21 5XB
tel. 44-1483-740090, fax 44-1483-776620, tel. 44-1483-251063

- *Services Offered:* expat health insurance

Goodhealth Worldwide Limited
Mill Bay Lane
Horsham, West Sussex, UK, RH12 1TQ
tel. 44-1403-230000, fax 44-1403-268429

- *Services Offered:* expat health insurance

International Health Insurance Danmark
64A Athol Street
Douglas, Isle of Man, IM1 1JE
tel. 44-1624-677412, fax 44-1624-675856

- *Services Offered:* expat health insurance

Medicare International Health Plan
One Hundred Whitechapel
London, UK, E1 1JG
tel. 44-1718-162000, fax 44-1718-162413

- *Services Offered:* expat health insurance

PPP International Health Plan
PPP House, 20 Upperton Road
Eastbourne, East Sussex, UK, N21 1LH
tel. 44-1323-410505, fax 44-1323-432208, tel. 44-1892-503311

- *Services Offered:* expat health insurance

William Russell International Health Care Plans
UK
tel. 44-1483-772245, fax 44-1483-747553

- *Services Offered:* expat health insurance

INFORMATION SOURCES

There are many excellent books and newsletters that provide information on tax havens, offshore investing, and personal privacy issues. The following companies offer a wide range of publications.

Information sources and contacts:

Alternative Inphormation
PO.Box 4
Carthage, TX, USA, 75633-0004
tel. 903-693-7824, fax 903-693-7824

- *Services Offered:* books or newsletters

Delta Press Ltd.
PO.Box 1625, 215 South Washington Street
El Dorado, AR, USA, 71731
tel. 501-862-4984, fax 501-862-9671, toll free 800-852-4445

- *Services Offered:* books or newsletters

Eden Press
PO.Box 8410
Fountain Valley, CA, USA, 92728

- *Services Offered:* books or newsletters, Books on every aspect of protection, security, and survival.

Expat World
PO.Box 1341
Raffles City, Singapore, 9117
tel. 65-466-3680, fax 65-466-7006, fax 65-339-7048

- *Services Offered:* books or newsletters

FEAR (Forfeiture Endangers American Rights)
20 Sunnyside, Suite A204
Mill Valley, CA, USA, 94941
tel. 415-380-9108

- *Services Offered:* books or newsletters

Freedom Publications
PO. Box 183
Douglas, Isle of Man
fax 44-1624-801380

- *Services Offered:* books or newsletters

International Bank Research
27 Lamar Park Center, Unit A
Corpus Christi, TX, USA, 78411
tel. 512-242-3170, fax 512-242-9768

- *Services Offered:* books or newsletters, Worldwide Directory of International Banks.

Mark Skousen Newsletter
PO.Box 2488
Winter Park, FL, USA, 32790

- *Services Offered:* books or newsletters

National Taxpayers Union
325 Pennsylvania Avenue Southeast
Washington, DC, USA, 20003
tel. 202-543-1300, fax 202-546-2086

- *Services Offered:* books or newsletters

Offshore Finance
1 Britannia Place, Bath Street
St.Helier, Jersey, Channel Islands
tel. 44-1534-25517, fax 44-1534-38889

- *Services Offered:* books or newsletters

Offshore Financial Review
fax 44-171-242-2439

- *Services Offered:* books or newsletters

Paladin Press
PO.Box 1307
Boulder, CO, USA, 80306
tel. 303-443-7250, fax 303-442-8741, toll free 800-872-4993

- *Services Offered:* camouflage passports, books or newsletters

Privacy Reports Inc.
26A Peel Street, Ground Floor
Central, Hong Kong
fax 852-2850-5502

- *Services Offered:* camouflage passports, books or newsletters

---

R.L. Polk & Company
1155 Brewery Park Blvd.
Detroit, MI, USA, 48207

- *Services Offered:* books or newsletters, International Bank Directory

---

Scope International Ltd.
Forestside House, Rowlands Castle
Hants, UK, P09 6EE
tel. 44-1705-631751, fax 44-1705-631322

- *Services Offered:* books or newsletters

Terra Libra
2430 E. Roosevelt #998EP3
Phoenix, AZ, USA, 85008
tel. 602-265-7627, fax 602-234-1281

- *Services Offered:* books or newsletters

The Freebooter
PO.Box 602
St.Peter Port, Guernsey, Channel Islands, GY1 6BZ
fax 44-0171-223-4295

- *Services Offered:* books or newsletters, The Freebooter newsletter for PT's.

The Freedom, Wealth & Privacy Report
2 Old Brompton Road, Suite 685, South Kensington
London, UK, SW7 3DQ
tel. 44-1714-139115, fax 44-1715-814445

- *Services Offered:* books or newsletters, The Freedom, Wealth & Privacy Report newsletter.

The Privacy Reporter
1575 Military Road
Niagara Falls, NY, USA, 14304-4706
tel. 905-333-3807, fax 905-333-2678

- *Services Offered:* books or newsletters, Financial Privacy Report newsletter

---

The Privacy Reporter
828 Elrick Place
Victoria, BC, Canada, V9A 4T1
tel. 250-383-1877, fax 250-385-0010

- *Services Offered:* books or newsletters, The Privacy Reporter newsletter

---

The Private Planner
Nauenstrasse 63a , 4052 Basel
Switzerland
tel. 41-61-272-2450, fax 41-610272-2502

- *Services Offered:* books or newsletters, The Private Planner newsletter.

The Private Planner
9986 N. Newport Highway, Suite 286
Spokane, WA, USA, 99218
tel. 509-325-9167, fax 509-326-8690, toll free 800-821-6075

- *Services Offered:* books or newsletters, The Private Planner newsletter.

Travel Document Advisors (UK) Ltd.
28 Grosvenor Street
London, UK, W1X 9FE
tel. 44-1719-179624, fax 44-1719-176002, toll free 800-844-9994

- *Services Offered:* books or newsletters

Uphill Publishing
190 Attwell Drive, Suite 400
Toronto, ON, Canada, M9W 6H8
toll free 800-363-4737, fax 416-798-2715

- *Services Offered:* books or newsletters, Tax Haven Roadmap, Take Your Money and Run, My Blue Haven

---

Voth Publication
215 Perreault Crescent
Saskatoon, SK, Canada, S7K 6B1
tel. 306-242-3193, toll free 800-815-5650

- *Services Offered:* books or newsletters, 10 Secrets Revenue Canada Doesn't Want You To Know!

SECURITY & SURVEILLANCE

There are some incredible products available to help you protect your privacy. These products range from bug detection and surveillance equipment to military and law enforcement technology. These contacts will help you find what you're looking for.

Security & Surveillance contacts:

Cabela's
812 13th Avenue
Sidney, NE, USA, 69160
tel. 800-237-4444, fax 308-254-2200, toll free 800-237-8888

- *Services Offered:* security devices

Communication Control Systems of NY
675 Third Ave., Suite 408
New York, NY, USA, 10017
tel. 212-557-3040, fax 212-983-1278

- *Services Offered:* surveillance equipment, Truth phone, recording system, hidden video, and scrambling systems.

Counter Spy Shop
360 Madison Avenue, 6th Floor
New York, NY, USA, 10017
tel. 212-557-3040, fax 212-983-1278, toll free 800-722-4490

- *Services Offered:* security devices, surveillance equipment

Counter Spy Shop
62 South Audley Street
London, UK, W1
tel. 071-408-0287, fax 071-629-9538

- *Services Offered:* security devices, surveillance equipment

Eagle Flight Financial Group
7127 E. Becker Lane
Scottsdale, AZ, USA, 85254
tel. 602-368-7229, fax 602-368-5568, toll free 888-690-7066

- *Services Offered:* travel services & information, mail forwarding, camouflage passports, security devices

---

Eavesdropping Detection Equipment
2480 Niagara Falls Boulevard
Tonawanda, NY, USA, 14150
tel. 716-691-3476, fax 716-691-0604

- *Services Offered:* surveillance equipment

Freedom Catalogue
UK
tel. 44-1225-427759, fax 44-1225-427759

- *Services Offered:* surveillance equipment

HiTek
490 El Camino Real
Redwood City, CA, USA, 94063
toll free 800-546-4448

- *Services Offered:* surveillance equipment, Bug detection equipment.

Information Unlimited
PO.Box 716
Amherst, NH, USA, 03031-0716
tel. 603-673-4730, fax 603-672-5406, toll free 800-221-1705

- *Services Offered:* surveillance equipment, Night vision equipment.

Johnson Smith Company
4514 19th Street Court East, PO.Box 2500
Bradenton, FL, USA, 34206-5500
tel. 813-747-2356, fax 813-746-7896

- *Services Offered:* books or newsletters, surveillance equipment

---

Major Surplus & Survival Inc.
435 W. Alondra
Gardena, CA, USA, 90248
tel. 310-324-8855, toll free 800-441-8855

- *Services Offered:* security devices, surveillance equipment

---

Quark Spy Centre
537 Third Ave.
New York, NY, USA, 10016
tel. 212-889-1808, fax 212-447-5510, toll free 800-343-6443

- *Services Offered:* security devices, surveillance equipment

---

Safe S.L.
Apartado 2227
Andorra la Vella, Andorra
tel. 376-837546, fax 376-837546

- *Services Offered:* security devices

Scanner Master
PO.Box 428
Newton Highlands, MA, USA, 02161
tel. 508-655-6300, fax 508-655-2350, toll free 800-722-6701

- *Services Offered:* surveillance equipment

Southern Ordnance
PO.Box 279
Babson Park, FL, USA, 33827
tel. 813-638-2486, fax 813-638-2499

- *Services Offered:* security devices, surveillance equipment

---

Sportsman's Guide
411 Farwell Avenue, PO.Box 239
St.Paul, MN, USA, 55075-0239
toll free 800-888-3006, fax 800-333-6933, toll free 800-888-5222

- *Services Offered:* security devices

Spy Supply
7 Colby Court, Suite 215
Bedford, NH, USA, 03110
tel. 617-327-7272

- *Services Offered:* security devices, surveillance equipment

---

The Edge Company
PO.Box 826
Brattleboro, VT, USA, 05302
toll free 800-732-9976, fax 802-257-2787

- *Services Offered:* security devices, surveillance equipment

---

The Privacy Connection
23133 Ventura Boulevard, Suite 103
Woodland Hills, CA, USA, 91364
tel. 818-225-8007, fax 818-225-7516

- *Services Offered:* surveillance equipment

The Survival Center
PO.Box 234
McKenna, WA, USA, 98558
tel. 206-458-6778, toll free 800-321-2900

- *Services Offered:* books or newsletters, security devices

U.S. Cavalry
2855 Centennial Ave.
Radcliff, KY, USA, 40160-9000
toll free 800-777-7732, fax 502-352-0266, tel. 502-351-1164

- *Services Offered:* security devices, surveillance equipment, military and adventure catalog.

USI Corporation
PO.Box 2052
Melbourne, FL, USA, 32902
tel. 407-725-1000, fax 407-727-1179

- *Services Offered:* surveillance equipment, Electronic lockpicks and tools.

CHAPTER 5

YOUR OFFSHORE STRUCTURE

There are several effective methods to utilize offshore tax havens for a wide variety of reasons. Following you will find outlines covering the most basic offshore bank account, company structure, and trust structure. Also included is an overview of a captive insurance structure. Care must be taken to ensure that using these structures does not violate the laws of the country in which you reside, or of which you are a citizen. The concepts discussed in this section are very general, and legal or tax professionals in your area should be able to create an offshore structure that complies with applicable legislation.

Common applications:

1. **Investments** - Using a properly set-up offshore entity, it is possible to earn interest, dividends, and capital-gains in a tax-free environment. This provides several advantages, including the ability to trade on international markets with complete anonymity. Generally dividend and interest payments would be subject to local taxation, however, there are a number of offshore jurisdictions which do not levy any type of taxation on these investments. To provide additional diversification, these investments may be held in most major currencies.
2. **Portfolio Management** - Many of the world's most outstanding investment opportunities are available only to those outside North America. Because of this, we also find that many of the world's most outstanding portfolio managers are also based in various "business-friendly" offshore jurisdictions. With today's communications technology, portfolio management decisions can be made on a real-time basis from just about anywhere around the globe. These benefits in turn accrue to the offshore entity.

3. **Professional Services** - Professional services entities are often established offshore by individuals who receive fees as consultants, authors, designers, entertainers, and so on, on the basis that they may have assigned or contracted with an offshore company the right to receive those fees. The offshore employment company may not have to pay tax on profits, which can be reinvested in a tax free climate to generate further income for the offshore entity. Payments to the individuals concerned can be structured in such a way as to minimize their tax liabilities.
4. **Personal Royalties** - Artists, authors, inventors, musicians, and actors are in the fortunate position of being able to assign royalty contracts to an offshore entity. This allows them to receive royalties on artistic works, books, inventions, music, and movies in a low tax environment, giving the advantage of being able to accumulate significant wealth offshore. Although the offshore entity may be subject to withholding taxes, this can be minimized by using appropriate tax treaty jurisdictions.
5. **Consulting and Employment** - Experts in many fields undertake short term contracts in different countries which can cause taxation and pension fund difficulties. By forming an offshore company the expert can be employed directly by that company, with fees paid to the company rather than directly to the expert. Similar arrangements are suitable for sports and media professionals.
6. **Property Owning** - Offshore property owning entities can offer quite significant tax advantages, including the avoidance of inheritance tax, capital gains tax, and complex probate procedures, depending upon the country in which the property itself is located. An additional benefit is the ease of sale achieved by transferring the ownership of the offshore entity rather than transferring the property owned by that entity, thereby reducing property purchase costs to buyers.
7. **Holding Company** - Holding companies have a number of personal and business applications. For example, holding companies may be used for the holding of precious metals and valuable collections. An individual with assets in a number of countries may

wish to hold the assets through a personal holding company to maintain complete privacy and to reduce or eliminate inheritance tax, capital gains tax and expensive probate fees. In many cases the sale of assets can be easily facilitated by transferring the shares in the company rather than transferring the assets owned by the company. Holding companies can also be used to finance the operation of subsidiaries in various countries so that the subsidiaries, for example, obtain the benefit of tax deductions on interest paid. If the holding company is located in an offshore area where there is no corporate taxation and no requirement that dividends must be paid, then the profits which are accumulated in the tax free climate can be used to fund the requirements of various domestic and offshore subsidiaries.

8. **Patents, Copyrights, and Licensing** - Typically an offshore entity would purchase (or be assigned the right to use) a patent, copyright, trademark or know-how by its original holders with the power to sub-licence. The offshore entity can then enter into agreements with licensees around the world, licensees who will be able to exploit that intellectual property right in various countries. It is preferable to acquire a patent at the patent pending stage, before it becomes very valuable, so that the capital payment for the acquisition can be set at a lower amount. Often royalties paid out of a high tax area attract withholding taxes at source. In many cases withholding taxes can be minimized by taking advantage of double taxation agreements (tax treaty tax havens), allowing a reduction in the rate of tax withheld.
9. **Import/Export** - An importing or exporting firm can take advantage of arms-length trading firms established in low tax offshore jurisdictions. By routing import/export transactions through the arms-length trading firm, profits arising out of the difference between the purchase and sale price would be accumulated in the offshore jurisdiction.
10. **Sales/Re-Invoicing** - An offshore company acting as a "middleman entity" may sell goods for related or unrelated parties throughout the world, accumulating profits in a tax free area for working capital or reinvestment.

11. **Management Services** - An offshore corporation can perform various management and administration services for individuals or companies in the U.S. and Canada, taking advantage of deductible tax write-offs on management and administration expenses.
12. **Accounts Receivable Factoring** - Often when products or services are sold, they are sold with terms allowing payment at some time in the future. A common practice is to sell the accounts receivables to an offshore "factoring" firm. The factor pays immediate cash for the receivable, at a discount based upon the length of the collection terms. For example, a net 60-day receivable may be sold at an 8% discount to a factoring firm, which will then collect the receivable in 60 days, retaining the 8% profit in the offshore jurisdiction. The benefit to the domestic operation is immediate cashflow, while the factoring firm earns tax-free income.
13. **Leasing** - Capital equipment may be purchased and leased by an offshore leasing company, taking advantage of deductible tax write-offs on lease payments. A leasing contract is usually structured with an interest rate that allows the leasing company to retain a profit. Adjusting the rate of interest will naturally determine the leasing firm's earnings. By locating the leasing firm in a low tax jurisdiction, these profits can be retained largely free of taxation. Of course, for the domestic company, lease payments are deductible under Canadian and US tax laws.
14. **Advertising** - For domestic companies that allocate a large portion of revenues to marketing and advertising, it may be beneficial to use the services of a marketing and advertising agency located in a low tax jurisdiction. Both the standard advertising agency commissions and the additional revenues generated by marketing activities can be retained by the offshore advertising agency at a reduced rate of tax. The marketing and advertising fees paid by domestic corporations are deductible under Canadian and US tax laws.
15. **Shipping** - Shipping companies are often established offshore to eliminate direct or indirect taxation on shipping. Profits on these shipping and ship charter operations can then be accumulated tax

free. Tax and legal requirements generally dictate that the offshore company owning a shipping vessel should be incorporated in the jurisdiction whose flag the ship flies. Owners of private vessels can take advantage of inexpensive yacht registration facilities available through many offshore centres.

16. **Captive Insurance** - In situations where the risk is quantified and known to either direct industry members or a group of companies in the same industry, it is often financially worthwhile to investigate the options presented by retaining the risks through a captive insurance company. In other cases, captive insurance companies are ideally suited for the insurance of risks which might otherwise be available only at prohibitive premiums.

OFFSHORE BANK ACCOUNT

The simplest, and least effective method of structuring your offshore activities is to open an offshore bank account in your own name. Although there is some degree of secrecy and confidentiality associated with such an account, provided the account is opened in a jurisdiction with bank secrecy, your only layer of "protection" is that jurisdiction's bank secrecy legislation.

When opening a personal offshore bank account, the following information will be required:

i] Bankers letter of introduction/reference (on bank's letterhead) for each signatory.

ii] Positive identification (copy of passport photo page or photo driving license) of all officers and signatories to the account.

iii] Witnessing of signatures by bank official or notary public.

iv] Signed and witnessed fax indemnity agreement.

v] International money order to open the account.

When opening an offshore corporate bank account, the bank will most likely ask for the following information, although some items are optional at some banks:

i] Certificate of incorporation.

ii] Copy of articles of association.

iii] Copy of memorandum of association.

iv] Bankers letter of introduction/reference (on bank's letterhead) for each signatory.

v] Positive identification (copy of passport photo page or photo driving license) of all officers and signatories to the account.

vi] Witnessing of signatures by bank official or notary public.

vii] Fax indemnity agreement with company seal.

viii] International money order to open the account.

The positive identification is required as part of the "know your customer" regulations adopted by financial institutions around the world.

This information is held confidentially in jurisdictions that offer banking and corporate secrecy, such as Anguilla, Antigua, Austria, Bahamas, Belize, British Virgin Islands, Cayman Islands, Cook Islands, Gibraltar, Liechtenstein, Luxembourg, Malta, Nauru, Panama, St.Kitts & Nevis, Switzerland, and the Turks and Caicos Islands.

Personal offshore bank account.

In this example, an individual opens an offshore bank account. Through this account, all normal banking activities can take place, including deposits, withdrawals, and wire transfers using the offshore bank's correspondent network. A debit card may be issued by the offshore bank, providing the account holder with immediate access to funds.

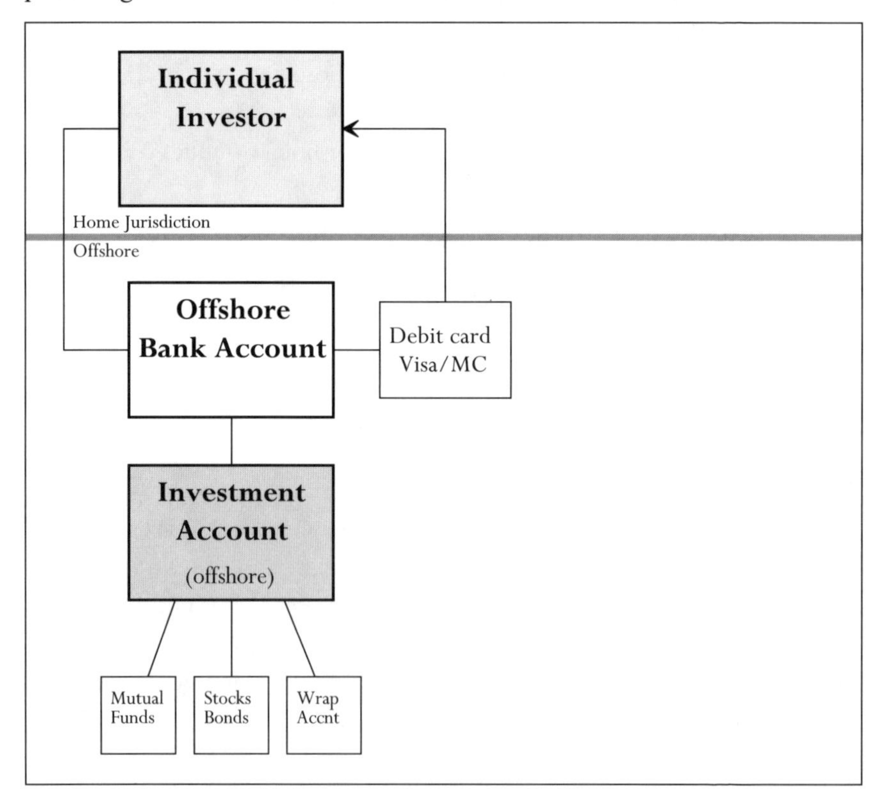

OFFSHORE COMPANY

Historically, the primary attraction of an incorporated company was to limit the liability of the investors to the extent of their investment. Limited liability is based on the principle that the company is a distinct legal entity from its shareholders. Creditors are, therefore, only able to attack the assets of the company, rather than the assets of the company's investors. Because the company is legally distinct from its shareholders, tax planning possibilities are immediately established.

In many countries, tax rates vary between individuals and corporations. It is possible that a shareholder resident in a high tax jurisdiction may hold an interest in a company incorporated in a low tax jurisdiction. Taking advantage of low tax jurisdictions allows certain opportunities for tax avoidance and tax deferral.

Offshore Limited Companies offer numerous advantages and benefits when formed in a jurisdiction with strict bank secrecy laws. Factors to consider when choosing a jurisdiction include:

1. Taxation. Low tax is good, no tax is better.
2. Confidentiality is very important. It is best to choose a jurisdiction with formal bank and commercial secrecy laws in place.
3. Legal System. English Common Law avoids forced-heirship laws, although some jurisdictions have modified statutes to avoid forced-heirship laws.
4. Look for a statute in place that prevents a new government or political party from implementing a sudden "new tax" within a certain limitation period.
5. Government stability is important. The jurisdiction chosen should be free from violent political swings or possible military coup.
6. There should be a good selection of qualified lawyers, accountants, investment advisors, and bankers. Be sure they can speak your language.
7. A developed infrastructure is necessary. It is helpful to use a jurisdiction in a time zone close to your own.

8. There should also be good telecommunications links and travel connections.

Advantages and benefits of forming an offshore limited company.

1. **Secrecy** - The beneficial ownership of an offshore company incorporated in a jurisdiction with secrecy laws can not be disclosed. Shares may be held by nominees representing the beneficial owners under a management agreement. This ensures that the names of the beneficial owners never become a matter of public record, nor are they divulged to third parties.
2. **Security** - The ownership of assets by an offshore company guarantees that these assets will be protected by the courts in that jurisdiction. This helps to protect the offshore company's assets against attack by foreign courts or government expropriation and confiscation.
3. **Taxation** - The absence of income, corporate or capital gains taxes ensures that the assets of the company will enjoy maximum growth.
4. **Management** - The companies laws in most jurisdictions require compliance with certain regulations to safeguard the assets. Many offshore firms are are bound by these regulations, providing safety to the company's assets.

Simple corporate structure.

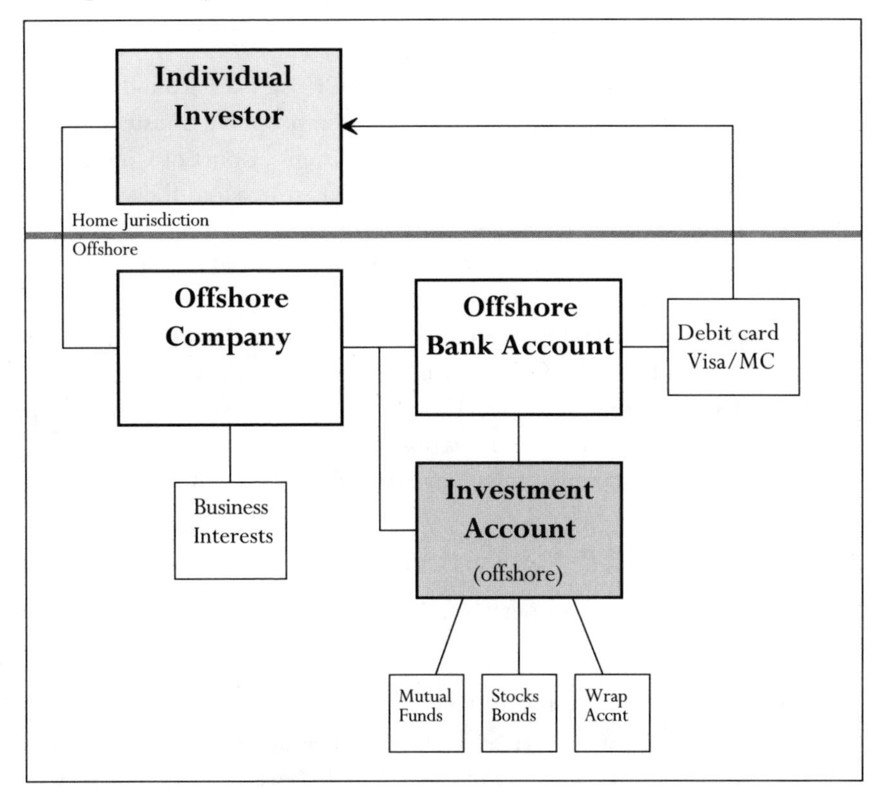

OFFSHORE TRUST

The Trust concept was developed in the British Isles around the Middle Ages, as a means of avoiding feudal taxes on property transfers and inheritance. It was the Court of Chancery (the King's "Court of Conscience" overseen by Churchmen) that developed the Trust to avoid the application of rigid laws relating to the succession of property. The Trust allowed the owner to pass legal title to a Trustee on behalf of his wife, child, or other person as Beneficiary. Trusts were not known in Roman or Civil Law, although they are becoming increasingly more popular, thanks to the Hague Convention of July 1, 1985. The Trust is a concept conceived and developed as a means of separating legal ownership from beneficial ownership. Trust law is found in all countries whose law is based on British common law, and in civil-law countries that have passed laws recognizing Trusts.

Components of a Trust.

A Trust is a right of property (real or personal), held by one party for the benefit of another.

There are four principal components to a Trust:

- The "Settlor" of a Trust is a person who creates the Trust by providing the initial property of the Trust. A Trust is created usually by means of a Declaration of Trust.
- The "Trustee" is the person who holds title for the benefit of another person. The Trustee may be an individual or a corporation.
- The "Beneficiary" is the person or persons who will benefit from the assets held by the Trust.
- The "Trust Asset" is the property being held by the Trust.

Occasionally there is a fifth component:

- The "Protector" who ensures the Settlor's wishes are carried out. The Protector may be an individual or a corporation.

Under a Trust, the original owner (Settlor) of the assets places the assets in the Trust, which is administered by the Trustee, who may be an individual, bank, trust company, etc. The Trustee becomes legal owner of the assets while the Beneficiary becomes the beneficial owner. Therefore, the ownership of the Trust Asset is vested in the Trustee who has no right or ability to enjoy the property, while those who do enjoy the property (the Beneficiaries) do not legally own it.

Types of Trusts.

Depending upon the result required, there are several types of Trusts that can be used to accomplish various goals, such as:

1. **Asset Protection Trust** - A form of Trust which provides the Settlor and the Beneficiaries with protection from creditors. To ensure creditor protection, an Asset Protection Trust should be established in a jurisdiction with specific asset protection legislation.
2. **Non-Discretionary (Fixed) Trust** - A form of Trust where the interest of the Beneficiaries is fixed, leaving the Trustee with no discretion as to how to distribute the income and/or capital of the Trust.
3. **Discretionary Trust** - A form of Trust where the interest of the Beneficiaries is not fixed, leaving the Trustee with the discretion as to how to distribute the income and/or capital of the Trust.
4. **Protective Trust** - A form of Trust where the object of the Trust is to provide income and/or capital to a Beneficiary suffering from some form of disability.
5. **Charitable Trust** - A form of Trust where one of the Beneficiaries is a charity or a charitable foundation.
6. **Spousal Trust** - A form of Trust where the only Beneficiary is the spouse of the Settlor.
7. **Revocable Trust** - A form of Trust where the Settlor has the ability at any time to revoke the Trust and, as a result, have title in the Trust Assets revert back to the Settlor.
8. **Irrevocable Trust** - A form of Trust where once the Settlor has transferred the property to the Trust, the Settlor has no ability to have the property transferred back to the Settlor.

A valid Trust requires at least two separate and distinct parties. It is not possible for the same person to be both the sole Trustee and the sole Beneficiary, since it is an established point of law that an individual cannot be under an equitable obligation to himself.

How does a Trust eliminate estate and inheritance taxes?

If a Trust is properly established, all Trust property belongs to the Trustee. Therefore, it does not form part of one's estate for estate tax purposes, or part of ones assets for wealth tax purposes. The death of the Settlor or the Trustee does not affect the ownership of the Trust assets. It cannot be included in an estate until the Trust terminates and the Trust assets are distributed to the Beneficiaries.

Can a Trust protect against creditors?

In most jurisdictions that offer bank secrecy, the Trustee is not allowed to disclose to creditors (or anyone else) what assets are held by the Trust, nor can the Trust be required to transfer assets to foreign creditors. An attack on the assets held by your foreign Trust will allow time to move the assets to another jurisdiction. Offshore Trusts do not, however, protect assets located in your home country, such as business holdings or real estate. There is nothing a foreign Trustee can do to keep assets away from creditors in your home country.

Fraudulent conveyance statutes prevent transfers to Trusts with the explicit intention to defraud current or anticipated creditors. The statute of limitations varies with the jurisdiction where the Trust was formed, but usually it is 2 years. After this time, the Trust will protect the assets from judgements, divorce, creditors, malpractice claims, lawsuit, and bankruptcy. If the establishment of a Trust contributes to bankruptcy, the Trust may be terminated as a fraudulent transfer to defraud creditors.

Trust assets are not liable for the personal debts of the Trustee. If the Trust funds are used to pay personal expenses of the Settlor or Trustee, or if Trust funds are commingled with personal funds, a court may rule that the Trust should be terminated. Proper management is critical to the effectiveness of the Trust.

Advantages and benefits of using a Trust.

Offshore Trusts offer several advantages and benefits when formed in a country with strict bank secrecy laws. To ensure complete compliance, research the following points with the offshore bank or trust company you wish to deal with. Advantages and benefits are as follows:

Holdings - The Trust may be used to hold any assets, such as cash, stocks, bonds, mutual funds, property (usually held through a company), or other assets.

Anonymity - The Trust deed is not a public document (unless it is registered, such as certain Asset Protection Trusts) and the Beneficiaries are known only to the Trustee. This ensures that the names of the Settlor and Beneficiaries will not be divulged to outside parties. Naturally, the use of an underlying investment company will provide even greater secrecy.

Security - Since your assets have to be delivered to the Trustee, you must have complete confidence in your chosen Trustee. The assets of the Trust may be held either directly by the Trustee or through an underlying investment company anywhere in the world. The assets may be held in the name of the Trustee or through nominees, ensuring greater security and anonymity. Provisions are also usually made for the Trust to be moved to another jurisdiction in the event of war, riot, or civil strife. While it may not be necessary to use these powers, they do give added security.

Planned Distribution - The Trust ensures that your assets will be administered in accordance with your wishes and will eventually be distributed as required. This will also prevent any forced heirship distribution. Therefore, it is not necessary for you to use any other estate planning techniques, such as wills, making periodic gifts, arranging for assets to be held in joint tenancies or leaving informal instructions. All these methods are complex, unreliable, or not legally enforceable and result in a loss of confidentiality and control.

The Trust mechanism also enables the Settlor to lay down specific instructions for the management and/or distribution of the assets after his death. For example, he may specify the following:

- income to his widow during her lifetime with no access to capital;

- income to the children when they reach the age of 21 and restricted access to capital when they reach age 25; and
- on their death before age 25, income to grandchildren, or distributions to other parties.

There are no stipulations as to distribution of assets on death, so the Settlor may specify any criteria he wishes.

Financial - The use of a completely tax free jurisdiction ensures that the value of the assets will not be eroded by probate costs and inheritance taxes. In addition, the income and capital of the Trust will also accumulate without suffering any additional income or capital gains taxes.

Flexibility - The Trust may be tailored to your specific needs and may even be varied as personal circumstances change. When the Settlor creates a Trust, he writes a "Letter of Wishes" to the Trustee, which describes the Settlor's intentions, the objects of the Trust, and his requirements as to the distribution of the assets. It is important to note that the Settlor may at any time vary the terms of the Trust or create an entirely new set of requirements of distribution.

Control - While it is necessary that the assets must be delivered to the Trustee, you may retain a right to direct investment strategy and may also retain a degree of control through a beneficial interest in the Trust or through the powers of a Trust Protector.

Political - The Trust may be used to protect the wealth of individuals residing in politically sensitive areas of the world. Passing the legal control of the assets to a Trust can allow the preservation and accumulation of wealth without exposure to adverse political risk.

Probate Disclosure - By placing the ownership of assets in a Trust, you can determine how and to whom these assets are to transfer to at death, avoiding public disclosure during probate.

Taxation - Business owners may find it beneficial to place some of their shares in developing companies into a Trust, in such a way that capital gains tax would be avoided on a future disposition of those shares (for example, if the business is successful and is acquired or goes public).

Currency Controls - Assets can be protected from confiscation, enforced repatriation, or loss of freedom of choice if currency controls are introduced in your home country.

Sample letter of wishes.

A typical Letter of Wishes, provided by Standard Private Trust Ltd. in Providenciales, Turks & Caicos Islands, reads as follows:

Standard Private Trust Ltd.
Caribbean Place, Leeward Highway
Providenciales, Turks & Caicos Islands, BWI

Dear Sirs,
You are the Trustees of the settlement dated _______ and known as the "Trust". Under the terms of the Trust you are empowered to administer the assets of the Trust and to distribute them to the beneficiaries as you in your sole and absolute discretion think fit. In the exercise of your duties it will assist you to know of my wishes with regard to the administration of the assets of the Trust.

During my lifetime I request that you consider my wishes relevant to any action you propose in the administration of the Trust or the distribution of its assets. In the event of my death I propose that the Trust assets be administered in accordance with the wishes of _______.

In the event of the death of _______, or if _______ should predecease me then, upon my death, I propose that the Trust assets be divided equally between my children. Each child who survives both _______ and myself should receive his or her portion upon attaining the age of 25.

In the event of any child predeceasing _______ and myself, without leaving issue, his or her portion should be divided equally among the other children or other issue per stirpes. In the event of any child predeceasing _______ and myself, leaving issue, such child's share should be distributed to his or her children or other issue per stripes.

Yours faithfully, _______.

Simple Trust Structure.

The following is a simple Trust structure that can shelter and retain family assets by providing confidentiality and anonymity, protecting against unreasonable income and capital gains taxes, possible forced heirship regulations, and claims that may be made against the Trust assets. This simple Trust structure provides an ideal asset protection, estate planning, and tax minimization vehicle.

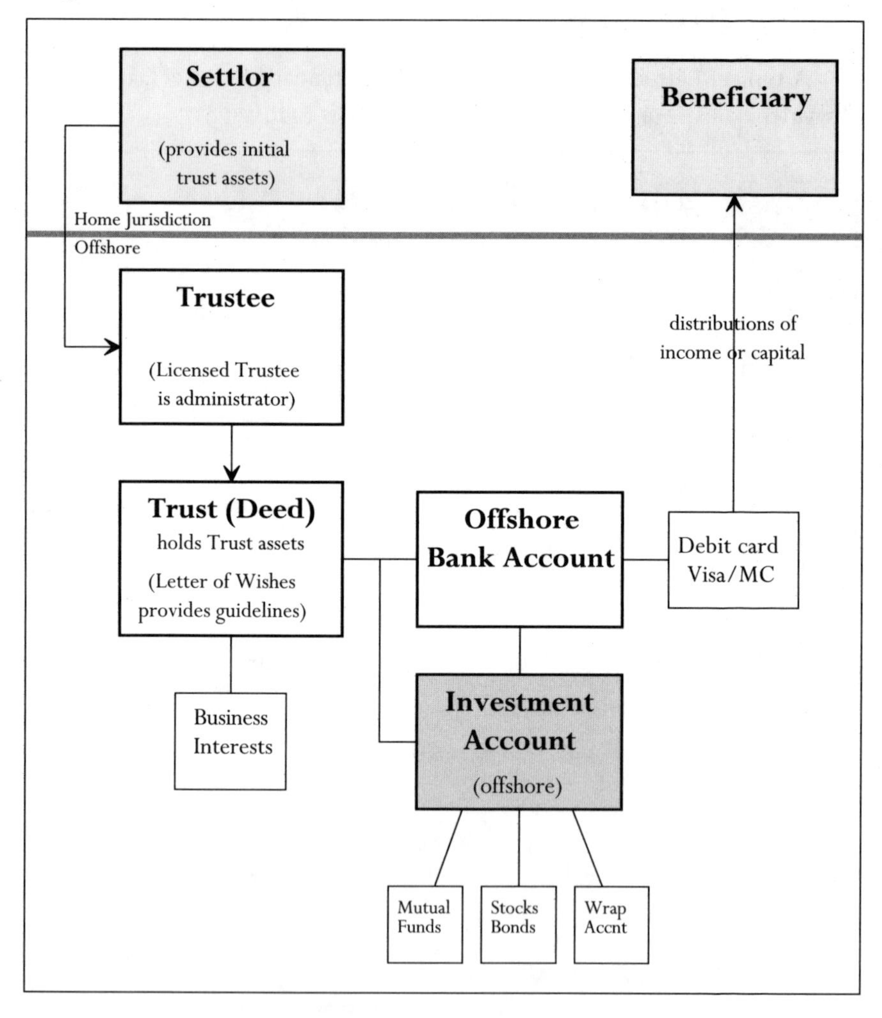

OFFSHORE CAPTIVE INSURANCE COMPANY

Many benefits, including substantial savings in premiums, can be achieved by the risk management technique of establishing a captive insurance company. Internationally, there has been substantial growth in this industry since the mid-1970's, with thousands of captive insurance companies formed world-wide. Captive insurance companies now play a significant role in the international insurance market. Several offshore locations have developed into established insurance centres.

Advantages and benefits of establishing an offshore captive insurance company.

The advantages and benefits of industrial or commercial groups forming a captive insurance company to underwrite some or all of their risk include:

- insurance at a lower cost;
- turning a cost centre (insurance expenditure) into a profit centre;
- gaining access to the more cost effective reinsurance market;
- having the ability to build reserves from pre-tax earnings;
- enhancing group cash flow;
- providing coverage not otherwise available;
- consolidation of group insurance programs; and
- acquiring the operations of other insurance companies to increase assets and reduce risk.

Premiums paid to insurance companies include a significant mark-up to meet the insurer's general expenses such as marketing overheads, profits, and commission payments to brokers. Premiums are usually paid annually in advance, with the insurance company retaining the premium until claims are paid, earning investment income that is not usually passed back to the client company.

Creating a captive insurance company enables the industrial or commercial group to "capture" the profits obtained by the insurer from pure underwriting and investment income, without the loss of coverage. Effectively this allows the captive insurance company to have direct access to the reinsurance markets where it will have the opportunity to secure coverage at more favorable rates.

A captive insurance company can also build up reserves to fund claims on a tax deductible basis with insurance premiums, rather than out of after-tax profits. Insurance costs can also be related to the claims' experience of the group, which can often lead to lower rates than are available on the open market.

In some cases, traditional insurance companies have been unable or unwilling to provide corporate insurance buyers with the coverage they need, or are unable to provide the required policy wordings. A captive insurance company can produce an insurance policy with the wording specifically designed to suit the parent and its affiliates, or to cover risks that conventional insurance companies may find unacceptable.

Finally, the establishment of a captive insurance company provides the industrial or commercial group with an opportunity to diversify its operations into insurance services. The choice of a tax-efficient offshore location also enables the reserves of the captive insurance company to accumulate at a faster rate than those of a domestic insurance company.

CHAPTER 6

SELECTING A TAX HAVEN

The surest way to avoid confiscatory taxes is to not own assets or receive any income. Choosing the wrong jurisdiction may grant you this wish when you find out all of your assets have disappeared, or have been "nationalized" by a new government or political party.

Tax Haven Roadmap explores each of the following tax haven jurisdictions in full detail to ensure that you can make an informed decision:

- Anguilla
- Antigua & Barbuda
- Austria
- Bahamas
- Barbados
- Belize
- Bermuda
- British Virgin Islands
- Cayman Islands
- Channel Islands - Guernsey and Jersey
- Cook Islands
- Gibraltar
- Hong Kong
- Isle of Man
- Liechtenstein
- Luxembourg
- Malta
- Monaco
- Nauru
- Niue
- Panama
- St.Kitts & Nevis
- Switzerland
- Turks & Caicos Islands

For each tax haven the following questions will be reviewed in detail:

- Does the country have any banking or corporate secrecy legislation?
- Does the country have a long history of legal stability?
- Is there an income tax in the country?
- Are there any other taxes in the country?
- Does the country maintain exchange controls?
- Does the country maintain any tax treaties?
- Does the country allow for the formation of corporate entities?
- Does the country allow the formation of Trusts?
- Does the country allow the formation of Captive Insurance Companies?
- Does the country allow the formation of Private Banking Companies?

A comprehensive list of contacts is also provided to guarantee that your information will be accurate and up-to-date.

Financial secrecy, privacy, and confidentiality begins with proper goal setting, planning, and implementation of a program that will best suit your needs.

ANGUILLA

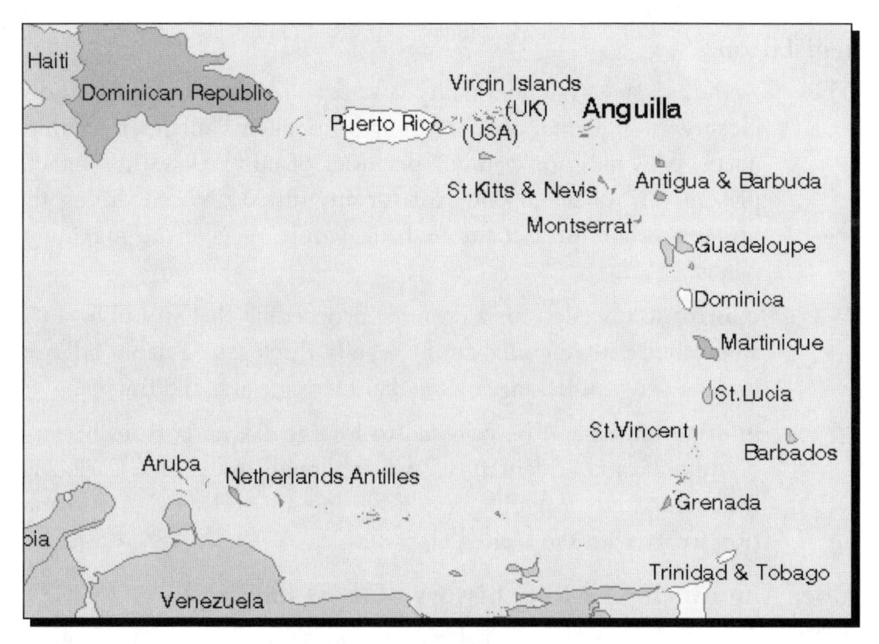

In the Caribbean (Leeward Islands). Caribbean island, 272 km south-east of Puerto Rico, 1,920 km south of Miami, population of approximately 8,000. Main languages are English and Creole English. Climate is tropical with relatively low humidity, average temperature 28°C.

Rich in pre-Columbian history. Archaeologists have determined there was a large settlement of Arawak Indians living on Anguilla. They called the island Malliouhana. The Spaniards who followed Christopher Columbus to the New World are said to have given the island its present name of Anguilla, because of its long eel-like shape.

The government of Anguilla is actively promoting the offshore banking and financial sector. A computerized filing system has been developed for the Anguilla Companies Registry allowing remote access filing and registration of companies by both local and overseas agents. The Companies Registry is scheduled to operate 24 hours a day, 365 days a year. In a determined effort to encourage offshore professionals to relocate to

Anguilla, the government is offering multi-year renewable work permits and other financial incentives.

Does Anguilla have any banking or corporate secrecy legislation?

YES. Anguilla's strict confidentiality laws prohibit the unauthorized disclosure of information pertaining to a clients affairs to a third party, providing for criminal penalties of up to US$50,000 and a prison term of up to one year for any disclosure concerning the business affairs of a client. A bank would receive the maximum penalty.

Information needed for a criminal proceeding that would be a triable offense in Anguilla can be legally disclosed. Triable offenses include drug trafficking, money laundering, theft and fraud.

Information cannot be released to foreign tax authorities because of Anguilla's confidentiality laws, although under the Caribbean Basin Initiative, Anguilla is considering an exchange of information treaty with the United States.

Does Anguilla have a long history of legal stability?

YES. Anguilla is a stable British colony administered by the Anguilla Constitution Order of 1982, a self-governing constitution that went into effect on April 1, 1982.

The legal system is administered by the Eastern Caribbean States Supreme Court, and is based on English common law supplemented by local statutes.

Is there an income tax in Anguilla?

NO. There is no income tax in Anguilla. Specific statutes have been enacted to ensure a perpetual tax exemption on IBCs, LLs, and Trusts. To qualify for this exemption, the IBC or LLC must not carry on business in Anguilla. To qualify as an exempt Trust, the Settlor and Beneficiaries may not be residents of Anguilla.

Are there any other taxes in Anguilla?

NO. There is no capital gains tax, gift tax, or estate tax in Anguilla. Historically, Anguilla has always been a no-tax jurisdiction with no personal or corporate taxation.

Does Anguilla maintain exchange controls?

NO. There are currently no exchange controls in Anguilla.

Does Anguilla maintain tax treaties with any other countries?

YES. Currently there is no tax treaty between the U.S. and Anguilla. Note that under the Caribbean Basin Initiative, Anguilla is considering an exchange of information treaty with the United States.

Anguilla maintains the UK Tax Convention with Denmark, New Zealand, Norway, Sweden, and Switzerland, allowing for a 15% withholding tax on dividends. Anguilla maintains double-taxation agreements with Barbados, Guyana, Jamaica, and Trinidad and Tobago.

Currently there is no tax treaty between Canada and Anguilla.

Does Anguilla allow for the formation of corporate entities?

YES. Limited Companies are governed by the Companies Ordinance of 1994 and the International Business Companies Ordinance of 1994. Both Ordinances were passed by the Anguilla House of Assembly on November 3, 1994, and proclaimed in force on January 1, 1995. Offshore companies can continue to be formed under the domestic Companies Ordinance as Anguillan private companies, or as offshore International Business Companies under the IBC legislation.

Companies Ordinance - The Companies Ordinance is based on the Caribbean Law Institute Draft Bill, based upon Ontario, Canada legislation. A prescribed three page Articles of Incorporation is used. Requirements and related benefits include:

- Only one shareholder and one director are required.
- Shareholder and director may both be nominees.
- Shareholders and directors may be of any nationality.
- All shares are of no par value.

- Companies must have a registered agent in Anguilla.
- Annual meetings need not be held in Anguilla.
- Annual returns listing shareholders, directors, registered office, and registered agent must be filed annually.

The Ordinance exempts a class of company called Specified Private Company (SPC) from certain financial recording requirements. To qualify as an SPC, the following conditions must be met:

- Maximum number of shareholders is 11.
- Restrictions on share transfers must be imposed.
- Shares may not be offered to the public.

International Business Companies Ordinance - The IBC Ordinance is based on the British Virgin Islands and revised Bahamas Acts, permitting the formation of an International Business Company by filing brief articles of incorporation.

Advantages of incorporating an IBC in Anguilla include:

- One person may incorporate.
- IBC's are exempt from filing accounts, although this information can be provided on an optional filing basis.
- Nominee shareholders and directors may be used.
- No par value shares are permitted.

The words Incorporated, Limited, Sociétè Anonyme and their abbreviations indicate limited liability.

Limited Liability Company Ordinance - Anguilla also offers the option of forming a Limited Liability Company (LLC), similar to American LLCs first formed in 1977 in the state of Wyoming. LLCs formed in Anguilla can be of limited duration or have a perpetual life. A Limited Liability Company is a hybrid company with the characteristics of both a company and a partnership, offering the following advantages:

- It is a separate legal entity, as a company.
- Limited liability is offered to shareholders.
- Has status as a "pass-through" entity for U.S. income tax purposes.

Limited Liability Companies are commonly used in joint ventures, venture capital investments, and real estate syndication.

Does Anguilla allow for the formation of Trusts?

YES. International Trusts are governed by the Trusts Ordinance, passed by the Anguilla House of Assembly on November 3, 1994, and proclaimed in force on January 1, 1995. Anguilla's new trust legislation uses the most current and innovative provisions found in the Bahamas, Belize, Bermuda, Cayman Islands, and Cook Islands Trusts Acts, and the Turks & Caicos Trusts Ordinance.

Under Section 6 of the Ordinance, the rule against perpetuities has been abolished, allowing the formation of trusts of perpetual duration. Under Section 14, the definition of Charitable Trusts has been expanded to include "any other purposes which are beneficial to the community." The new Trust legislation has made it possible to create a Commercial Purpose Trust, which is a non-charitable Trust created for a specific purpose, and has also allowed for the creation of Spendthrift Trusts.

Under Section 16 of the Ordinance, a Trust Protector may be appointed for any type of Trust, and is a mandatory requirement for a Commercial Purpose Trust. The Trust Protector has the power to enforce the trust, and under the terms of the Trust can also be authorized to remove and appoint Trustees.

Under Part IX, Choice of Governing Law, "a term of the Trust expressly selecting the laws of Anguilla to govern the Trust is valid, effective and conclusive regardless of any other circumstances." Under Part XII, an optional facility to file and register a Trust with the Registrar of Companies is provided.

A Trust formed with the Settlor and Beneficiaries not resident in Anguilla is declared to be an Exempt Trust, specifically exempt from any form of taxation for an indefinite period. Exempt Trusts may not hold land in Anguilla.

The Fraudulent Dispositions Ordinance is similar to the Cayman and Bahamas Acts, which prevents transfers to Trusts with the explicit intention to defraud current or anticipated creditors. The burden of proof of establishing such an intent to defraud is upon the creditor who has a period of 3 years to make an application from the date of relevant disposition. After this time, the Trust will protect the assets from creditors. The statute of limitations is 3 years.

Does Anguilla allow for the formation of Captive Insurance Companies?

YES. The statute governing the licensing and operation of insurance companies in Anguilla is the Insurance Ordinance of 1994.

To form an insurance company, the applicant must complete an Application for Registration, Certificate of Solvency, Balance Sheet, Profit and Loss Account, and Appointment of Agent. Additionally, the Application for Registration must include:

- Confirmation shareholders not involved with an insolvent company.
- 2 references for each shareholder, 1 from a banker.
- Qualifications and experience of each director.
- Clean record and financial background for each director.
- Details of all directorships in the past 5 years.
- The insurance company's auditors, bankers and lawyers must confirm in writing that they are willing to act on behalf of company.
- Details of all reinsurance arrangements.
- Copies of audited accounts for the past 5 years.
- Business plan and investment strategy for the next 5 years.

Does Anguilla allow for the formation of Private Banking Companies?

YES. Anguilla is a suitable jurisdiction for the formation of Banking Companies.

Financial institutions and contacts:

Anguilla Registry of Companies
The Secretariat, PO.Box 60
The Valley, Anguilla, B.W.I.
tel. 264-497-5881, fax 264-497-5872

- *Services Offered:* government services

Antilles International Management Services Ltd.
PO.Box 970
The Valley, Anguilla, B.W.I.
tel. 264-497-3660, fax 264-497-3096

- *Services Offered:* corporate services

AXA Offshore Mangement Services Co. Ltd.
PO.Box 687
The Valley, Anguilla, B.W.I.
tel. 264-497-2069, fax 264-497-3012

- *Services Offered:* corporate services

Bank of Nova Scotia
PO.Box 250
The Valley, Anguilla, B.W.I.
tel. 264-497-3333, fax 264-497-3344, telex 9333

- *Services Offered:* retail banking

Banx Professional Services Ltd.
PO.Box 20
The Valley, Anguilla, B.W.I.
tel. 264-497-2388, fax 264-497-3286

- *Services Offered:* company formation, corporate services

Caribbean Commercial Bank
PO.Box 23
The Valley, Anguilla, B.W.I.
tel. 264-497-2571, fax 264-497-3570

- *Services Offered:* retail banking

Caribbean Juris Chambers
PO.Box 328
The Valley, Anguilla, B.W.I.
tel. 264-497-3470, fax 264-497-3177

- *Services Offered:* company formation, law office

FINSCO Limited
Victoria House , PO.Box 58
The Valley, Anguilla, B.W.I.
tel. 264-497-2060, fax 264-497-3096

- *Services Offered:* corporate services

Fitzroy Bryant
PO.Box 50
The Valley, Anguilla, B.W.I.
tel. 264-497-2910, fax 264-497-2910

- *Services Offered:* company formation, law office

International Corporate Management Services
PO.Box 249
The Valley, Anguilla, B.W.I.
tel. 264-497-3540, fax 264-497-3544

- *Services Offered:* corporate services

IPS (Anguilla) Ltd.
PO.Box 801
The Valley, Anguilla, B.W.I.
tel. 264-497-4053

- *Services Offered:* company formation, trust formation

Keithley F. T. Lake
PO.Box 14
The Valley, Anguilla, B.W.I.
tel. 264-497-2069, fax 264-497-3012

- *Services Offered:* company formation, law office

Lombard Management Services Ltd.
PO.Box 206
The Valley, Anguilla, B.W.I.
tel. 264-497-2988, fax 264-497-5714

- *Services Offered:* company formation, corporate services

Myrna R. Walwyn & Associates
The Valley, Anguilla, B.W.I.
tel. 264-497-2484, fax 264-497-3076

- *Services Offered:* company formation, law office

National Bank of Anguilla
PO.Box 44
The Valley, Anguilla, B.W.I.
tel. 264-497-2101, fax 264-497-3310

- *Services Offered:* retail banking

Pannell Kerr Foster (F. Fleming & Co.)
PO.Box 206
The Valley, Anguilla, B.W.I.
tel. 264-497-2988, fax 264-497-5714

- *Services Offered:* accounting services

Rathbone (Anguilla) Ltd.
PO.Box 136
The Valley , Anguilla, B.W.I.
tel. 264-497-3400, fax 264-497-3544

- *Services Offered:* company formation, corporate services

Spectrum Management Services
PO.Box 136
The Valley, Anguilla, B.W.I.
tel. 264-497-3400, fax 264-497-3755

- *Services Offered:* company formation, corporate services

Suisse & Harman Inc.
PO.Box 1054
The Valley, Anguilla, B.W.I.

- *Services Offered:* mutual fund manager

West Indies Corporate Services Ltd.
PO.Box 617, No. 17 Caribbean Commercial Centre
The Valley, Anguilla, B.W.I.
tel. 264-497-5599, fax 264-497-5310

- *Services Offered:* corporate services

ANTIGUA & BARBUDA

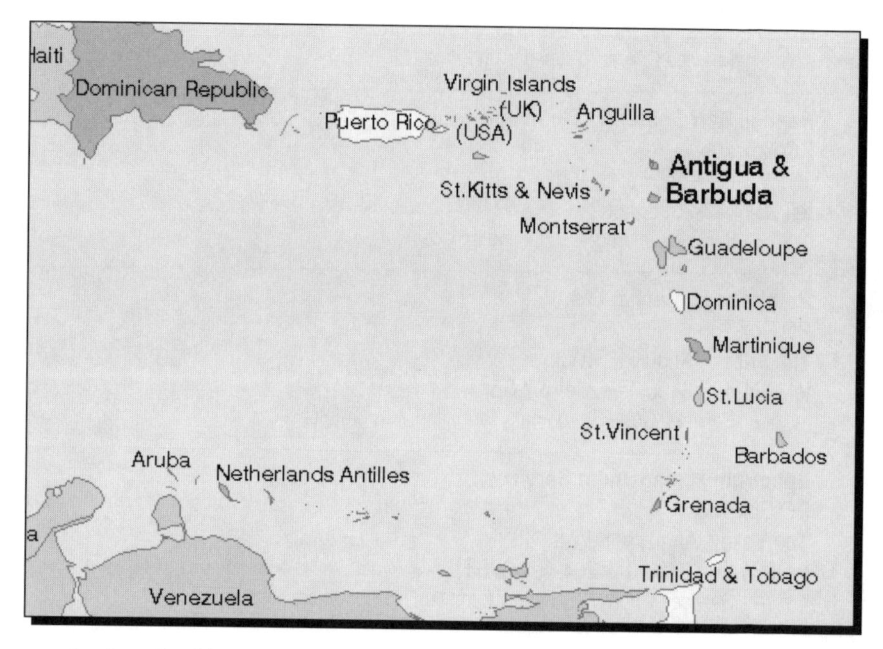

In the Caribbean. 108 square miles, 320 km southeast of Puerto Rico in the Leeward Islands. Population is approximately 65,000, with approximately 20,000 living in St.John's, the capital. Lying to the north of Antigua and covering 75 square miles is the island of Barbuda, with a population of 1,500. Main language is English. Temperature averages between 70°F and 86°F, with low humidity.

Columbus discovered Antigua in November 1493, on his second voyage to the new world, finding it inhabited by Carib Indians. For 135 years following Columbus' sighting of Antigua, neither the French, nor the major colonial powers in the region, the Dutch, made any serious attempts to colonize the island. This was primarily due to its lack of fresh water and the continual Carib raids. The island was occupied by the French for six months in 1652, while the British settled later that year and established sugar plantations during the 17th and 18th centuries. To protect their interests they built several forts, the ruins of which are still seen today. Antigua & Barbuda were granted Associate State status in 1956 at a constitutional conference held in London. Full independence was granted on November 1, 1981.

Does Antigua have any banking or corporate secrecy legislation?

YES. Antigua's Offshore Banking Secrecy Act and the International Business Corporation Act (28/1982 sub section 244 1-5 "Confidential matters protected") prohibits the unauthorized disclosure of information pertaining to a clients affairs to a third party. The Act provides criminal penalties of up to US$50,000 or a prison term not to exceed one year for any inquiry or disclosure concerning the business affairs of a client or transaction involving an IBC bank or trust company.

The Act does not prohibit the disclosure of confidential information upon court order in connection with an authorized investigation, or with the giving of evidence on an alleged criminal offense triable within Antigua or which would have been so triable if it had been committed within Antigua.

Foreign tax authorities can only obtain information related to a triable criminal offense. Note that tax evasion is not a criminal offense in Antigua.

Does Antigua have a long history of legal stability?

YES. Antigua was a British colony from 1653 to 1967, attaining the status of a self-governing island under Associated Statehood in 1967. Antigua gained its independence on November 1, 1981 from Britain, but remains a member of the British Commonwealth of Nations.

Antigua enacts their own independent legislation based on British Common Law. The legal system is administered by the Eastern Caribbean States Supreme Court.

Is there an income tax in Antigua?

NO. No personal income tax. No income tax on assets held by an IBC, as a Trustee, for a minimum period of 50 years. Local businesses are required to pay a 40% income tax.

Are there any other taxes in Antigua?

NO. No personal capital gains tax. No capital gains tax on assets held by an IBC, as a Trustee, for a minimum period of 50 years. No personal inheritance tax. No inheritance tax on assets held by an IBC, as a Trustee, for a minimum period of 50 years. There is no gift tax in Antigua, except duties charged by Customs on certain gifts imported.

Does Antigua maintain exchange controls ?

NO. There are currently no exchange controls in Antigua. The official currency is the East Caribbean Dollar.

Does Antigua maintain tax treaties with any other countries?

YES. There is no double-taxation agreement between the U.S. and Antigua, although Antigua maintains double-taxation agreements with Australia, New Zealand, Singapore, and the United Kingdom.

There is no double-taxation agreement between Canada and Antigua.

Does Antigua allow for the formation of corporate entities?

YES. An IBC (International Business Corporation) is a company limited by shares which is not allowed to engage in any active trade or business within Antigua, except for those activities which are solely in support of its business outside Antigua. An IBC falls under the provisions of the International Business Corporations Act of 1982.

The incorporator must either be a resident of Antigua together with a member of the Bar, or a trust company empowered by the Cabinet of Antigua to act as an incorporator. Most banking and trust companies in Antigua function as incorporators.

Every IBC must have a registered office and a resident agent in Antigua. The Company must be managed by a Board of Directors consisting of at least one director which may be corporate.

Incorporating in Antigua brings certain advantages:

- There is a guarantee that an IBC is not liable for taxation for 50 years.

- There are no requirements to have paid-up capital. There is no time limit in which the authorized capital must be fully paid (except for banks and insurance companies).
- There are no requirements to file any corporate reports with the government regarding any offshore activities.
- There are no citizenship or residence requirements for directors, officers, stockholders, or incorporators.
- Officers and directors need not be shareholders.
- Only one director is required and nationality is not an issue. The director can be a corporation.
- Meetings of directors and shareholders may be held in any country.
- The books of the corporation may be kept in any country.
- The corporation may increase or decrease its authorized capital by means of an amendment to its Articles of Incorporation.
- Share certificates can be issued in bearer form or nominee form, with or without par value.
- There are no currency restrictions of any type for Antiguan Offshore Corporations.
- Incorporation and annual government fees are a flat US$300 and not based on capital. This is very cost effective for highly capitalized corporations.

Important points to consider when forming an Antiguan Offshore Corporation include:

- The name of the corporation must end in the words Limited, Incorporated, Corporation, Société Anonyme, Sociedad Anonima, or their abbreviations. The use of the words Trust, Bank, Insurance, Fiduciary, Reinsurance, or any of their derivatives is restricted by law, unless licensed as such.
- The full names of the officers of the corporation may be the same persons that are appointed as directors. One person can hold more than one office and officers need not be shareholders.

Does Antigua allow for the formation of Trusts?

YES. No income, capital gains or inheritance tax may be levied against assets held by an IBC as a Trustee on behalf of a non-resident of Antigua for a period of 50 years from the IBC's incorporation date.

Although there is no requirement that a Trust instrument be recorded, it may be recorded in the non-public records of the Director of IBCs, who will issue a certificate of record attached to an original of the Trust instrument. There are no restrictions on accumulations by Trusts. The Rule Against Perpetuities has been abolished. The governing law of Trusts is the British common law which was adopted by Antigua as a colony and re-affirmed upon independence.

Does Antigua allow for the formation of Captive Insurance Companies?

YES. Any company incorporated under the laws of Antigua may, when permitted by its Articles of Incorporation, apply for permission to register as an international insurance company. The following restrictions apply to the formation of an international insurance company:

- An international insurance company may engage in any insurance business other than domestic insurance.
- The Superintendent of International Insurance Corporations is empowered to revoke or suspend any license when he is of the opinion that the continued registration of the international insurance company is detrimental to the public interest.
- The law requires that an insurance company have a local director.
- The licensing application must include resumes for all shareholders, officers and directors of the insurance company.
- The required start-up capital is US$100,000.

- An international insurance company is required to appoint an auditor and file annual reports with the Superintendent of International Insurance Corporations.

Does Antigua allow for the formation of Private Banking Companies?

YES. Any IBC, when permitted by its Articles of Incorporation, may apply for an international banking license. IBC Banks are exempt from the restrictions of the Exchange Control Act of 1958 and the one percent (1%) levy on foreign currency transactions imposed by the Foreign Currency Levy Act of 1976.

The following restrictions apply to the formation of an international banking company:

- The minimum capital required for a banking license is US$5,000,000.
- Biographical information for each director, officer and subscriber of 5% or more of the IBC's stock must be submitted. This information must show that the directors and officers have banking experience and have the ability to operate the bank. A police record is also required for each director.
- Audited corporate and personal financial statements of the organizer must be submitted before final approval.
- The granting of an international banking license is solely within the discretion of the Supervisor of Banks and Trust Corporations, who may revoke the license at any time if in his opinion the revocation is in the public interest.
- IBC banks are required to appoint an auditor and file unaudited quarterly and audited annual returns with the Supervisor of Banks and Trust Corporations.

Does Antigua allow the formation of Shipping Companies?

YES. The Department of Marine Services and Merchant Shipping can advise on specific inquiries. Offshore shipping companies use the provisions of the International Business Corporations Act of 1982. Following are several important points:

- Antigua provides full convention registration and has entered bilateral trading agreements with major sea trade countries.
- No age restrictions are in force, providing the vessels class status is current. Exemptions from the class requirements can be made under certain conditions for cargo vessels under 500GRT, yachts, fishing vessels, and vessels in coastal trade only. Vessels of over 14 years old will be inspected by an appointed surveyor prior to acceptance.
- Antigua registered vessels can be owned by non-citizens, but a nationality waiver must be obtained. Incorporations of offshore companies are invited at very competitive costs (offshore companies in Antigua are not liable for taxation for 50 years).
- Bare boat registration is permitted.
- Vessels under the flag of Antigua will be liable to an annual safety inspection, prior to re-registration.
- Full-term registration will be issued after receiving a certificate of deletion from the previous register.

Special thanks to Mr. McAlister Abbott and Mrs. Carole Schlott-Donelan of Antigua Overseas Bank Ltd. / ABI Trust Ltd., telephone 268-480-2723, for their assistance in the preparation of this section.

Financial Institutions:

Antigua Overseas Bank Ltd. / ABI Trust Ltd.
High Street & Corn Alley, PO.Box 1679
St.John's, Antigua, W.I.
tel. 268-480-2723, fax 268-480-2750, tel. 268-480-2734, email: aob@candw.ag

- *Services Offered:* company formation, trust formation, bank formation, private banking, retail banking, loans and credit, deposit backed MC/Visa

---

Blue Chip Capital Management Limited
St.John's, Antigua, W.I.
tel. 888-265-6661, fax 800-560-0645

- *Services Offered:* investment advisor, mutual fund manager, private banking, global investing information, deposit backed MC/Visa, insurance-based investments

---

CIBC (Canadian Imperial Bank Commerce)
High Street and Corn Alley
St.John's, Antigua, W.I.
tel. 268-462-0998, fax 268-462-4439

- *Services Offered:* retail banking, loans and credit, safekeeping services

---

Czerlau & Associates Limited
High Street
St.John's, Antigua, W.I.
tel. 800-226-5703, fax 242-356-0223

- *Services Offered:* company formation, trust formation, corporate services, estate planning services, deposit backed MC/Visa

---

Terrance M. F. Small, M.A.
High Street, PO.Box 2655
Antigua, W.I.
tel. 268-462-9577, fax 268-462-9578

- *Services Offered:* law office

AUSTRIA

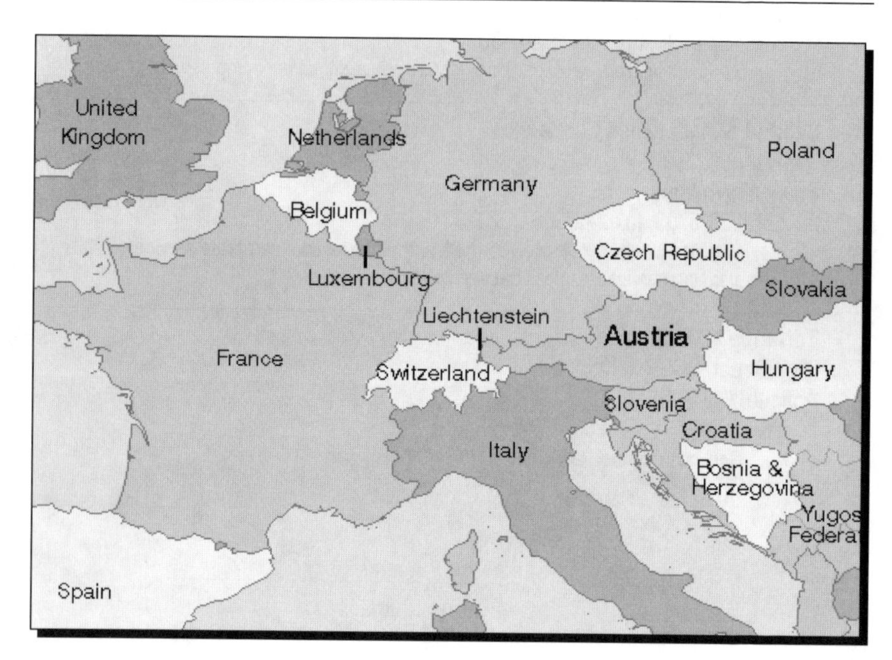

In Western Europe. Borders with Germany to the north, Italy to the south, Switzerland to the west, and Hungary to the east. Population is approximately 8 million. Main language is German, although English is spoken.

Until 1918 Austria was the heart of the vast Hapsburg Empire, encompassing the Danube Basin and much of the Balkans. Austria is now a democratic republic based upon the German speaking parts of the former empire.

Does Austria have any banking or corporate secrecy legislation?

YES. Bank secrecy is certified by the Austrian Banking Act, Section 23, which states:

"*The banks, their shareholders, their partners, members of their various bodies, employees as well as all other persons in any way acting for the banks may not disclose or make use of secrets which have been entrusted or made accessible to them solely due to the business relationships with customers. The obligation to maintain secrecy shall apply without time restriction. Whoever discloses or makes use of facts which are subject to bank secrecy in order to obtain financial benefit for himself or a third party, or to cause disadvantages to another, shall be sentenced by the court to imprisonment of up to one year or a penalty of up to 360 days court rates."*

Instead of using numbered accounts, Austrian banks offer password accounts, providing an added level of secrecy protection.

Bank secrecy may be lifted under certain extreme conditions relating to national security. The obligation to maintain bank secrecy does not exist:

- In context with commenced criminal court proceedings for fiscal violations, not including fiscal petty offenses.
- In case of probate procedures as against the probate court and the notary public acting as court commissioner.
- In case the client is of minor age or is otherwise granted curatorship.
- If the client explicitly and in writing authorizes the disclosure of the secret.
- To the extent the disclosure is necessary for clarification of legal matters originating from the relationship between the credit institution and the client.
- With regard to the reporting obligation pursuant to the Inheritance and Gift Tax Law (applying to residents of Austria).

Bank secrecy is protected by the Austrian Banking Act, and prohibits the release of financial information for foreign tax investigations.

Does Austria have a long history of legal stability?

YES. Austria is a neutral, democratic federal republic, with the United States, Russia, France and Britain as signatory powers to its neutrality. Government is a parliamentary democracy divided into three branches; the executive branch (including federal president, chancellor, and cabinet), the legislative branch (federal assembly), and judicial branch (constitutional, administrative, and supreme court).

The legal system based on civil law and is governed by the Federal Constitutional Act of 1920.

Is there an income tax in Austria?

YES. Austrian tax laws focus primarily on Austrian residents. Non-resident banking income is free of Austrian income, inheritance or capital gains taxes. No Austrian taxes are levied on the interest from either Austrian or foreign bonds or mutual funds held by non-residents. International Certificates of Deposit (ICDs) are also tax free. Precious metals can be bought tax-free if stored outside Austria.

Are there any other taxes in Austria?

YES. There is a 20% withholding tax on share dividends and participation capital dividends.

Does Austria maintain exchange controls?

NO. Non-residents can freely transfer funds or exchange currencies in Austria. Currency is the Austrian Schilling.

Does Austria maintain tax treaties with any other countries?

YES. The tax treaty between the U.S. and Austria is modeled after the standard Organization for Economic Cooperation and Development (OECD) model treaty. Austria also maintains tax treaties with Argentina, Australia, Belgium, Brazil, Bulgaria, Canada, Denmark, Egypt, Finland, France, Germany, Greece, Hungary, India, Indonesia, Ireland, Israel, Italy, Japan, Korea, Liechtenstein, Luxembourg, Malta, the Netherlands, Norway, Pakistan, the Philippines, Poland, Portugal, Spain, Sweden, Switzerland, Thailand, Tunisia, Turkey, and the United Kingdom.

The tax treaty between Canada and Austria is modeled after the standard OECD model treaty.

Does Austria allow for the formation of corporate entities?

YES. Both a limited company (Gesellschaft mit beschrankter Hftung - GesmbH), and a stock corporation (Aktiengesellschaft - AG) are subject to certain taxes.

Does Austria allow for the formation of Trusts?

NO. Civil law does not readily support the formation of International Trusts.

Does Austria allow for the formation of Captive Insurance Companies?

YES. Although Captive Insurance Companies can be formed in Austria, there are other jurisdictions with lower costs and friendlier legislation.

Does Austria allow for the formation of Private Banking Companies?

YES. Although Banking Companies can be formed in Austria, there are other jurisdictions with lower costs and friendlier legislation.

Financial Institutions:

Citibank (Austria) AG
Lothringerstrasse 7
Vienna, Austria, A-1015
tel. 43-1-717-170, fax 43-1-713-9206

- *Services Offered:* private banking, retail banking

ING Bank(Vienna) - Trade and Commodity Finance
Tuchlauben 8, 4th Floor
Vienna, Austria, A-1010
tel. 43-222-531640, fax 43-222-5316499

- *Services Offered:* trust formation, private banking, corporate services

BAHAMAS

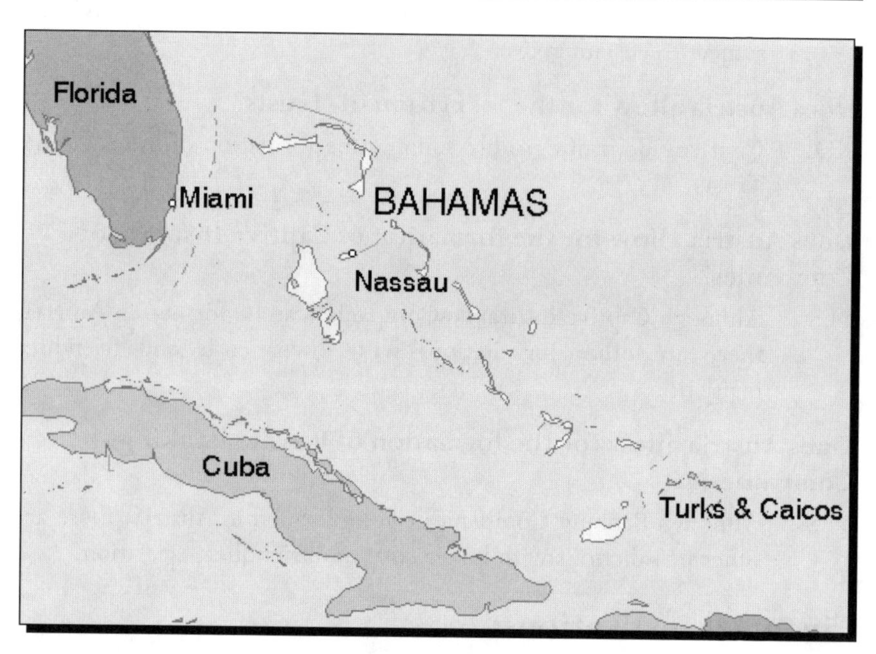

In the Caribbean, 60 miles southeast of Florida, north of Haiti. An archipelago of approximately 700 islands and 2,500 cays stretching from 60 miles east of Palm Beach Florida nearly to the Turks & Caicos Islands, over 500 miles away. Population is approximately 350,000. Main language is English. Climate is semi-tropical, with temperatures averaging 85°F in summer and 73°F in winter.

The Bahamas was initially settled in 1640 by the Eleutheran Adventurers, a group of Englishmen who sailed from Bermuda. The Bahamas has had a Parliamentary government since 1729, and became an independent nation in July, 1973.

The Bahamas Investment Authority, operating out of the office of the Prime Minister, was created to stimulate growth in the financial sector and promote foreign direct investment.

The Bahamas recently had a test of their secrecy legislation, and came through (so far) with flying colors. A US court has levied a fine of US$1.8

million against an investor who used Royal Bank of Canada's Bahamian trading arm to profit illegally in options of Duracell International Inc. just days before it was bought by Gillette Co. The Federal Court in Manhattan seized US$603,275 in profit and levied the fine against the unidentified client of the Nassau-based bank after the Securities & Exchange Commission found suspicious trades in what it called "virtually worthless" Duracell options. This was just before the US$7.3 billion takeover was made public. An SEC investigator said the SEC did not find out who made the trades through Royal Bank's Nominees (Bahamas) Ltd. but that its investigation was continuing. Royal Bank was not accused of doing anything illegal and sources said the unnamed investor is no longer a client of the bank. Royal had no comment on the court's decision. The SEC investigated two major trades in September 1996 in which options were bought from the Bahamas and through a Swiss trader. About US$1 million in profit was made before the funds were seized. The New York court did not levy a fine against investors who also bought options through Lennox SA, a Swiss firm, because it co-operated with the investigation. The SEC investigator admitted that the court is unlikely to ever collect the fine "unless we find there are assets we can reach." The SEC claimed that several people used offshore securities dealers to illegally profit on insider information that Gillette was about to make a premium takeover offer for Duracell. "The purchases were out-of-the-money call options that were near expiration and permitted the defendants to turn an investment of approximately US$120,000 in what appeared to be virtually worthless options into profits of over US$1 million," the SEC said in documents. The SEC has become more aggressive in trying to crack down on illegal insider trading done through offshore tax havens that offer clients secrecy. As of the time of writing, no information has ever been released to the SEC.

Does the Bahamas have any banking or corporate secrecy legislation?

YES. The Bahamas Bank and Trust Company Regulatory Act prohibit the unauthorized disclosure of information pertaining to a clients affairs to a third party, without the customer's written permission. The secrecy laws are imposed on all Bank and Trust companies, their directors, officers, employees, attorneys, auditors, and outside agents. Only by Supreme Court Order can information be supplied about any account. A fine of US$5,000 applies to any person disclosing details of accounts contrary to the Bank and Trust Company Regulatory Act.

The commitment to bank secrecy was reaffirmed by Mr. Orville A. Turnquest, Minister of Justice and Foreign Affairs, on June 10, 1993, who stated that "*Bahamas is not only committed to the bank secrecy laws, but to the prevention of intrusion by foreign governments.*"

There is a requirement to report bank deposits of more than US$100,000 to the Bahamas government, although this information is protected by the Bahamas Bank and Trust Company Regulatory Act. It is possible for foreign law enforcement agencies to obtain a court order demanding production of documents in criminal matters, although a very high standard of proof is required. An example of bank secrecy being lifted is the case of Dennis Levine, an American who was suspected of insider trading. Under pressure from U.S. authorities, Bahamian banks violated secrecy laws and released information, even though no crime had been committed in the Bahamas. This example casts a negative view of Bahamian bank secrecy, indicating that if you absolutely require secrecy, look elsewhere. Political pressure seems to weigh heavily on the validity of bank secrecy laws.

Tax evasion in the Bahamas or in any other jurisdiction is not a criminal matter in the Bahamas, therefore any bank account or financial record is protected by the Bahamas Bank and Trust Company Regulatory Act.

The following quote is from a Government of Bahamas publication covering the banking industry: "*Tax evasion is not illegal in the Bahamas, since we do not have income, capital gains or inheritance taxes. Tax evasion is not considered suitable grounds for ordering access to information about an account.*"

Does the Bahamas have a long history of legal stability?

YES. The Bahamas became an independent nation in 1973, although it remains a member of the British Commonwealth of Nations. A Governor General appointed by the British Government is responsible for defense, external affairs and internal security. An elected Prime Minister consults with a Cabinet of nine ministers chosen from the Legislature.

The Bahamas enacts their own Independent Legislation based on British Common Law, supplemented by local statutes. The Supreme Court is responsible for major criminal and civil cases. The Court of Appeals handles appeals, while the Magistrate's Court is responsible for civil and criminal cases. The ultimate Court of Appeal is the Privy Council of the United Kingdom.

Is there an income tax in the Bahamas?

NO. No personal income tax. No tax on personal, business or company profits. No income tax on assets held by an IBC for a minimum period of 20 years. No taxes payable on the holding, income from, or transfer of IBC shares.

Are there any other taxes in the Bahamas?

NO. No personal capital gains tax. No capital gains tax on assets held by an IBC for a minimum period of 20 years. No gift or distribution tax. No personal estate, probate, or inheritance tax.

The government derives its income from tourism, import and stamp duties, and license fees on companies.

Does the Bahamas maintain exchange controls?

YES. An exchange control is exercised over citizens of the Bahamas to keep their funds in the local currency. Offshore entities use other currencies and are exempted from exchange controls. The official currency is the Bahamian Dollar. The Bahamian Dollar is at par with the U.S. dollar.

Does the Bahamas maintain tax treaties with any other countries?

NO. There is no tax treaty between the U.S. and the Bahamas, although there is an exchange of information agreement applied if drug trafficking is suspected.

There is no double-taxation agreement between Canada and the Bahamas.

Does the Bahamas allow for the formation of corporate entities?

YES. Offshore companies are known as International Business Companies. An IBC (International Business Corporation) falls under the provisions of the International Business Companies Act of 1989, which came into force on January 15, 1990. Internal Companies are governed by the Companies Act of 1992, which came into force on August 1, 1992. An IBC is a company limited by shares which is not allowed to engage in any active trade or business within the Bahamas except for those activities which are solely in furtherance of its business outside Bahamas. IBCs are governed by the following:

- The Company must be managed by a Board of Directors consisting of at least one director which need not be a natural person.
- The name of the company must include either Limited, Corporation, Incorporated, GmbH, Société Anonyme, Sociedad Anonima or their abbreviations.
- The name of the company may not include the words Bank, Building Society, Chamber of Commerce or any word that may indicate a connection with the Government or the Royal family.
- The Memorandum of Association may include the standard objects clause "*the company is allowed to engage in any act or activity which is not prohibited under any law for the time being in the Bahamas.*"
- An IBC must always have a registered office and a registered agent in the Bahamas.
- An IBC requires a minimum of two shareholders, although this may be reduced to one shareholder after incorporation.
- There must be at least one director who may be an individual or a corporation. A director may appoint an alternate. Other officers may be appointed.
- Subject to the Memorandum and Articles, the directors may call meetings inside or outside the Bahamas.

IBCs incorporated in the Bahamas offer the following advantages:

- To reduce annual tax (which is based on authorized capital), an authorized capital of US$5,000 is often used. This results in an annual fee payable to the Registrar of Companies of only US$100.
- An IBC is guaranteed to be exempt from any taxes for 20 years.
- The shares may be with or without par value, in bearer or registered form, and issued in any currency.
- There is no requirement to file annual returns or accounts.
- No public record is maintained of the identities of the shareholders or directors.
- There is no requirement for an annual general meeting.
- Company names can be set out in script applicable to Japanese, Chinese, Thai, Arabic, and other languages.

Any Bahamian company can empower any person as its attorney to execute deeds on its behalf in any place not situated in the Bahamas. Every deed signed by the attorney on behalf of the company and under his seal shall be binding on the company, and have the same effect as if it were under the common seal of the company.

Does the Bahamas allow for the formation of Trusts?

YES. International Trusts have had a long and stable record in the Bahamas, being governed by the Trustee Act of 1893 and amendments. Trusts formed in the Bahamas offer the following benefits:

- There is no requirement to register the Trust.
- A stamp duty payable upon declaration of Trust. This establishes the existence of the Trust and Trust deed for legal purposes.
- Assets held by an IBC as a Trustee on behalf of a non-resident of the Bahamas is guaranteed to be exempt from income, capital gains and inheritance tax at least until the year 2035.

The Trust (Choice of Governing Law) Act of 1989 protects Trusts established in the Bahamas from attack from other jurisdictions.

Does the Bahamas allow for the formation of Captive Insurance Companies?

YES. Any IBC, when permitted by its Articles of Incorporation, may apply for a re-insurance license, and may engage in any insurance business other than domestic insurance.

Does the Bahamas allow for the formation of Private Banking Companies?

YES. Any IBC, when permitted by its Articles of Incorporation, may apply for an international banking license.

Financial institutions and contacts:

Alexiou, Knowles & Co.
St.Andrews Court, Frederick Street, PO.Box N-4805
Nassau, Bahamas

- *Services Offered:* law office

Apax Bank & Trust Co. Ltd.
PO.Box N-4915, Charlotte House, Charlotte Street
Nassau, Bahamas
tel. 242-322-4456, fax 242-326-2280

- *Services Offered:* private banking

Arthur Young & Co.
PO.Box N-3231
Nassau, Bahamas
tel. 242-322-3805

- *Services Offered:* accounting services

Bahamas Development Bank
PO.Box N-3034, Cable Beach, West Bay Street
Nassau, Bahamas
tel. 242-327-5780, fax 242-327-5047, telex NS-297

- *Services Offered:* retail banking

Banco CCF Brazil SA (Nassau Branch)
PO.Box N-8710, Saffrey Square, Suite 204
Nassau, Bahamas
tel. 242-356-5851, fax 242-356-5850

- *Services Offered:* private banking

Bank Leu
PO.Box N-3926
Nassau, Bahamas
tel. 242-328-1444, fax 242-323-8828tel. 242-326-5054

- *Services Offered:* private banking

Bank of Boston Trust Co. (Bahamas) Ltd.
PO.Box N-3930, Charlotte & Shirley Streets
Nassau, Bahamas
tel. 242-322-8531, fax 242-328-2750

- *Services Offered:* private banking

Bank of Nova Scotia Trust Company (Bahamas) Limited
PO.Box N-3016, Scotiabank Building
Nassau, Bahamas
tel. 242-356-1500, fax 242-326-0991, telex 2-0247

- *Services Offered:* private banking, loans and credit, safekeeping services

---

BankAmerica Trust & Banking Corporation (Bahamas) Ltd.
PO.Box N-9100, BankAmerica House, East Bay Street
Nassau, Bahamas
tel. 242-393-7411, fax 242-393-3030, telex 20-159

- *Services Offered:* retail banking

Barclays Bank PLC
PO.Box N-8350, Shirley & Charlotte Streets
Nassau, Bahamas
tel. 242-322-4921, fax 242-328-7979

- *Services Offered:* private banking, retail banking, loans and credit, safekeeping services

---

Blue Chip Capital Management Limited
Bahamas Financial Centre, 3rd Floor, Shirley & Charlotte Streets
Nassau, Bahamas
tel. 888-265-6661, fax 242-356-0223

- *Services Offered:* investment advisor, mutual fund manager, private banking, global investing information, deposit backed MC/Visa, insurance-based investments

Britannia Assurance Internacionale, Inc.
PO.Box CB-13482, West Bay Centre, West Bay Street
Nassau, Bahamas
tel. 242-327-1480, fax 242-327-1483

- *Services Offered:* insurance-based investments

British West Indies Securities Company Limited
PO.Box F-42886
Freeport, Bahamas
tel. 242-351-5040, fax 242-351-5549, fax 242-327-4128

- *Services Offered:* investment advisor, company formation, trust formation, captive insurance formation, corporate services

British-American Bank
PO.Box N-3744, West Bay Street
Nassau, Bahamas
tel. 242-327-5170, fax 242-327-5166

- *Services Offered:* retail banking

Butler & Taylor Chartered Accountants
PO.Box N-7777, 29 Retirement Road
Nassau, Bahamas
tel. 242-393-0224, fax 242-393-7570

- *Services Offered:* accounting services

Cassar and Co. Counsel & Attorney
PO.Box CB-11683, Norfolk House Annex II, Market & Frederick Streets
Nassau, Bahamas
tel. 242-356-7015, fax 242-328-4694

- *Services Offered:* company formation, law office

Central Bank of The Bahamas
PO.Box N-4868, Frederick St.
Nassau, Bahamas
tel. 242-322-2193, fax 242-322-4321

- *Services Offered:* retail banking, government services

Chase Manhattan Private Bank
PO.Box N-1576
Nassau, Bahamas
tel. 242-323-6811, fax 242-326-8814

- *Services Offered:* private banking

Citco Fund Services (Bahamas) Limited
Bahamas Financial Centre, Third Floor, Charlotte Street, PO.Box CB-13136
Nassau, Bahamas
tel. 242-356-5928, fax 242-356-0223

- *Services Offered:* mutual fund manager, company formation

Cititrust (Bahamas) Limited
PO.Box N 1576, Thompson Blvd
Nassau, Bahamas
tel. 242-322-4240, fax 242-325-0716

- *Services Offered:* retail banking

Commonwealth Bank
PO.Box SS-5541, East Bay Street
Nassau, Bahamas
tel. 242-328-1854, fax 242-325-8765

- *Services Offered:* retail banking

Czerlau & Associates Limited
Bahamas Financial Centre, 3rd Floor, Shirley & Charlotte Streets
Nassau, Bahamas
tel. 800-226-5703, fax 242-356-0223

- *Services Offered:* company formation, trust formation, captive insurance formation, corporate services, estate planning services, deposit backed MC/Visa, safekeeping services, telephone calling cards, mail forwarding, books or newsletters, data encryption, security devices, surveillance equipment

---

Darier, Hentsch Private Bank & Trust Ltd
PO.Box N-4938, Charlotte Street
Nassau, Bahamas
tel. 242-322-2721, fax 242-326-6983

- *Services Offered:* private banking

Dupuch & Turnquest & Co. Chambers
PO.Box F2578
Freeport, Bahamas
tel. 242-352-8134, fax 242-352-5687

- *Services Offered:* law office

Dupuch & Turnquest & Co. Chambers
Bankamerica House, 308 East Bay Street, PO.Box N-8181
Nassau, Bahamas
tel. 242-393-3226, fax 242-393-6807

- *Services Offered:* law office

E.Dawson Roberts Higgs & Co.
PO.Box N-918, Magna Carta Court, Parliament & Shirley Street
Nassau, Bahamas
tel. 242-322-4782, fax 242-322-2048

- *Services Offered:* law office

Ernst & Young
PO.BoxN3231
Nassau, Bahamas
tel. 242-322-3805, fax 242-326-8180

- *Services Offered:* accounting services

Euro-Caribbean Management Services Limited
104B Saffrey Square, Bank Lane & Bay St, PO.Box N-1612
Nassau, Bahamas
tel. 242-356-5280, fax 242-356-5281

- *Services Offered:* investment advisor, company formation, corporate services

---

Ferrier Lullin Bank & Trust (Bahamas) Ltd.
Swiss Bank House - East Bay Street, PO.Box N-4890
Nassau, Bahamas
tel. 242-394-91-00, fax 242-394-91-40

- *Services Offered:* trust formation, private banking

Geneva Private Bank & Trust Bahamas Ltd.
PO.Box N-9204, Charlotte Street
Nassau, Bahamas
tel. 242-323-7211, fax 242-323-7918

- *Services Offered:* private banking

Handels Bank NatWest (Overseas) Ltd.
Beaumont House, PO.Box N-4214
Nassau, Bahamas
tel. 242-325-5534, fax 242-326-8807

- *Services Offered:* retail banking

Handelsfinanz-CCF Bank International Ltd.
PO.Box N-10441, Maritime House, Frederick Street
Nassau, Bahamas
tel. 242-328-8644, fax 242-328-8600

- *Services Offered:* retail banking

Harry B. Sands and Company
PO.Box N-624, 50 Shirley Street
Nassau, Bahamas
tel. 242-322-2670, fax 242-323-8914

- *Services Offered:* company formation, trust formation, law office

---

Higgs & Johnson
PO.Box N-3247, Sandringham House, 83 Shirley Street
Nassau, Bahamas
tel. 242-322-8571, fax 242-328-7727

- *Services Offered:* company formation, trust formation, law office, corporate services

---

International Investors Group, Ltd.
Marlborough House, Third Floor, Cumberland Street, PO.Box N-4922
Nassau, Bahamas
tel. 242-356-0107, fax 242-322-1612

- *Services Offered:* company formation, trust formation

KPMG Peat Marwick
Centreville House, Collins Avenue, PO.Box N-123
Nassau, Bahamas
tel. 242-322-8551, fax 242-326-5622

- *Services Offered:* accounting services

Leu Trust & Banking (Bahamas) Limited
PO.Box N-3926, Norfolk House
Nassau, Bahamas
tel. 242-326-5054, fax 242-323-5825

- *Services Offered:* retail banking

MeesPierson (Bahamas) Limited
PO.Box SS-5539, 308 East Bay Street
Nassau , Bahamas
tel. 242-393-8777, fax 242-393-0582

- *Services Offered:* private banking

Mossack Fonseca & Co. (Bahamas) Ltd.
Saffrey Square, Suite 205, Bank Lane, PO.Box N-8188
Nassau, Bahamas
tel. 242-322-7601, fax 242-322-5807

- *Services Offered:* company formation

Pictet Bank & Trust Ltd.
PO.Box N-4837, Charlotte House, Charlotte Street
Nassau, Bahamas
tel. 242-322-3938, fax 242-323-7986, fax 242-326-8355

- *Services Offered:* retail banking

Sheffields Counsel & Attorneys-at-Law
PO.Box CB-11986, Suite 303, East Street North
Nassau, Bahamas
tel. 242-322-7404, fax 242-322-7168

- *Services Offered:* law office

Swiss Bank Corporation (Overseas) Ltd.
PO.Box N-7757, East Bay Street, Swiss Bank House
Nassau, Bahamas
tel. 242-322-7570, fax 242-394-9333, fax 242-323-8953

- *Services Offered:* investment advisor, private banking

United Management Services Limited
Cumberland House, Cumberland Street, PO.Box N-629
Nassau, Bahamas
tel. 242-323-7585, fax 242-323-7284

- *Services Offered:* company formation, corporate services

Westpac Bank and Trust (Bahamas) Ltd.
PO.Box N-8332, Charlotte House, Charlotte Street
Nassau, Bahamas
tel. 242-328-8064, fax 242-326-0067, telex 20621 WBTL BS

- *Services Offered:* private banking

BARBADOS

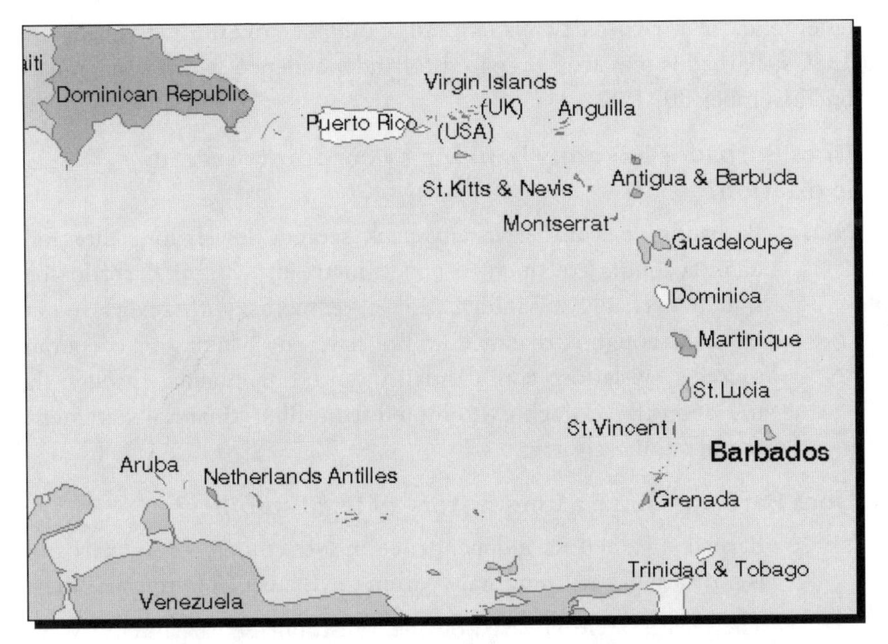

In the Caribbean (Windward Islands). A 166 square mile island that is the most easterly of the Caribbean Islands, and the most easterly part of the West Indies. Population is approximately 260,000. Main language is English and Bajan Creole. Tropical climate tempered by ocean breezes.

The first inhabitants of the island were Arawak and Carib Indians. Portuguese sailors stopped in 1536 on the way to Brazil, calling the island Los Barbados, after the ficus trees whose aerial roots look like beards. The English arrived in 1625, found the island uninhabited and claimed it for King James I of England. Settlers arrived in 1627 at the site which is now known as Holetown. During the next two decades the population grew dramatically due to political unrest in England between Oliver Cromwell and Charles I, causing the arrival of many English subjects. The introduction of sugar cane as the island's main crop brought slaves from Africa. English law and tradition took hold so fast that soon the island was called "Little England." The first Parliament was held in 1639 making it the third oldest in the Commonwealth, after the British House of Commons and the

Bermuda House of Assembly. Barbados moved toward the formation of an independent society with the freeing of slaves on 1834, enfranchisement of women in 1944, and the universal adult suffrage in 1951. With the emergence of a two-party system and a cabinet government during the 1950's, Barbados was well prepared for independence which was granted on November 30, 1966.

Does Barbados have any banking or corporate secrecy legislation?

NO. Barbados does not have any bank secrecy legislation, therefore bank accounts are open to government inspection. Barbados has signed exchange of information agreements with several countries. Although Barbados does not have any banking or corporate secrecy legislation, confidentiality can be maintained through the use of an IBC, which is exempted from filing financial statements in the public registry.

Does Barbados have a long history of legal stability?

YES. Barbados gained its independence in November, 1966. Barbados is now a self-governing state within the British Commonwealth.

The legal system is based on the Westminster parliamentary system of government. Judicial, political, and administrative institutions are closely modeled on the British system.

Is there an income tax in Barbados?

YES. Maximum rate of 2.5% of net income for International Business Companies, Investment Companies, and Offshore Banks.

Shipping Corporations receive a 10-year tax holiday.

No withholding taxes on dividends, interest and management fees and royalties paid to non-residents.

Are there any other taxes in Barbados?

NO. There is no capital gains tax in Barbados. Exempt Insurance Companies pay no capital gains tax.

Full tax exemption from all dividends, royalties, interest, fees and management fees paid to a non-resident person or to another IBC.

Full tax exemption for Foreign Sales Corporations doing business outside of Barbados and for Captive Insurance Companies.

There are no estate taxes or death duties payable in Barbados.

Does Barbados maintain exchange controls?

NO. There are currently no exchange controls in Barbados. The official currency is the Barbados Dollar.

Does Barbados maintain tax treaties with any other countries?

YES. There is a double-taxation agreement signed between Barbados and the U.S. Barbados also maintains double-taxation agreements with Denmark, Norway, Switzerland, and the United Kingdom.

There is a comprehensive double-taxation agreement signed between Barbados and Canada.

Does Barbados allow for the formation of Corporate Entities:

YES. Legislation to provide for the creation of International Business Companies was enacted in 1965, but saw little activity until 1986. In March 1992 Barbados enacted a new International Business Companies Act and brought into force supporting regulations.

Barbados IBCs have the following features, benefits, and restrictions:

- beneficial owners are not required to be disclosed to the government;
- registered shareholders are not required to be disclosed to the public, although records must be kept at the registered office;
- financial statements are not required to be filed with the government authorities;
- legislation does not provide for the use of bearer shares;
- the minimum number of shareholders required is 1;
- shareholders may be corporate;
- shareholders are not required to be resident in Barbados;
- the minimum number of directors is 1;
- directors are not required to be resident in Barbados;
- the corporate secretary may be corporate;

- an IBC's Register of Shareholders is available for inspection only by shareholders or by order of the Barbados Courts;
- meetings of shareholders and directors may be held in any country; and
- company names must end with the following words or their abbreviations: Limited, Corporation, Incorporated, Société Anonyme, or Sociedad Anonima.

An IBCs operations are restricted from the following activities:

- the IBC may not do business with residents of Barbados; and
- the IBC may not own real estate in Barbados.

Other benefits of the International Business Companies Act include:

- Option of ministerial guarantee that the benefits and exemptions granted will apply for 15 years from the IBC becoming a licensee.
- Simplification of the rules so that an IBC will be deemed to be resident in Barbados if it is incorporated or registered in Barbados.
- Option to offset foreign taxes against taxes due, provided that the net tax payable in Barbados is not less than 1% of taxable profits.
- Ability to negotiate special tax rates, provided that the net tax payable in Barbados is not less than 1% of taxable profits.
- Facility for companies engaged in manufacturing products for export outside of the Caribbean, to be licensed as IBCs.
- Complete exemption from taxation for IBCs owned by a resident Trust managed by an offshore bank, provided that the IBC is engaged only in the holding or dealing in securities.
- Legislation allows IBCs the option to carry on the business of international manufacturing under the IBC regime for the life of the company or under the Fiscal Incentives regime which offers tax holidays for a specific period.

- There are no restrictions on foreign ownership of business enterprises.
- Barbados offers tax holidays, concessions, and other incentives for manufacturing and information service companies.

Foreign Sales Corporation (FSC) - A Foreign Sales Corporation is a corporation specifically developed to assist U.S. exporters. FSC legislation emerged as part of the 1984 Tax Reform Act. In order to qualify for the partial U.S. tax exemption, the FSC is required to maintain a foreign presence and to earn export income outside of U.S. customs territories. In response to the 1984 Tax Reform Act, the Barbados Parliament passed the Barbados Foreign Sales Corporation Act of 1984. The Act contains the following restrictions:

- No person may engage in foreign trade transactions from within Barbados without license under the Act.
- No license may be issued other than to a company that is incorporated under the Companies Act, whose principal object and activity is designated as a foreign sales corporation under the laws of the US, including the Commonwealth of Puerto Rico.

Does Barbados allow for the formation of Trusts:

YES. Trusts are governed by the International Trusts Act 1995. International Trusts have the following features, benefits, and restrictions:

- the Trust is a private document and there is no requirement for it to be registered (unless the Trust holds Barbados land titles);
- the terms of the Trust may direct the accumulation of all or part of the income for a period not exceeding 100 years from the creation of the Trust;
- rule against perpetuities does not apply;
- the use of a Protector is provided for in the legislation;
- the Trust can specify that the laws of another jurisdiction are to apply to the interpretation and settlement of the Trust;

- forced heirship rules are avoided;
- the Trust may allow for the addition of future Beneficiaries;
- the Trust may exclude a Beneficiary from certain Trust assets; and
- the Trust may require certain terms & conditions to be met before distributing Trust assets.

The International Trusts Act also allows the formation of an Asset Protection Trust, where if a Settlor (who is solvent at the time and not planning to become insolvent) transfers assets to the Trust and subsequently becomes insolvent, the Trust would not be declared void upon application by a creditor. The fraudulent dispositons limit is 3 years. An advantage of the Asset Protection Trust is that the intent of the Settlor in establishing the Asset Protection Trust is irrelevant to any attack against Trust assets.

Does Barbados allow for the formation of Captive Insurance Companies?

YES. International insurance companies are governed by the Exempt Insurance Act of 1983. Barbados captive insurance companies have the following features, benefits, and restrictions:

- Exemption from all corporate taxes on income or capital gains or any tax on the transfer of assets or securities to any person.
- Exemption from withholding tax on any dividends, interest or other returns to shareholders.
- Dividends paid to a Canadian company out of income earned from a captive insurance business in Barbados are considered exempt earnings and are not subject to Canadian taxes, providing the risks insured are non-Canadian or third party risks.
- Business convention expenses incurred by U.S. corporations and organizations are deductible in the U.S. against U.S. taxes.
- Simple statutory filing requirements.
- Minimum capitalization of US$125,000. Annual license fee of US$2,500.

- 35% of earnings tax free by resident expatriate employees.
- Exemption from exchange control regulations.

Does Barbados allow for the formation of Private Banking Companies?

YES. International banking companies are governed by the Offshore Banking Act of 1979.

Financial institutions and contacts:

Altamira International Bank (Barbados) Inc.
3rd Floor, International Trading Centre, Warrens
St.Michael, Barbados, W.I.
tel. 246-425-4940, fax 246-425-4944, email: altabank@caribsurf.com, net: www.altabank.com

- *Services Offered:* investment advisor, private banking, mutual fund manager, trust services, global investing information, safekeeping services

---

Bank of Nova Scotia
PO.Box 202, Broad Street
Bridgetown, Barbados, W.I.
tel. 246-431-3000, fax 246-426-0969

- *Services Offered:* retail banking, loans and credit, safekeeping services

---

Barbados International Bank & Trust Co.
Price Waterhouse Centre, Collymore Rock, PO.Box 634C
St.Michael, Barbados, W.I.
tel. 246-436-7000, fax 246-436-7057

- *Services Offered:* retail banking

Barbados Investment & Development Corp.
Pelican House, Princess Alice Highway
Bridgetown, Barbados, W.I.
tel. 246-427-5350, fax 246-426-7802

- *Services Offered:* government services

Barbados National Bank
No.1 Broad Street, PO.Box 1009
Bridgetown, Barbados, W.I.
tel. 246-431-5800, fax 246-426-5037, telex 2271 WB

- *Services Offered:* private banking, retail banking, loans and credit

---

Barbados Supervisor of Insurance
Ministry of Finance & Economic Affairs, Treasury Building, 6th floor
Bridgetown, Barbados, W.I.
tel. 246-426-3815, fax 246-436-2699

- *Services Offered:* government services, Booklet: Barbados - A Guide For Investors in the Exempt Insurance Industry.

Caribbean Captive Insurance Managers, Inc. (CCIM)
PO.Box 84W, Worthing
Christ Church, Barbados, W.I.
tel. 809-436-8826, fax 809-436-8821

- *Services Offered:* captive insurance formation

Central Bank of Barbados
PO.Box 1016
Bridgetown, Barbados, W.I.
tel. 246-436-6870, fax 246-427-9559

- *Services Offered:* government services

International Insurance Management Ltd.
CGM Building, Collymore Rock
Bridgetown, Barbados, W.I.
tel. 809-426-1442, fax 809-426-7336

- *Services Offered:* captive insurance formation, captive insurance management

---

Royal Bank of Canada (Caribbean) Corporation
2nd Floor, Building #2, Chelston Park, Collymore Rock
St.Michael, Barbados, W.I.
tel. 246-429-4923, fax 246-429-4948

- *Services Offered:* private banking, estate planning services

BELIZE

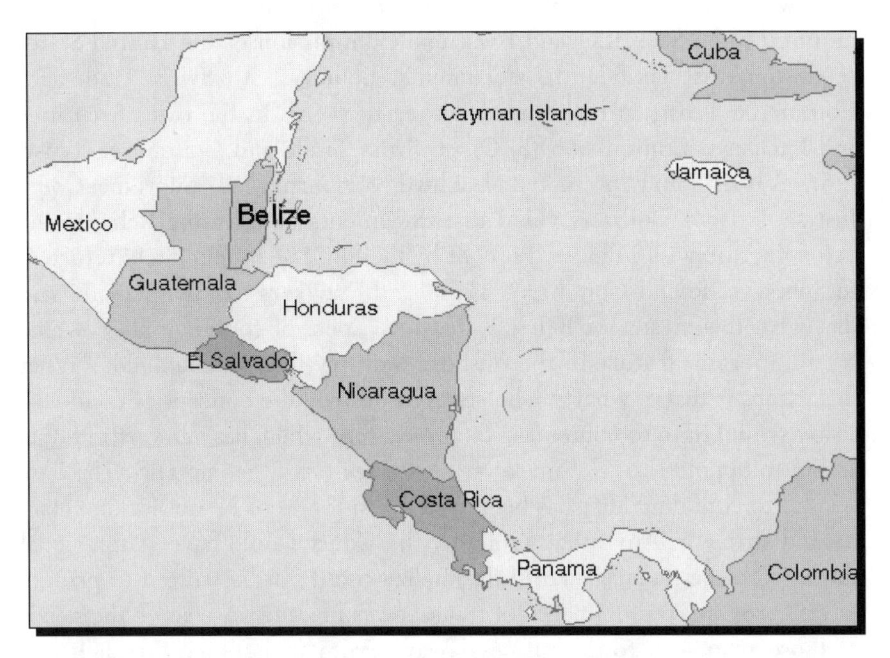

In Central America. On the east coast of Central America bordering Mexico to the north and Guatemala to the west and south. Belize is 174 miles long and 68 miles wide, covering an area of 8,865 square miles. Population is approximately 240,000 with approximately 60,000 living in Belize City, the capital. Main language is English and Spanish. Climate is sub-tropical.

Formerly known as the British Honduras, Belize became a British Crown Colony in 1862. The name was changed from British Honduras to Belize in 1973. Belize became an independent self ruling republic on September 21, 1981. A British military garrison remains, however, to protect against Guatemala which has claimed Belize.

You must live in Belize one year to be granted permanent residency. Upon entering Belize, apply for residency, and then renew your tourist visa every 30 or 90 days until residency is granted.

In a decision asserting Belize's sovereignty as an offshore financial jurisdiction, the Supreme Court of Belize upheld the country's confidentiality laws (January 20, 1995) by revoking a previous court order set in motion by the Securities and Exchange Commission of the United States requesting that confidential documents, belonging to Swiss Trade and Commerce Trust, Ltd., be handed over to them. In the case, Securities and Exchange Commission (SEC) vs. Swiss Trade and Commerce Trust, Ltd., Banner Fund International, Lloyd Winburn et al, Supreme Court Justice Troadio Gonzalez ruled that documents held by the Belize court belonging to Swiss Trade and sought by the SEC, be immediately returned to Swiss Trade and Commerce Trust, Ltd. Lawyers for Swiss Trade said that what this means for Belize is that this aspect of confidentiality, which is an important feature of the offshore industry, has been upheld. "What this means is that any party who seeks to destroy the concept of confidentiality would have to contend with our system, which has demonstrated its ability to uphold the relevant laws," Attorney Oscar Sabido said. The Law related to confidentiality has been tested and found to be not lacking clarity and strength. Any other ruling by the Court would have sent a signal throughout the financial world that Belize could not be trusted to protect assets, provide confidentiality of transactions or otherwise serve the needs of those who seek to do business away "From their home jurisdiction." The decision clearly shows that the SEC stepped out of bounds in trying to obtain confidential information, the matter having been urged on both sides by learned Queen's Council. The case arose after the SEC appeared at Swiss Trade's office on March 3, 1994 with the expectation that they would be able to just take the files and leave the country with them, with no regard whatever to Belizean law. The quick reaction of company employees prevented any further disregard for the law on the part of the SEC and their Belizean lawyer, Eamon Courtenay, who previously had been the lawyer for Swiss Trade.

Does Belize have any banking or corporate secrecy legislation?

YES. Belize's secrecy laws prohibit the unauthorized disclosure of information, providing for criminal penalties of up to US$50,000 and a prison term of up to one year for any disclosure concerning the business affairs of a client. A bank would receive the maximum penalty.

Although Belize has imposed strict bank secrecy laws, the law does not apply to activities that are considered crimes in Belize, such as illegal drug activities, theft, or fraud.

Although the secrecy laws protect against unauthorized disclosure to foreign tax authorities, confidential information has been released in the past through an exchange of information agreement between the U.S. and Belize. The new Trust Act, enacted in May 1992, has further enhanced secrecy, hopefully preventing any further compromising of bank secrecy.

Does Belize have a long history of legal stability?

YES. Formerly under British rule as the British Honduras, the republic of Belize became an independent country with its own constitution in 1981. Government is a parliamentary democracy based on the Westminster model. The cabinet, under the leadership of the Prime Minister, directs the policy of the government which consists of the Prime Minister and ministers chosen by him from an elected house of representatives. Belize is a member of the British Commonwealth and the United Nations.

The legal system is based on the Westminster model and is supplemented by local statutes. The court system is also similar to that in England. Contract and commercial law is based on the English model.

Is there an income tax in Belize?

NO. Both a Belize Trust and an IBC are exempt from any form of income tax in the country if they do not produce income in Belize. IBC's are exempt from capital gains tax, inheritance tax, and stamp duties.

For residents of Belize, pension and social security income received in Belize is tax free. Other income from outside Belize is taxed at 5% on the first Bz$1,000, graduated up to 50% on income over Bz$60,000.

Are there any other taxes in Belize?

NO. There is no capital gains taxes, gift taxes, or estate taxes in Belize for an IBC or Trust.

Does Belize maintain exchange controls?

NO. There are currently no exchange controls in Belize. The official currency is the Belize dollar which is tied to the U.S. dollar with a fixed exchange rate of Bz$2.00 = US$1.00.

Does Belize maintain tax treaties with any other countries?

NO. There is no double-taxation agreement between the U.S. and Belize, although there is an exchange of information agreement in certain tax cases.

There is no double-taxation agreement between Canada and Belize.

Does Belize allow for the formation of corporate entities?

YES. The International Business Companies Act 1990, based on the British Virgin Islands Act, created a special class of company called an IBC. The law was enacted to permit asset protection and tax minimization at competitive rates. Some advantages of Belize IBCs are as follows:

- Total exemption from all forms of local taxation including stamp duty.
- Only one shareholder (who could be corporate) is required.
- An IBC may have bearer shares or registered shares.
- The person creating the corporation can remain secret by appointing nominee shareholders and directors.
- IBCs require only one director. Directors can be corporate and need not be resident in the country.
- Meetings of shareholders and directors can be held in any country, at any time and they may attend meetings by proxy.
- No accounts or information pertaining to the identity of shareholders or directors need be filed on public record. An IBC's Register of Shareholders is available for inspection only by shareholders or by order of the Belize Courts at the request of a shareholder.

- Limited filing requirements, mainly certificate of incorporation, memorandum and articles of association, registered office and name and address of registered agent.
- The process of incorporation is simple, requiring the filing of a memorandum and articles of association, and the fee paid to the relevant registrar.
- The annual filing fee may be as low as US$100.

You are restricted from forming an IBC only under two conditions: if that IBC would be doing business with residents of Belize or if it would own real estate in the country. Company names must end with the following words or their abbreviations: Limited, Corporation, Incorporated, Société Anonyme, or Sociedad Anonima.

Public Investment Company - Belize also offers a Public Investment Company (PIC) that grants additional benefits, such as the right to manage funds belonging to Belize residents. A PIC is guaranteed exemption from all forms of taxes and duties for up to 30 years. Dividends paid to shareholders are not subject to withholding tax. PIC shares must be listed on an approved international stock exchange.

Does Belize allow for the formation of Trusts?

YES. The Belize Trusts Act of 1992 was enacted in May 1992 to offer innovative programs in the areas of Trusts and taxation. The new Belize trust and incorporation legislation is perhaps the cleanest and most user-friendly in the world. The Belize Trusts Act allows you to achieve a high level of asset protection, protecting from both Belize taxation and your local taxation. The Trust Act avoids any restrictions placed on what the Trustee can do with the money. Belize Trusts offer the following advantages:

- The maximum life for a Belize Trust is 120 years.
- Trusts of a finite duration can convert to charitable Trusts of indefinite duration.
- Trust can be registered, which may appeal to residents of civil law countries.

The cost of registering a Trust is US$100 and the process takes one to two weeks.

Does Belize allow for the formation of Captive Insurance Companies?

YES. A Belize IBC may apply for an insurance license.

Does Belize allow for the formation of Private Banking Companies?

YES. A Belize IBC may apply for a banking license.

Financial institutions and contacts:

Belize Trust Company Limited
60 Market Square, PO.Box 1764
Belize City, Belize
tel. 501-2-72660, fax 501-2-70983

- *Services Offered:* private banking

Butterfield, Reimer & Associates S.A.
1632 Buttonwood Bay Blvd., PO.Box 2098
Belize City, Belize
tel. 501-2-34274, fax 501-2-34306

- *Services Offered:* investment advisor, company formation, trust formation, global investing information, deposit backed MC/Visa

---

Glenn D. Godfrey Barrister-at-Law
PO.Box 1074, 2A King Street
Belize City, Belize
tel. 501-2-72457, fax 501-2-78909

- *Services Offered:* law office

Government of Belize
Belmopan, Belize
tel. 501-8-22423, fax 501-8-22662

- *Services Offered:* government services

Magna Charta Society of Business Administrators Limited
PO.Box 1113, 4-1/2 Mile North Highway
Belize City, Belize
tel. 501-2-33338, fax 501-2-33338

- *Services Offered:* company formation, trust formation

Pannell Kerr Forster
Regent House, 35 Regent Street, PO.Box 280
Belize City, Belize

- *Services Offered:* accounting services

The Belize Bank Limited (Corporate Services)
60 Market Square, PO.Box 1764
Belize City, Belize
tel. 501-2-72390, fax 501-2-77018, telex 158 BZE BANK BZ

- *Services Offered:* company formation, trust formation, private banking, retail banking, loans and credit

BERMUDA

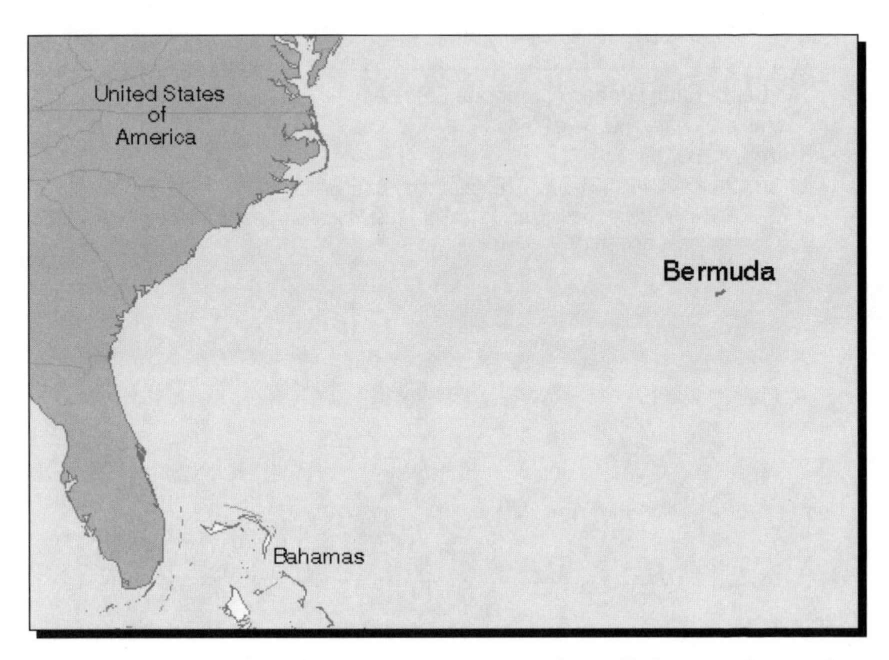

In the Western Atlantic Ocean, 570 miles off the North Carolina coast, and 774 miles southeast of New York. Over 150 small islands, the seven largest connected by bridges and causeways. Population is approximately 60,000. Main language is English. The climate is semi-tropical and frost free, and humid due to the warming effect of the Gulf Stream. Average temperatures are 89°F in summer and 47°F in winter.

In the 16th Century Spaniard Juan de Bermudez discovered the islands. He visited there in 1503 but failed to claim them for his country. It wasn't until July 28, 1609 that British Admiral Sir George Somers, leading a fleet on its way to the struggling colony of Virginia with his flag ship "Sea Venture," was shipwrecked on Bermuda's treacherous reefs. It was a mishap which led to the British colonization in 1612 what is officially known today as the Bermudas, or Somers Island. Bermuda has remained under the flag of Great Britain, and Bermudans are proud of the fact that their country is the oldest British colony with a House of Assembly elected by the people.

Bermuda has now signed a double-taxation agreement with the United States that includes exchange of information. The Florida branch of the Bank of Nova Scotia was hit with a fine of US$25,000 per day until it released information on clients of its Bermuda branch. Switzerland's Banca dela Svizzera Italiana was fined US$50,000 per day until it revealed information about Kuwaiti investors for whom it had bought stock (because the clients volunteered the information, the Swiss bank did not have to disclose any information).

Does Bermuda have any banking or corporate secrecy legislation?

NO. There are no bank secrecy laws in Bermuda, although the Bermudan government will not allow disclosure of confidential bank information in cases strictly involving tax evasion.

A tax treaty ratified in July 1986 provides U.S. law enforcement agencies with financial information concerning U.S. civil and criminal tax cases.

Does Bermuda have a long history of legal stability?

YES. Since 1684 Governors of Bermuda, acting on behalf of Her Majesty, have been appointed by the Crown. The Bermuda Constitution Order, effective June 8, 1968, provides for internal self-government. The UK, through the Governor, is responsible for external affairs, defense, internal security, and the police.

As the oldest British colony with a House of Assembly elected by the people, the legal system is based on English Acts of general application which were in force on July 11, 1612. These Acts have been subject to Amendments since 1612 that have repealed, modified, and amended those laws. The judicial system incorporates the Court of Appeals, Supreme Court, Magistrate's Court, and Special Court.

Is there an income tax in Bermuda?

NO. There are no income taxes, profit taxes, withholding taxes or capital gains taxes in Bermuda. Under the Exempted Tax Protection Act, Exempted Companies can obtain a guarantee of exemption from any taxes that may be imposed in the future, until

March 29, 2016. It is expected that as this date approaches, the guarantee will be further extended. No income tax, gift tax, business, property, capital gains, sales, estate, or any other kind of tax, except for certain annual fees.

The government receives revenue from customs duties, an employment tax of 7%, a hotel occupancy tax of 6%, an annual land tax on properties ranging from 1.5% to 22.5% of assessed ARV (Annual Rental Value), and a $15 departure tax when departing from Bermuda. There is a tax on payrolls and a charge for estates probated in Bermuda.

Are there any other taxes in Bermuda?

YES. There is a charge for estates probated in Bermuda There are no capital gains taxes or gift taxes in Bermuda.

Does Bermuda maintain exchange controls?

YES. An exchange control is exercised over Bermuda's citizens, subject to the controls imposed by the Exchange Control Act, 1972. Legislation provides for the formation of companies which are exempted from the 60% Bermudan ownership requirement on condition that they carry on business outside Bermuda. Since February 6, 1970, the official currency has been the Bermuda dollar. The Bermuda Dollar is at par with the U.S. dollar.

Does Bermuda maintain tax treaties with any other countries?

YES. A tax treaty ratified in July 1986 provides U.S. law enforcement agencies with financial information concerning U.S. civil and criminal tax cases.

There is no tax treaty between Canada and Bermuda.

Does Bermuda allow for the formation of corporate entities?

YES. Bermuda companies are governed by the Companies Act, 1981, and the Companies Amendment Act, 1992, stating that:

- A minimum of two directors are required who need not be shareholders.
- The issue of bearer shares is prohibited.

- A public offering requires a prospectus that complies with the terms of the Act.

Two types of companies can be incorporated in Bermuda, Local Companies and Exempted Companies.

Local Companies - Local Companies may carry on commercial activity within Bermuda, and must have at least 60% of the voting shares owned by Bermudans.

Exempted Companies - Exempted Companies are exempt from statutes applying to local companies, including exchange controls, and can trade in any currency other than Bermuda dollars. No Exempted Company can hold titles to Bermuda land, and are prohibited from trading within Bermuda. The Companies Act, 1981 and Companies Amendment Act, 1992 require that:

- Exempted Companies must have a registered office in Bermuda where corporate records (minute book, corporate seal, share certificate book, share register, and incorporation documents) are maintained.
- A minimum of one shareholder is required.
- A minimum of two directors resident in Bermuda are required. Directors need not be shareholders.
- An Exempted Company must elect a president and vice-president from among its directors.
- A secretary must be appointed who may be a director.

Advantages of a Bermuda Exempted Company include:

- A nominee or nominee company may hold shares and provide directors.
- No financial statements of a private company are open to public inspection, and there is no reporting to any authority.
- Exempted companies can obtain a guarantee of exemption from any taxes that may be imposed in the future, until March 29, 2016.
- Annual meetings need not be held in Bermuda.

- Exempted Companies may provide financial assistance for their employees to buy shares.

Does Bermuda allow for the formation of Trusts?

YES. Bermuda Trusts are governed by the Trustee Act 1975, the Trust (Special Provisions) Act 1989 and the Perpetuities and Accumulations Act 1989, which incorporate most of the provisions of the English Trustee Act 1925.

Bermuda's modern Trust law allows for no limit on the income accumulation within the 100 year perpetuity period. Bermuda Trust law allows "Purpose Trusts" permitting the establishment of Trusts for the benefit of business, scientific, or charitable purposes. Advantages include:

- The Trust may be governed by the laws of any jurisdiction.
- The governing laws of the Trust may be changed to the laws of another jurisdiction at any time.
- No Bermuda Trust may be set aside if the laws of a foreign jurisdiction do not recognize the concept of a Trust. Forced heirship provisions are ignored.
- Accumulation of income is permitted throughout the Trust period.
- Bermuda allows the formation of Discretionary Trusts, Fixed Trusts, and combinations thereof.
- A Trust may be revocable or irrevocable.
- There are no filing requirements for Trusts.

The Stamp Duties Amendment Act 1993 abolished the maximum stamp duty (US$250 plus 0.1% of assets up to US$4,000) if the Trust is administered by a Bermudan Trustee.

Does Bermuda allow for the formation of Captive Insurance Companies?

YES. Under the Insurance Act, 1978, insurance companies must have a minimum paid-up capital of US$120,000 for general business, US$250,000 for long-term business, or US$370,000 for both general and long-term business. Applications for registration are reviewed in detail by the Bermuda Monetary Authority, the Registrar of Companies and the Insurers Admissions Committee.

Insurance companies are required to prepare annual audited financial statements to be filed with the Registrar of Companies consisting of:

- An approved auditor's report.
- A certificate of solvency.
- Declaration of statutory ratios.

Long-term business includes the following additional requirements:

- Insurers must appoint an approved actuary.
- An actuarial certificate is required to be filed every year.
- Long-term business must be segregated with appropriate accounting.

The Minister of Finance has the power to investigate the affairs of an insurer. If there is a risk of insolvency, he has the power to restrict the operations of the insurer by restricting new business, restricting investments to specific classes, and requiring liquidation of certain investments.

Does Bermuda allow for the formation of Private Banking Companies?

YES. Because the definition of "banking business" in Bermuda is narrow, it is possible to carry on many banking activities from Bermuda which in many other jurisdictions would require a banking license.

Financial institutions and contacts:

Bank of N.T. Butterfield & Son Ltd.
PO.Box HM 195, 65 Front Street
Hamilton, Bermuda, HM AX
tel. 441-295-1111, fax 441-292-4365, telex 321 FIELD BA

- *Services Offered:* investment advisor, company formation, trust formation, private banking, retail banking, safekeeping services

---

Bermuda Chamber of Commerce
PO.Box HM 655
Hamilton, Bermuda, HM CX
tel. 441-295-4201

- *Services Offered:* government services

Bermuda Ministry of Finance
Government Administration Building, 30 Parliament Street
Hamilton, Bermuda, HM 12

- *Services Offered:* government services

GT (Bermuda) Ltd.
Hamilton, Bermuda
tel. 441-292-5415, fax 441-292-5810

- *Services Offered:* mutual fund manager

Orbis Investment Management Limited
4/F, LPG Building, 34 Bermudiana Road
Hamilton, Bermuda, HM 2
tel. 441-292-6666, fax 441-292-6500

- *Services Offered:* mutual fund manager

Standard Life-Bermuda
PO.Box HM 1125
Hamilton, Bermuda, HM EX
tel. 441-296-0333, fax 441-295-6209

- *Services Offered:* insurance-based investments

BRITISH VIRGIN ISLANDS

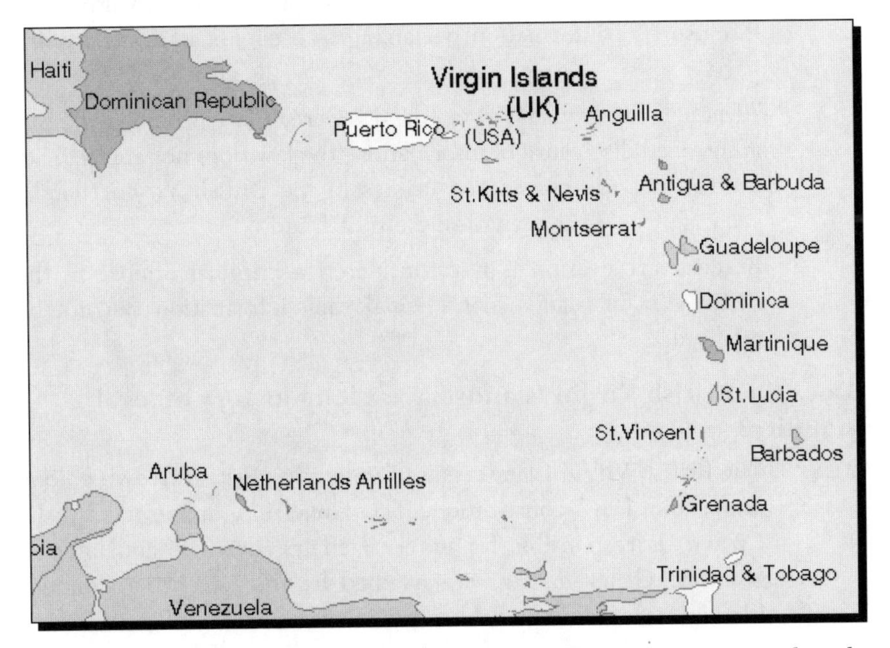

In the Caribbean. An archipelago of over 60 islands, cays and rocks spread over 58 square miles. The British Virgin Islands are 90 miles east of Puerto Rico, neighboring the U.S.Virgin Islands. Population is approximately 12,000. Main language is English.

On November 16, 1493, while en route to Puerto Rico, Christopher Columbus discovered the islands. He anchored and spent the night southeast of the island that became known as Virgin Gorda. He named the entire group of islands "Las Once Mil Virgines," after St.Ursula and her legendary 11,000 martyred companions. At that time the indigenous population consisted mainly of Carib Indians. In 1672 Britain claimed Tortola, while Denmark claimed St.Thomas and St.John in that same year. The Danish islands were then sold to the U.S. for $25 million in 1917. The British Virgin Islands became a self-governing colony with its own constitution in 1967.

Does the British Virgin Islands have any banking or corporate secrecy legislation?

YES. The British Virgin Islands' secrecy laws prohibit the unauthorized disclosure of information pertaining to a clients affairs to a third party.

Although the British Virgin Island's secrecy law prohibits the unauthorized disclosure of information, the law does not apply to activities that are considered crimes in the British Virgin Islands, such as illegal drug activities, theft, or fraud.

Because tax evasion is not considered a criminal offense in the British Virgin Islands, confidential bank information can not be released.

Does the British Virgin Islands have a long history of legal stability?

YES. The British Virgin Islands is a self-governing British Crown colony under the 1967 constitution. The Governor, appointed by the Crown, is responsible for external affairs, defense, and internal security. Other matters are handled by the Executive Council. Elections are normally held every five years.

The legal system was established by the British, and is based on English Common Law. The supreme court is the West Indies Associated States Supreme Court, with High Court of Justice and Court of Appeal branches. Lower courts are the Court of Summary Jurisdiction and the Magistrate's Court.

Is there an income tax in the British Virgin Islands?

NO. There is no income tax in the British Virgin Islands on income earned outside the islands. Personal income derived from the islands is taxed at a maximum rate of 20%. Corporate income derived from the islands is taxed at a flat rate of 15%.

Are there any other taxes in the British Virgin Islands?

NO. There is no capital gains tax, gift tax, death duty, or estate tax in the British Virgin Islands.

Does the British Virgin Islands maintain exchange controls?

NO. There are currently no exchange controls in the British Virgin Islands. The official currency is the U.S. dollar.

Does the British Virgin Islands maintain tax treaties with any other countries?

YES. The tax treaty with the U.S. was terminated in January 1, 1983 because negotiators could not agree on a suitable arrangement, although an exchange of information agreement is a distinct possibility in the near future. An exchange of information agreement was signed with the U.S. in 1987 allowing bank accounts to be examined if there is evidence of them being used for drug trafficking or money laundering. Double taxation agreements exist with Japan and Switzerland.

The tax treaty between the UK (extended to cover the British Virgin Islands) and Canada was terminated in 1972.

Does the BVI allow for the formation of corporate entities?

YES. There are two types of companies that can be incorporated in the British Virgin Islands - Companies Act Companies and International Business Companies.

Companies Act Company - A Companies Act Company is designed to be operated within the British Virgin Islands, carrying on business with persons in the BVI.

International Business Company (IBC) - IBCs are governed by the International Business Companies Act 1984, enacted August 1, 1994. An IBC provides the following advantages and benefits:

- It is exempt from BVI taxes and stamp duty.
- There are no minimum capitalization requirements.
- Only one shareholder is required.
- The company requires only one director. No residency or nationality requirements for directors exist. Alternate directors are permitted. Directors may be corporate.
- Bearer shares, no par value shares, treasury shares, and different classes of shares are permitted.

- An IBC may purchase and own shares.
- Directors meetings may be held in any jurisdiction.
- There is no requirement to hold an annual general meeting.
- Disclosure of beneficial ownership is not required.
- The IBC laws provide for the transfer of registration of a company to another accommodating jurisdiction.
- In its title an IBC may use the word or an abbreviation of Limited, Incorporated, Corporation, Société Anonyme, or Sociedad Anonima.
- Companies incorporated in foreign jurisdictions may continue under the IBC Ordinance without the need for reciprocal arrangements with the jurisdiction of incorporation.
- Full compensation of officers or agents of an IBC from corporate funds is permitted.
- The directors are empowered to protect the assets of an IBC for the benefit of the IBC, its creditors and its members, and for any person having direct or indirect interests in the IBC by transferring the assets of the IBC in trust to Trustees or another company or legal entity, for the benefit of the IBC, its creditors or members.
- The filing of annual accounts is not required.
- The annual license fee is only US$300.

The only public record consists of the current certificate of incorporation, the Memorandum and Articles and amendments, the name and address of the registered agent, and the record of payments of the annual fees.

There is no public record identifying the shareholders or directors. However, an IBC may elect to maintain a register of directors, a share register and a register of mortgages and charges. Additionally, the International Business Companies (Amendment) Act 1990 created an optional registration facility so that shareholder and director reports can be filed with the Registrar of Companies.

IBCs may be managed and controlled from the British Virgin Islands, although they are prohibited from:

- Trading within the British Virgin Islands.
- Owning land titles in the British Virgin Islands.
- Carrying on banking, trust, insurance, or company management business without a license.

Where a foreign government expropriates or imposes confiscatory taxes upon the shares or other interests in the IBC, the IBC or any person holding shares or other interests therein, may apply to the court for an order that the IBC disregard the action of the foreign government and continue to treat as members or interest holders, those persons or shares or interests were subject to the action by the foreign government.

Does the BVI allow for the formation of Trusts?

YES. The British Virgin Islands is a suitable jurisdiction for the formation of International Trusts.

Does the BVI allow for the formation of Captive Insurance Companies?

YES. An IBC may apply for an insurance license, allowing it to carry on insurance business outside the British Virgin Islands.

Does the BVI allow for the formation of Private Banking Companies?

YES. An IBC can carry on banking or trust business if licensed under the Banks and Trust Companies Act 1990.

Financial institutions and contacts:

Allgemeines Treuunternehmen-ATU General Trust (BVI) Limited
65 Main Street, PO.Box 3463
Road Town, Tortola, British Virgin Islands
tel. 284-494-1100, fax 284-494-1199

- *Services Offered:* company formation, trust formation, estate planning services

---

Bank of Nova Scotia
PO.Box 434
Road Town, Tortola, British Virgin Islands

- *Services Offered:* private banking, retail banking, loans and credit

---

Blue Chip Capital Management Limited
Road Town, Tortola, British Virgin Islands
tel. 888-265-6661, fax 800-560-0645

- *Services Offered:* investment advisor, mutual fund manager, deposit backed MC/Visa, insurance-based investments

---

British Virgin Islands Financial Services
Road Town, Tortola, British Virgin Islands
tel. 284-494-6430

- *Services Offered:* government services

Commonwealth Trust Co. Ltd.
PO.Box 3321, Drake Chambers, Main Street
Road Town, Tortola, British Virgin Islands
tel. 284-494-4541, fax 284-494-3016, net: cowlth@caribsurf.com

- *Services Offered:* investment advisor, company formation, trust formation, corporate services, confidential securities trading

---

Czerlau & Associates Limited
Road Town, Tortola, British Virgin Islands
tel. 800-226-5703, fax 242-356-0223

- *Services Offered:* company formation, trust formation, estate planning services

---

Government of British Virgin Islands
Road Town, Tortola, British Virgin Islands
tel. 284-494-4190, fax 284-494-5016

- *Services Offered:* government services

Mossack Fonseca & Co. (BVI) Ltd.
Akara Building, 24 De Castro Street, PO.Box 3136
Wickhams Cay, Tortola, British Virgin Islands
tel. 284-494-4840, fax 284-494-5884

- *Services Offered:* company formation

CAYMAN ISLANDS

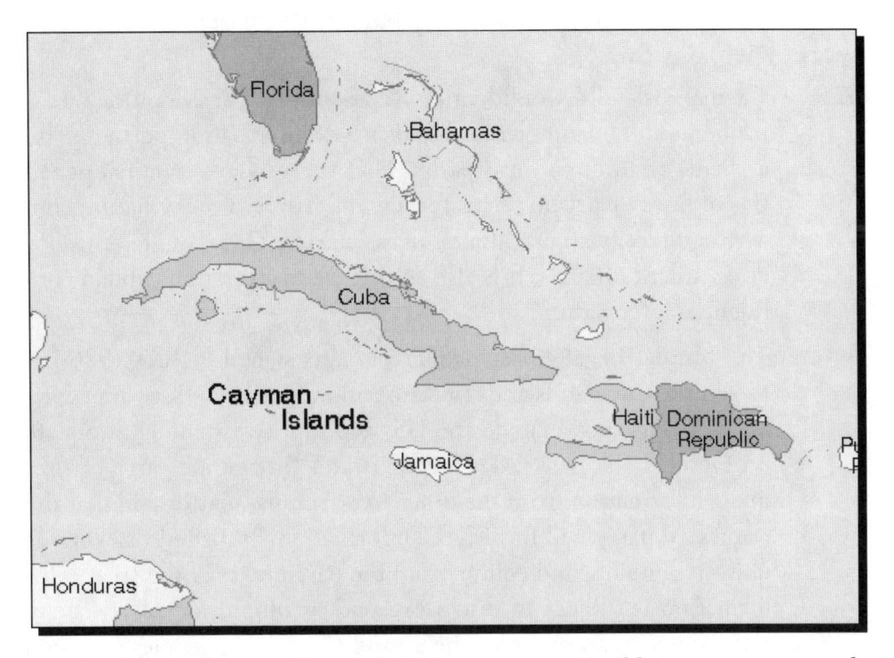

In the Caribbean. Situated in the western Caribbean, approximately 475 miles south of Miami, Florida and 180 miles northwest of Jamaica, and south of Cuba. Main language is English. They consist of three small islands with a total area of 100 square miles. Population is approximately 30,000 with the majority living on Grand Cayman. Climate is tropical with relatively low humidity, average temperature 82°F in summer and 72°F in winter.

Discovered by Columbus on May 10, 1503 during his fourth and last West Indian voyage, the trio of islands were named "Las Tortugas" after the turtles which surrounded them. By 1530 they were called "Caymanas," after the iguanas which roamed the islands. The Caymanas were ceded to Britain by Spain in 1670, and served as a favorite refuge for pirates and mariners until colonization began during the 1700's. For centuries the Caymans were associated politically with the British Colony of Jamaica. When Jamaica became independent in 1962, the Caymans chose to become a British Crown Colony. They have consistently rejected all offers of independence.

Does the Cayman Islands have any banking or corporate secrecy legislation?

YES. Cayman Island's Confidential Relationships (Preservation) Law prohibits the unauthorized disclosure of information pertaining to a clients affairs to a third party. The Act provides criminal penalties of fines or prison terms for any disclosure of information concerning the business affairs of a client. This law extends to government officials. It is also an offense to attempt to obtain confidential information.

The Mutual Legal Assistance Treaty was signed in July 1986 between the Cayman Islands (in association with the UK as appropriate sovereign power) and the US, and ratified by the U.S. Senate on October 24, 1989. This treaty states that either party can request information from the other in a criminal matter and that the requested party will furnish the information if satisfied that the request is genuine, and conforms to the parameters of the treaty. Information is subject to disclosure under compulsion of law or in satisfaction of an order of the Grand Court. The crimes included are all mutually recognized crimes drawing a sentence of one year or more, together with certain American offenses, such as insider trading and securities fraud. Tax matters are specifically excluded.

A typical Bank or Trust Company "Information Waiver" reads as follows:

```
The Confidential Relationships (Preservation) Law of
the Cayman Islands subjects (This Bank) to strict
regulations concerning the confidentiality of client
affairs. However, if and to the extent that (This
Bank) shall consider that non-disclosure would result
in the assets, operations, or personnel of (This
Bank) becoming liable to seizure, interference or
prejudice in the United States of America, (This
Bank) reserves the right to make disclosures. In all
other respects the rule of confidentiality remains
applicable and unaffected.
```

This "Information Waiver" is required by many of the Cayman banks. Although the Cayman Island's Confidential Relationships (Preservation) Law prohibits the unauthorized disclosure of information, the law does not apply to activities that are considered crimes in the Cayman Islands, such as illegal drug activities, theft, or fraud.

Confidential information can only be released if there is suspected criminal activity such as illegal drug activities, theft, or fraud. Tax matters are specifically excluded under the Mutual Legal Assistance Treaty with the U.S.

Does the Cayman Islands have a long history of legal stability?

YES. The present constitution was adopted August 22, 1972. The Government is headed by a resident British Governor, appointed by and responsible to the Crown. Through him, the British Government retains direct responsibility for internal and external security, the judiciary, and external relations. The Cayman Islands internal government is provided by a Legislative Assembly, responsible for enacting the local laws.

There are no political parties and no trade unions. There is no desire for independence and the Islands are considered politically, economically, and racially stable.

The legal system is based on English Common Law and is supplemented by local statutes. Modern company and trust statutes have been enacted together with legislation to control the activities of banks, trust companies and insurance businesses. Modern legislation, including the preservation of secrecy, has been specifically tailored to meet the needs of an offshore financial centre on a foundation of no direct taxation. The Financial Secretary maintains a standing Advisory Committee of members from all of the sectors of the financial industry to advise on any amendments which may be desirable to keep legislation current and competitive.

Is there an income tax in the Cayman Islands?

NO. There are no direct taxes on individuals or corporations. An exempted company is guaranteed to not be taxed for a period of 30 years. An ordinary company is guaranteed to not be taxed for a period of 20 years (even though there are currently no Cayman Island taxes).

Customs duties are levied on certain goods imported into the Islands, and stamp duty is charged on documents such as transfers of land, mortgages, debentures, leases, and promissory notes.

Are there any other taxes in the Cayman Islands?

NO. There are no direct taxes on individuals or corporations. There is no income tax, corporate tax, capital gains tax, capital or wealth tax, gift tax, inheritance tax or estate duty, property or estate tax, sales tax, payroll tax, business tax, withholding or dividend tax, or profits tax.

Does the Cayman Islands maintain exchange controls?

NO. All forms of exchange control in the Cayman Islands were abolished in 1980. The local currency is the Cayman Islands Dollar, which is tied to the U.S. Dollar at a rate of CI$1.00 = US$1.20.

Does the Cayman Islands maintain tax treaties with any other countries?

NO. No tax treaty has been signed between the U.S. and the Cayman Islands, although the Cayman Islands has signed the Mutual Legal Assistance Treaty with the U.S. The Mutual Legal Assistance Treaty covers narcotics trafficking and other specified crimes. Information may only be requested for use in the Cayman Islands or the US, and taxation is specifically excluded.

No tax treaty has been signed between Canada and the Cayman Islands. There are no exchange of information agreements with any other jurisdiction.

Does the Cayman Islands allow for the formation of corporate entities?

YES. The Cayman Islands Companies Law provides for the incorporation of two types of company - the Ordinary Company and the Exempted Company. Companies may be limited by guarantee or unlimited. Companies may also be established by a private act of the Legislative Assembly, but this is a rare occurrence. There is no legal distinction between private and public companies.

Ordinary Limited Company - An ordinary company limited by shares may be incorporated for any legal purpose by any person of legal age subscribing his name to a Memorandum of Association and agreeing to take up at least one share in the company. The Memorandum must contain:

- The name of the company.
- The address of its registered office.
- Objects of the company.
- A statement that the liability of the members is limited.
- Authorized capital, number of shares, and par value.

It is usual for companies to file articles of association prescribing regulations for the company, but it is not a legal requirement. Articles may be filed at any time. In the absence of articles of association, Table A in the schedule to the Companies Law will apply. There are no nationality or residence requirements for shareholders nor are there restrictions on where meetings of shareholders may be held. An annual general meeting of shareholders is required. The shareholders may attend in person or be represented by a proxy. Bearer shares may be issued by an exempted company but not by an ordinary company.

Every company is required to maintain a registered office in the Cayman Islands at which there must be located:

- The register of members, directors and officers, together with a register of mortgages and charges.
- The name of the company is required to be displayed outside the registered office and any change of location, authorized by resolution of the directors, must be advised to the Registrar of Companies.

In January each year, a company must file a return with the Registrar of Companies giving details of its capital structure, its shareholders, directors and officers. This return is accompanied by a registration fee based on authorized capital. There are no statutory audit requirements other than for banks, trust companies, and insurance companies.

Exempted Company - The Companies Law provides for the incorporation of exempted companies. These are incorporated in a similar manner to ordinary companies. A meeting of the board of directors must be called in the Cayman Islands at least once each year, but the meeting may be conducted by alternate directors or by properly authorized proxies. Certain exemptions and privileges apply to exempted companies:

- The words Limited, Incorporated, Société Anonyme, or their abbreviations need not appear in the name.
- The name of an Exempted Company may be in a foreign language.
- Annual general meetings of shareholders are not required.
- Bearer shares and shares of no par value may be issued.
- Annual returns to the Registrar of Companies, accompanied by appropriate fees, take the form of a declaration by a director or the secretary that the company has complied with provisions of the Companies Law. The return does not identify shareholders, directors, or officers and these names are not a matter of public record.
- Names of shareholders of an Exempted Company are not required to be filed with the Registrar of Companies.
- An Exempted Company must hold a directors meeting at least once every year in the Cayman Islands.
- A guarantee may be obtained from the Government that no income or capital taxes will be imposed on a company for a period of up to thirty years (in practice guarantees are issued for twenty years in the first instance).
- Shares and debentures issued by a company are similarly exempted from the future imposition of estate or inheritance taxes.

An Exempted Company may not carry on business in the Cayman Islands, and is prohibited from public offering in the Cayman Islands to subscribe for any of its shares or debentures.

Foreign Company - A company incorporated outside the Cayman Islands that establishes a place of business, or carries on business, in the Cayman Islands must register in compliance with the Companies Law. Registration is accomplished by filing a certified copy of the Memorandum and articles of association (or equivalent incorporation documents) with the Registrar of Companies, together with a certified list of the directors and officers giving their names, addresses and occupations. A foreign company must have an agent in the Cayman Islands authorized to accept notices or service of process.

Partnerships - The Partnership Law 1983, as amended, is virtually identical to the English Partnership Act 1890 and permits the formation of Limited Partnerships.

Does the Cayman Islands allow for the formation of Trusts?

YES. Trusts in the Cayman Islands are governed by the Trusts Law of 1967, which is similar to the English Law of Trusts. Trusts are generally created by deed, and impose upon a Trustee a duty to hold and administer assets for a Beneficiary named in the deed. Unlike a corporation, a Trust is not a separate legal entity. The law relating to Trusts has developed over centuries and serves to enforce the duties of Trustees and the rights of Beneficiaries.

A Trust may be created in the Cayman Islands by a resident of any country. The relevant deed may be signed by the Settlor in a location of his choice. The deed will normally specify:

- The powers and duties of the Trustees.
- The perpetuity period (or period of existence) of the Trust.
- The name of (or otherwise identify) the Beneficiaries.
- Direct the Trustees in relation to the distribution of the income and capital of the Trust.

There are no statutory restrictions on income accumulations. Trustees of Cayman Islands Trusts will normally be resident in the islands.

Trusts may be revocable or irrevocable. The most common form of Trust is the Discretionary Trust, where the assets are administered by the Trustees for the benefit of the Beneficiaries, as the Trustees in their absolute discretion may decide. Assets of Trusts may be located anywhere in the world but will remain under the control of the Trustees. It is usual, however, for the Trust deed to include a clause to facilitate a change in the jurisdiction if at any time this should prove to be necessary or desirable.

The Trusts (Foreign Element) Law of 1987 permits the creation of a Cayman Island Trust by a foreign Settlor of full age and capacity (as defined in Cayman Law) so that moveable property settled in the Trust governed by Cayman Law is protected against any forced heirship rules which may exist in the Settlor's domicile.

Trusts may not continue indefinitely. Trust assets must be distributed within 21 years following the death of a person living at the Trust formation date.

Exempted Trusts - The Trusts Law provides for a form of Trust known as an Exempted Trust. Similar in form to the ordinary Trust, it may continue in existence for up to 100 years. An Exempted Trust must be registered with the Registrar of Trusts who retains the original deed and issues a certificate of registration. The Trustees of an Exempted Trust may obtain a guarantee from the government against the imposition of income or capital taxes for a period of up to 50 years. Fees are payable upon registration and annually thereafter.

Mutual Funds and Unit Trusts - Investment funds may be established by Trust deed or by a limited liability company. If a fund is established by Trust deed the creator of the Trust will usually be a management company. The management company empowers Trustees to safeguard the investments purchased, and to receive the proceeds of Trust units sold.

The purchasers of units are the Beneficiaries of the fund. Each unit represents an individual interest in the net assets. The value of each unit is established by dividing the current net asset value of the fund by the number of units in issue. The powers and duties of the Trustees are set forth in the Trust deed, which also details:

- The manner in which units may be issued or redeemed.
- The investment powers, including the nature of the investments which may be acquired.
- The remuneration of the Trustee and manager.
- Units may be issued to a bearer.

If a fund is created by the incorporation of a limited liability company, the name and objects of the fund, together with details of its capital structure, will be detailed in the Memorandum of Association. Regulations governing the issue, redemption and valuation of shares and the operations of the company must be directed in the Articles of Association.

Does the Cayman Islands allow for the formation of Captive Insurance Companies?

YES. The business of insurance and reinsurance companies, insurance managers, and agents and brokers dealing in the domestic market, is regulated by the terms of the Insurance Law 1979 as amended. The law requires that no insurance, or insurance related business, as defined in the law, may be conducted in the Cayman Islands other than by the holder of a valid license issued by the Governor in Council. Three categories of license are available to insurance and reinsurance companies:

Class "A" License - permits domestic business.

Class "B" Unrestricted License - permits the holder to carry on business, other than domestic business, from within the Cayman Islands.

Class "B" Restricted License - permits the holder to carry on business outside the Cayman Islands with its shareholders or such other persons where the insurer is constituted through partnership, share holding, or other acceptable mutual association by one or more persons having a common trade, profession, affinity or other special interest.

License applications must be submitted in a statutory form. The minimum net worth requirements prescribed by the Insurance Law are:

- Companies writing short term general business (property and casualty) CI$100,000 (US$120,000).
- Companies writing long term business CI$200,000 (US$240,000).
- Companies writing both short and long term business CI$300,000 (US$360,000).

The corporate and financial records of a licensee are required to be maintained in the Cayman Islands. Audited accounts must be filed each year within six months of the end of the financial year, together with a Certificate of Compliance signed by either the Company's auditor or Insurance Manager attesting to the activities of the licensed insurer or reinsurer.

Does the Cayman Islands allow for the formation of Private Banking Companies?

YES. Bank and trust business is strictly regulated in terms of the Banks and Trust Companies Regulation Law (Revised) and the underlying Banks and Trust Companies (License Applications) Regulations (Revised). The law requires that no banking or trust business may be conducted in or from the Cayman Islands other than by a holder of a valid license granted by the Governor in Council. Applications for licenses are carefully reviewed by the Inspector of Banks and every attempt is made to preserve the high standard for which the Cayman Islands have become known in international financial circles. Types of licenses are:

Category "A" - permits unrestricted domestic and overseas business and is usually only granted to a branch or affiliate of a major international bank. The applicant must maintain a fully staffed office in the Cayman Islands.

Category "B" Unrestricted - permits the operation of banking business anywhere in the world except the Cayman Islands. Transactions may be carried out within the Cayman Islands for clients outside the Islands.

Category "B" Restricted - This further restricts the business permitted under the Category B license and limits the holder to a small number of named clients.

Although the law stipulates a minimum capital requirement of CI$200,000, the Governor in Council currently requires a minimum paid up capital of US$500,000. For a restricted License the minimum capital requirements are CI$20,000 (US$24,000).

Does the Cayman Islands allow the formation of Shipping Companies?

YES. George Town, Grand Cayman is a British port of registry. Registration is regulated by the British Merchant Shipping Act 1988.

Ships registered in the Cayman Islands are required to have certification under the major maritime conventions, including the 1966 International Convention on Loadlines, the 1969 International Convention on Tonnage Measurement, the 1972 International Convention on Regulations for Preventing Collisions at Sea, the 1973 International Convention for the Preventing of Pollution from Ships, and the 1974 International Convention for the Safety of Life at Sea.

To be registered on the Cayman Register, majority ownership of the ship must be by British citizens or a company incorporated in the Cayman Islands, UK, or any other British dependency. Benefits include exemption from U.S. Federal Income Tax for vessels trading there, Royal Navy protection, no national crewing requirements, and assistance of British Consular service world-wide.

Financial institutions and contacts:

Aall Trust & Banking Corporation Ltd.
PO.Box 1166
Grand Cayman, Cayman Islands, B.W.I.
tel. 345-949-5588, fax 345-949-8265

- *Services Offered:* company formation, private banking, corporate services

---

ABN AMRO Trust Company (Cayman) Limited
PO.Box 2506
Grand Cayman, Cayman Islands, B.W.I.
tel. 345-949-6470, fax 345-949-7230

- *Services Offered:* private banking

Alexander Insurance Managers (Cayman) Ltd.
PO.Box 1125, Anderson Square, George Town
Grand Cayman, Cayman Islands, B.W.I.
tel. 345-945-2888, fax 345-945-2889

- *Services Offered:* captive insurance formation

Alexandria Bancorp Limited
PO.Box 2064
Grand Cayman, Cayman Islands, B.W.I.
tel. 345-945-1111, fax 345-945-1122

- *Services Offered:* private banking

Amex International Trust (Cayman) Limited
PO.Box 674
Grand Cayman, Cayman Islands, B.W.I.
tel. 345-949-8806, fax 345-949-0261
- *Services Offered:* private banking

Aston Corporate Managers Ltd.
PO.Box 1981, Elizabethan Square
Grand Cayman, Cayman Islands, B.W.I.
tel. 345-949-5586, fax 345-949-8099
- *Services Offered:* company formation, corporate services

Bank in Liechtenstein (Cayman) Ltd.
Grand Cayman, Cayman Islands, B.W.I.
tel. 345-949-7676, fax 345-949-8512
- *Services Offered:* private banking

Bank of Nova Scotia
PO.Box 689, Scotiabank Building
Grand Cayman, Cayman Islands, B.W.I.
tel. 345-949-7666, fax 345-949-0020
- *Services Offered:* private banking

BankAmerica Trust and Banking Corporation (Cayman) Limited
PO.Box 1092, Anchorage Centre, George Town
Grand Cayman, Cayman Islands, B.W.I.
tel. 345-949-7888, fax 345-949-7883
- *Services Offered:* captive insurance formation, private banking

---

Barclays Finance Corporation of the Cayman Islands Limited
PO.Box 1321
Grand Cayman, Cayman Islands, B.W.I.
tel. 345-949-4310, fax 345-949-7179
- *Services Offered:* private banking

Bessemer Trust Company (Cayman) Limited
PO.Box 694
Grand Cayman, Cayman Islands, B.W.I.
tel. 345-949-6674, fax 345-949-6064
- *Services Offered:* private banking

British American Bank Ltd.
PO.Box 914, First Home Tower
Grand Cayman, Cayman Islands, B.W.I.
tel. 345-949-7822, fax 345-949-6064

- *Services Offered:* private banking, retail banking

Caledonian Bank & Trust Limited
PO.Box 1043, Caledonian House, George Town
Grand Cayman, Cayman Islands, B.W.I.
tel. 345-949-0050, fax 345-949-8062

- *Services Offered:* captive insurance formation, private banking

---

Cayman Corporate Services (1995) Limited
PO.Box 490
Grand Cayman, Cayman Islands, B.W.I.
tel. 345-949-7533, fax 345-949-8419

- *Services Offered:* private banking

Cayman General Insurance Co. Ltd.
PO.Box 2171, Zephyr House, George Town
Grand Cayman, Cayman Islands, B.W.I.
tel. 345-949-7028, fax 345-949-7457

- *Services Offered:* captive insurance formation

Cayman Islands Government - Finance and Development
Government Administration Bldg, George Town
Grand Cayman, Cayman Islands, B.W.I.
tel. 345-949-7900, fax 345-949-8650

- *Services Offered:* government services

Cayman Islands Government - Financial Services Department
Harbour Centre
Grand Cayman, Cayman Islands, B.W.I.
tel. 345-949-7999, fax 345-949-8487

- *Services Offered:* government services

Cayman Islands Government - Government Information Services
George Town
Grand Cayman, Cayman Islands, B.W.I.
tel. 345-949-8092, fax 345-949-5936

- *Services Offered:* government services

Cayman Islands Government - Internal and External Affairs
Government Administration Bldg, George Town
Grand Cayman, Cayman Islands, B.W.I.
tel. 345-949-7900, fax 345-949-7544

- *Services Offered:* government services

Chandler Insurance Management Ltd.
PO.Box 1854, Anderson Square, George Town
Grand Cayman, Cayman Islands, B.W.I.
tel. 345-949-8177, fax 345-949-8376

- *Services Offered:* captive insurance formation

Citco Trust Company (Cayman Islands) Limited
PO.Box 31106
Grand Cayman, Cayman Islands, B.W.I.
tel. 345-949-3977, fax 345-949-3877

- *Services Offered:* private banking

Cititrust (Cayman) Limited
PO.Box 170
Grand Cayman, Cayman Islands, B.W.I.
tel. 345-949-0355, fax 345-949-0360, tel. 345-949-5405

- *Services Offered:* private banking

Coopers & Lybrand Chartered Accountants
PO.Box 219, Butterfield House
Grand Cayman, Cayman Islands, B.W.I.
tel. 345-949-7000, fax 345-949-8154, telex 4220 COLYBRA CP

- *Services Offered:* company formation, trust formation, captive insurance formation, bank formation, accounting services

---

First Cayman Bank
PO.Box 1113, West Bay Road
Grand Cayman, Cayman Islands, B.W.I.
tel. 345-949-5266, fax 345-949-5398

- *Services Offered:* private banking, retail banking

Five Continents Financial Limited
PO.Box 30715 SMB, 2nd Floor, Anchorage Centre
Grand Cayman, Cayman Islands, B.W.I.
tel. 345-949-3022, fax 345-949-3177

- *Services Offered:* mutual fund manager, company formation, corporate services

---

Giglioli & Company
PO.Box 1316, Scotiabank Building
Grand Cayman, Cayman Islands, B.W.I.
tel. 345-949-0999, fax 345-949-4093

- *Services Offered:* law office

HSBC International Trustee Limited
PO.Box 484
Grand Cayman, Cayman Islands, B.W.I.
tel. 345-949-9555, fax 345-949-9554

- *Services Offered:* private banking

HSBC Trustee (Cayman) Limited
PO.Box 484
Grand Cayman, Cayman Islands, B.W.I.
tel. 345-949-9555, fax 345-949-7634

- *Services Offered:* private banking

Insurance Services International Ltd. (ISIL)
PO.Box 1345, Elizabethan Square, George Town
Grand Cayman, Cayman Islands, B.W.I.
tel. 345-949-5499, fax 345-949-8747

- *Services Offered:* captive insurance formation

International Risk Management (Cayman) Ltd.
PO.Box 69, British American Tower, George Town
Grand Cayman, Cayman Islands, B.W.I.
tel. 345-949-0155, fax 345-949-0002

- *Services Offered:* captive insurance formation

Jeffrey M. Parker & Co.
PO.Box 1782, Clarion Grand Pavillion
Grand Cayman, Cayman Islands, B.W.I.
tel. 345-949-5758, fax 345-949-7707

- *Services Offered:* accounting services

Julius Baer Bank and Trust Company Ltd.
P.O.Box 1100
Grand Cayman, Cayman Islands, B.W.I.
tel. 345-949-7212, fax 345-949-6096

- *Services Offered:* private banking

Maples & Calder
PO.Box 309, Ugland House, South Church Street
Grand Cayman, Cayman Islands, B.W.I.
tel. 345-949-8066, fax 345-949-8080, telex 4212

- *Services Offered:* law office

Mercury Bank & Trust Limited
PO.Box 2424
Grand Cayman, Cayman Islands, B.W.I.
tel. 345-949-0800, fax 345-949-0295

- *Services Offered:* private banking

Myers & Alberga Attorneys-at-Law
PO.Box 472, Midland Bank Building
Grand Cayman, Cayman Islands, B.W.I.
tel. 345-949-0699, fax 345-949-8171

- *Services Offered:* company formation, trust formation, law office, corporate services, safekeeping services

---

Neville W. Levy & Associates
PO.Box 2177, Thompson Building
Grand Cayman, Cayman Islands, B.W.I.
tel. 345-949-5429

- *Services Offered:* law office

Offshore Incorporations (Cayman) Limited
PO.Box 309, Ugland House
Grand Cayman, Cayman Islands, B.W.I.
tel. 345-949-8066, fax 345-949-8080

- *Services Offered:* company formation, corporate services

Paul Harris & Co.
PO.Box 61, Genesis Building
Grand Cayman, Cayman Islands, B.W.I.
tel. 345-949-2914, fax 345-949-8635

- *Services Offered:* accounting services

Price Waterhouse
PO.Box 258, First Home Tower, Jennett Street, British-American Centre
Grand Cayman, Cayman Islands, B.W.I.
tel. 345-949-7944, fax 345-949-7352, telex CP 293 4 329

- *Services Offered:* company formation, trust formation, accounting services, safe-keeping services

---

Ramon Alberga, QC
PO.Box 731, Thompson Bldg.
Grand Cayman, Cayman Islands, B.W.I.
tel. 345-949-4145

- *Services Offered:* law office

Schroder Cayman Bank and Trust Company Limited
PO.Box 1040
Grand Cayman, Cayman Islands, B.W.I.
tel. 345-949-2849, fax 345-949-5409

- *Services Offered:* private banking

Sedgewick Management Services (Cayman) Limited
PO.Box 1109, Midland Bank Trust Bldg, George Town
Grand Cayman, Cayman Islands, B.W.I.
tel. 345-949-7755, fax 345-949-7634

- *Services Offered:* captive insurance formation

State Street Cayman Trust Company, Ltd.
PO.Box 1984
Grand Cayman, Cayman Islands, B.W.I.
tel. 345-949-6644, fax 345-949-8178

- *Services Offered:* private banking

UBS International Trustees Ltd.
PO.Box 2325
Grand Cayman, Cayman Islands, B.W.I.
tel. 345-949-6099, fax 345-949-6907

- *Services Offered:* private banking

Union Bank of Switzerland
PO.Box 1043
Grand Cayman, Cayman Islands, B.W.I.

- *Services Offered:* private banking, retail banking

VIB Bank & Trust Co.
PO.Box 454
Grand Cayman, Cayman Islands, B.W.I.
tel. 345-949-6917, fax 345-949-8017

- *Services Offered:* private banking

W.S. Walker & Co. Attorneys-at-Law
Caledonian House, PO.Box 265
Grand Cayman, Cayman Islands, B.W.I.
tel. 345-949-2444, fax 345-949-6100

- *Services Offered:* company formation, trust formation, law office

---

Woodward Terry & Co.
PO.Box 822, Caribbean Home Insurance Building
Grand Cayman, Cayman Islands, B.W.I.
tel. 345-945-2800, fax 345-945-2727

- *Services Offered:* law office

CHANNEL ISLANDS - GUERNSEY AND JERSEY

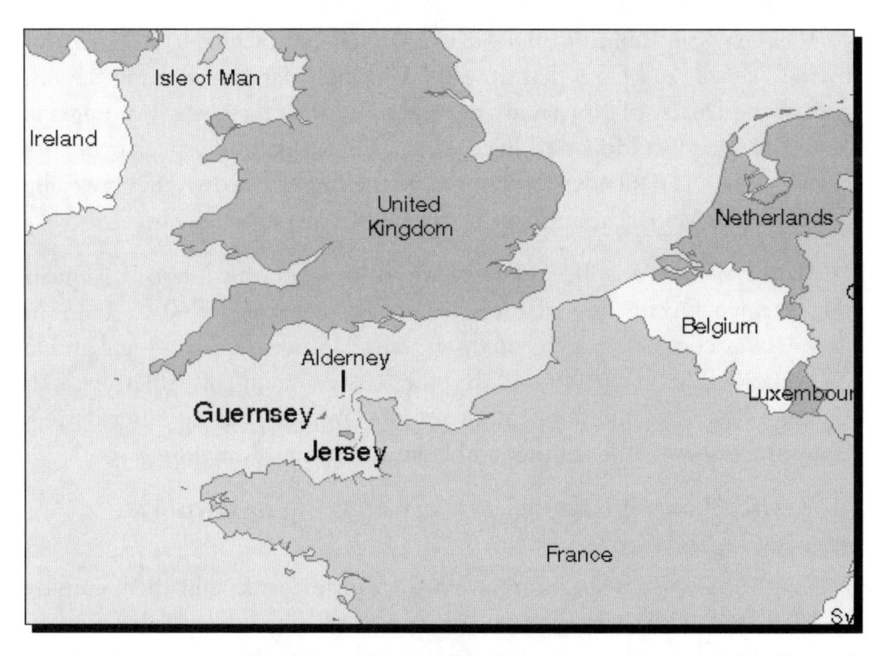

In Europe. South of Britain, North of France, in the English Channel. The two main islands Guernsey and Jersey. The smaller Channel Islands include Alderney, Herm, and Sark. Main language is English.

Guernsey

25 square miles, 30 miles west of the Cherbourg peninsula and 80 miles south of England. Population is approximately 55,000.

Jersey

The largest of the Channel Islands at 62 square miles. Jersey is 12 miles from the coast of Normandy and 90 miles south of England. Population is approximately 85,000. The official language of Jersey is French, although French is only used on ceremonial occasions.

In view of their close proximity to the French mainland it is not surprising to find that the Channel Islands originally formed a part of the Duchy of Normandy from 933. When William, Duke of Normandy, conquered England in 1066, England came under the same rule as the Channel Islands. The constitutional position then remained unaltered until 1204 when King John of England was driven out of mainland Normandy by the French, and from that time the Channel Islands have been the only part of the Duchy of Normandy to remain loyal to the Crown of England. Successive English Monarchs have given charters granting special constitutional status. As dependent territories of the English Crown they owe allegiance to the Monarch, but have no direct link with parliament.

Until World War II, Alderney was a jurisdiction of its own. During the German Occupation of the Channel Islands from 1940 to 1945 Alderney was completely evacuated, and in 1948 new constitutional and legal relationships were forged by the Government of Alderney. The Channel Islands are quite distinct from one another, having different legal systems from both one another and from the United Kingdom.

Does the Channel Islands have any banking or corporate secrecy legislation?

NO. Although English common law requires banks and their employees to maintain secrecy, no specific bank secrecy legislation has been passed, although it is technically very difficult to breach current bank secrecy. The English common law rule of confidentiality (imposed upon a bank in its relationship with its clients) applies in the Channel Islands.

Guernsey

Guernsey has no defined bank secrecy law. Secrecy is assured by the Common Law principle of confidentiality, and by the absence of any official disclosure requirements. If a Guernsey company is formed, the shareholders have their names forwarded to the Guernsey Financial Services Commission. This information is not released to the public.

Mr. Graham S. Basham, Manager, Private Banking, at CIBC Bank and Trust Company (Channel Islands) Limited provided this quote: "*Guernsey does not have any exchange of information treaties with regard to tax and therefore we certainly would not provide information concerning accounts held by ourselves.*"

Jersey

Details of a beneficial ownership of an Exempt Company must be disclosed to the appropriate local authority. This information is not available as a matter of public record, and there is no requirement for financial statements to be filed.

The only way information can be obtained by a third party is for the Royal Court to issue this authority. The Royal Court would only give this authority if proof of drug trade, arms trade, or money laundering could be established. The Basle Statement of Principles on Money Laundering was circulated by the Bank of England in January 1989. The Statement does not restrict itself to drug-related money laundering, but extends to all aspects of laundering money derived from illegal activities, such as robbery, terrorism, fraud or drugs.

Confidential information relating to taxation is not available to foreign authorities.

Professional advisors may only reveal confidential information by order of the Royal Court, and no order of a foreign court directing a professional advisor to disclose information can be applied locally.

Does the Channel Islands have a long history of legal stability?

YES. Although the Channel Islands are closely associated with the United Kingdom and part of the British Commonwealth, they are not directly a part of the UK, nor are they a colony. Alderney, Guernsey, Jersey, and Sark's constitution dates back to 1066, when Duke William of Normandy became King William I of England. In 1204 England lost the Normandy part of her Kingdom but the Channel Islands have remained loyal to the Crown of England since then. The Channel Islands have retained the right to legislate independently on domestic issues and taxation.

When the United Kingdom was admitted to the EEC, the Channel Islands were integrated with the Community, but granted a special status. This status states that they are included in the Community for the purposes of freedom of movement of goods and must apply the common external tariff, but they are not subject to the harmonization of taxes and social policies, and there is no value added tax in the Islands.

The legal system is based on Norman law, although the local legislature enacts laws directly influenced by English common law. In matters of real property law and inheritance the common law is the ancient customary law of Normandy, but in other areas the courts have adopted the concepts of the common laws of England. Trust law has developed very similarly to English Trust law.

Is there an income tax in the Channel Islands?

YES. All of the Channel Islands collect various forms and rates of tax.

Guernsey

The tax rates of the income and profit of an IC will be at a rate determined by the administrator of Income Tax who will review the business plan of the company in determining the appropriate tax rate. The rate of tax would be subject to review every five years. The rate of tax is subject to individual agreement and must be above 0% and no more than 30%. Dividend payments are subject to a withholding tax of 20%.

Investment income on shareholders' funds is taxable as follows:

- Up to £250,000 rate of tax 20%.
- Next £250,000 rate of tax 1%.
- Next £250,000 rate of tax 0.5%.
- Next £250,000 rate of tax 0.3%
- Excess 0.1%.

There are no capital gains, gift or estate taxes in Guernsey.

Jersey

Non-resident companies incorporated in Jersey are treated as resident for tax purposes (standard rate 20%) unless they are defined as an "exempt company," paying only a flat tax of £500 per year. The meeting place of the directors of a company does not constitute an established place of business so that the directors may meet (and conclude contracts) in the Islands without exposing profits to local tax.

Interest paid by an IBC is payable without deduction of Jersey tax, as are dividends and director's fees. There is no capital gains tax, gift tax or estate tax in Jersey.

Are there any other taxes in the Channel Islands?

NO. There are no capital gains taxes, wealth taxes, gift taxes, or estate duties charged on Company or Trust assets in the Channel Islands.

Does the Channel Islands maintain exchange controls?

NO. As of October 23, 1979, all exchange control regulations in the Channel Islands were abolished.

Does the Channel Islands maintain tax treaties with any other countries?

YES. There is no tax treaty between the U.S. and the Channel Islands, although there are double-taxation agreements between the UK and the Channel Islands. The Double Taxation Agreements between Guernsey & Jersey in 1956 and the UK in 1952 provide for exchange of information, but only to the revenue authorities, and not to outsiders.

There is no tax treaty between Canada and the Channel Islands.

Does the Channel Islands allow for the formation of corporate entities?

YES. The procedures to form either a Guernsey or Jersey Company are to:

- Obtain formal approval for the proposed name, and then for the formation of the company.

- Disclose the names of the registered shareholders, who may be nominees acting on behalf of the beneficial owners of the company.
- Disclose on a confidential basis to the island authority the names and addresses of the beneficial owners so that the island authority can satisfy itself that a company is not being formed for the benefit of undesirable persons.
- The minimum number of registered shareholders is two.
- If required a company can have only one beneficial owner with the registered shareholders acting as nominees.

In addition, Guernsey and Jersey Companies are required to:

- Maintain a register of members at its registered office, available for inspection by members of the public, together with a copy of its last annual return of shareholders.
- Make a return in January of each year stating the capital structure and the names and addresses of registered shareholders as of January 1. Guernsey companies must also supply the names of the directors.

Ad valorem stamp duty is payable on the incorporation of a company based upon the authorized share capital, subject to a minimum of £50. The company's registered office must be at an address in the island in which the company is incorporated.

Guernsey

The Guernsey Financial Services Commission regulates financial activity on the island.

International Company - The International Company (IC) was introduced in 1993 to include Guernsey incorporated companies, foreign incorporated companies, the Guernsey branch of a non-resident company and Limited Partnerships.

The identity of the beneficial owners must be disclosed to the Financial Services Commission to satisfy requirements that an IC is not be beneficially owned by residents of the Channel Islands. This information is not made public, and is not available to the

Island's tax authorities. Information must also be provided regarding any changes in beneficial ownership.

The tax rates of the income and profit of an IC will be at a rate determined by the administrator of Income Tax who will review the business plan of the company in determining the appropriate tax rate, subject to review every five years. The tax rate will be above 0% but not more than 30%. Dividend payments are subject to a withholding tax of 20%. The advantage of an IC is that a company with global operations can use a Guernsey IC as part of a strategy to optimize tax payments in other jurisdictions.

Guernsey Exempt Companies - Any company incorporated in Guernsey may apply to be registered as exempt from Guernsey income tax. Details of beneficial ownership must be disclosed to the Financial Services Commission. This information is not made public, and is not available to the Island's tax authorities.

Exempt Companies are regarded as non-resident for taxation purposes. The exempt company fee is £500 per year. Exempt companies are not required to file a copy of their annual accounts with the Income Tax authorities.

Jersey

International Business Company - The International Business Company (IBC) was introduced in 1993 to provide non-residents with a company that pays tax on its income at a maximum of 2.0% (subject to a minimum of £1,200 annually). Interest paid by an IBC is payable without deduction of Jersey tax, as are dividends and director's fees. Disclosure of beneficial ownership must be made to the Financial Services Department.

Jersey Exempt Companies - A company may claim to be an Exempt Company and be treated as non-resident if it is in the beneficial ownership of non-residents. The identity of the beneficial owners must be disclosed to the Financial Services Commission to satisfy requirements that an IBC is not beneficially owned by residents of the Channel Islands. The exempt company election must be submitted by March 31 of each year, and must include a confirmation that the Registrar of Companies has been kept informed of changes in beneficial ownership. These disclosure requirements came into full force in 1991.

Exempt companies are not required to file a copy of their annual accounts with the Income Tax authorities. The exempt company fee is £500 per year.

Jersey Foreign Companies - Foreign incorporated companies managed and controlled in the Islands which are beneficially owned by non-residents may apply for exempt status. Filing requirements will then be similar to companies incorporated in the Islands.

Jersey Collective Investment Schemes - A Collective Investment Scheme may also be treated as an Exempt Company. Any Exempt Company that is a Collective Investment Scheme must deduct tax from the payment of dividends to any Jersey resident shareholders. It must also provide the name, address and share holdings of any persons resident in Jersey. A clearance procedure exists for persons having Jersey addresses, but not residence in Jersey.

The main requirements of a Jersey company are that the Memorandum of Association must specify:

- The name of the company ending with the words Limited or Avec Responsibilite Limitee.
- The amount of authorized capital (minimum £50).
- It is possible for nominee subscribers to sign blank transfers and declarations of Trust in favor of the beneficial owners for their retention. The shares may be transferred into the names of the beneficial owners or into the names of other nominees as may be required.
- The subscribers to the Memorandum of Association appoint, in writing, the first directors of the company.
- The law does not require directors of a Jersey company to be resident in Jersey, nor does it provide that they must also be shareholders.
- The minimum number of directors is one.

- A Jersey company must hold its annual general meeting in Jersey.

Does the Channel Islands allow for the formation of Trusts?

YES. There are three main types of Trust and several variations on each type may be built into the Trust document:

Discretionary Trust - The most common form of Trust used in the Channel Islands is a discretionary Trust, where the Trustee has discretion to exercise his own judgement as to the manner and amount by which Beneficiaries of the Trust might benefit from the Trust assets. The beneficiaries have no legal rights to any portion of the Trust fund. It is usual for the Settlor to indicate to the Trustee his wishes as to the disposal of the Trust fund and his expression of wishes, while not legally binding, does give the Trustee guidance on the distribution of the Trust assets.

Fixed Trust - It is possible to make a Trust in a fixed form so that the Trustee has no discretionary powers when distributing the Trust assets to Beneficiaries, as the deed will specify how the assets are to be made available to the Beneficiaries.

Protective Trust - A protective Trust may be either discretionary, or fixed, or a combination of the two. Under such a Trust the Trustee will be required to benefit an individual, or alternatively to withhold benefit on the happening of an event specified within the Trust deed. Protective Trusts are most commonly set up for children, disabled or mentally handicapped persons.

In both Guernsey and Jersey the Trust deed does not have to be registered and is not available for inspection. It remains a private document between the Settlor and the Trustee.

Guernsey

Trusts are governed by the Trusts Law 1989, which outlines the duties and obligations of the Trustees and gives the Royal Court certain powers which it can exercise on application from a Settlor, Trustee, Beneficiary or Protector. The Trusts (Amendment) Law 1990 was enacted to protect the assets of a Trust from foreign rules of forced heirship.

Jersey

Revocable Trusts can be arranged in Jersey so that upon a written instruction from the client the Trust is revoked and the assets automatically pass back to the client.

Does the Channel Islands allow for the formation of Captive Insurance Companies?

YES. Captive Insurance Companies may be set up in Jersey and are generally not taxable on their underwriting profits, but are subject to tax on other income. Reinsurance Companies may also be formed.

Guernsey

Insurance companies must be licensed under the Insurance Business (Guernsey) Law, 1986. Insurance law requires certain information regarding insurers to be made available to the public, such as:

- Nominal and issued share capital.
- The location of the registered office.
- The name and address of all directors, shareholders, and secretary.
- Stamp duty is capped at £5,000, regardless of the size of business.

Accounts of insurance companies are not filed for public record but must be presented to the Income Tax Office to support audited tax returns. The 300th captive insurance operation was licenced in Guernsey in 1995.

Does the Channel Islands allow for the formation of Private Banking Companies?

YES. Although the Channel Islands allows the formation of Banking Companies, the strict requirements make them impractical for tax planning purposes. The Guernsey Financial Services Commission (GFSC) requires each bank requesting registration to be part of a well established organization from a jurisdiction with high levels of supervison. Under the Banking Supervision Law, which came into effect in September 1994, the GFSC is able to attach conditions to banking licenses and make directions if a license is revoked.

Financial institutions and contacts in Guernsey:

Abacus Financial Services Limited
Coopers & Lybrand Chartered Accountants, PO.Box 626, Le Truchot
St.Peter Port, Guernsey, Channel Islands, GY1 4PW
tel. 44-1481-726921, fax 44-1481-711075

- *Services Offered:* investment advisor, company formation, trust formation, private banking, accounting services, estate planning services, safekeeping services

---

ANZ Bank (Guernsey) Limited
PO.Box 153, Frances House, Sir William Place
St.Peter Port, Guernsey, Channel Islands, GY14ES
tel. 44-1481-726771, fax 44-1481-727851

- *Services Offered:* investment advisor, private banking, retail banking, safekeeping services

---

Bachmann Trust Company Limited
PO.Box 175, Frances House, Sir William Place
St.Peter Port, Guernsey, Channel Islands, GY1 4HQ
tel. 44-1481-723573, fax 44-1481-715544

- *Services Offered:* investment advisor, private banking, safekeeping services

---

Bank of Butterfield International (Guernsey) Limited
PO.Box 25, Roseneath, The Grange
St.Peter Port, Guernsey, Channel Islands, GY1 3AP
tel. 44-1481-711521, fax 44-1481-714533, telex 4191362 FIELD G

- *Services Offered:* private banking, retail banking, loans and credit, deposit backed MC/Visa

---

Banque Generale du Luxembourg Trustees Ltd
PO.Box 357, 26 Glategny Esplanade
St.Peter Port, Guernsey, Channel Islands, GY13XH
tel. 44-1481-728877, fax 44-1481-728712

- *Services Offered:* private banking, retail banking

Barclays Private Bank & Trust Limited
PO.Box 184, Barclaytrust House, South Esplanade
St.Peter Port, Guernsey, Channel Islands
tel. 44-1481-724706, fax 44-1481-728376

- *Services Offered:* investment advisor, company formation, trust formation, private banking, loans and credit, deposit backed MC/Visa, safekeeping services

---

Blue Chip Capital Management Limited
Le Bordage
St.Peter Port, Guernsey, Channel Islands
toll free 888-265-6661, fax 800-560-0645

- *Services Offered:* investment advisor, mutual fund manager, private banking, global investing information, deposit backed MC/Visa, insurance-based investments

---

Channel Islands Insurance Consultants
PO.Box 627, 26 Cornet Street
St.Peter Port, Guernsey, Channel Islands, GY1 4PP
tel. 44-1481-724212, fax 44-1481-710696

- *Services Offered:* captive insurance formation, corporate services, captive insurance management

---

Czerlau & Associates Limited
St.Peter Port, Guernsey, Channel Islands
toll free 800-226-5703, fax 242-356-0223

- *Services Offered:* company formation, trust formation, corporate services, estate planning services, deposit backed MC/Visa

---

Ernst & Young
14 New Street, PO.Box 236
St.Peter Port, Guernsey, Channel Islands, GY1 4LE
tel. 44-1534-723232, fax 44-1534-713901

- *Services Offered:* company formation, trust formation, accounting services, estate planning services, safekeeping services

---

Guernsey Financial Services Commission
Valley House, Hirzel Street
St.Peter Port, Guernsey, Channel Islands
tel. 44-1481-712706, fax 44-1481-712010

- *Services Offered:* government services

Guernsey Financial Services Commission
Valley House, Hirzel Street
St.Peter Port, Guernsey, Channel Islands
tel. 44-1481-712706, fax 44-1481-712010

- *Services Offered:* government services

Guinness Flight and Calder Private Trustees
Guinness Flight House, PO.Box 250
St.Peter Port, Guernsey, Channel Islands, GY1 3QH
tel. 44-1481-710404, fax 44-1481-728848

- *Services Offered:* company formation, trust formation

Helveticum Management Services Limited
Helvetia Court, PO.Box 290
St.Peter Port, Guernsey, Channel Islands, GY1 3RP
tel. 44-1481-719196, fax 44-1481-724968

- *Services Offered:* captive insurance formation, private banking, corporate services

---

International Risk Management Limited
2 Grange Place
St.Peter Port, Guernsey, Channel Islands, GY1 2QA
tel. 44-1481-727220, fax 44-1481-712443

- *Services Offered:* captive insurance formation, corporate services, captive insurance management

---

Lazard Fund Managers (Channel Islands) Limited
1 St. Julian's Avenue
St.Peter Port, Guernsey, Channel Islands
tel. 44-1481-710461, fax 44-1481-711438

- *Services Offered:* mutual fund manager

Leopold Joseph & Sons (Guernsey) Ltd.
PO.Box 244, Albert House, South Esplanade
St.Peter Port, Guernsey, Channel Islands, GY1 3QB
tel. 44-1481-712771, fax 44-1481-727025

- *Services Offered:* private banking

LGT Asset Management Ltd.
PO.Box 366, Town Mills
St.Peter Port, Guernsey, Channel Islands, GY1 4NE
tel. 44-1481-722746, fax 44-1481-722679

- *Services Offered:* mutual fund manager

MeesPierson (CI) Limited
PO.Box 253, Le Bordage
St.Peter Port, Guernsey, Channel Islands, GY1 3QJ
tel. 44-1481-728921, fax 44-1481-710665

- *Services Offered:* investment advisor, trust formation, private banking, safekeeping services

---

Mercator Trust Company Limited
PO.Box 336, Anson Court, La Routes Des Camps
St.Martins, Guernsey, Channel Islands, GY1 3UQ
tel. 44-1481-721896, fax 44-1481-724500

- *Services Offered:* private banking

Midland Bank Trustee (Guernsey) Limited
PO.Box 156, 22 Smith Street
St.Peter Port, Guernsey, Channel Islands, GY1 4EU
tel. 44-1481-717717, fax 44-1481-717850, telex 419-1586

- *Services Offered:* investment advisor, company formation, trust formation, private banking, loans and credit, estate planning services, safekeeping services

---

Rothschild Asset Management Limited
PO.Box 242, St.Peter Port House, Sausmarez Street
St.Peter Port, Guernsey, Channel Islands
tel. 44-1481-713713, fax 44-1481-711511

- *Services Offered:* investment advisor, mutual fund manager

---

Royal Bank of Scotland PLC
St.Andrew's House, Le Bordage, 22 High Street
St.Peter Port, Guernsey, Channel Islands, GY1 4BQ
tel. 44-1481-710051, fax 44-1481-715431

- *Services Offered:* captive insurance formation, private banking, retail banking, corporate services

---

Wilde & Co. Limited, Fiduciaries
PO.Box 112, Pollet House, Lower Pollet
St.Peter Port, Guernsey, Channel Islands, GY1 4EA
tel. 44-1481-726446, fax 44-1481-711156

- *Services Offered:* company formation, captive insurance formation

Financial institutions and contacts in Jersey:

Abacus Financial Services Limited
Coopers & Lybrand Chartered Accountants, La Motte Chambers
St.Helier, Jersey, Channel Islands, JE1 1BJ
tel. 44-1534-602000, fax 44-1534-602002, telex 4192231 COLY JY G

- *Services Offered:* company formation, trust formation, private banking, accounting services, estate planning services, safekeeping services

---

ABC Corporate Services Ltd.
20 Britannia Place, Bath Street
St.Helier, Jersey, Channel Islands, JE2 4SU
tel. 44-1534-24024, fax 44-1534-27272

- *Services Offered:* trust formation

Advent Management Company
La Motte Chambers, La Motte Street
St.Helier, Jersey, Channel Islands
tel. 44-1534-602000, fax 44-1534-602002

- *Services Offered:* company formation

AIB Fund Managers (CI) Limited
AIB House, Grenville St., PO.Box 468
St.Helier, Jersey, Channel Islands
tel. 44-1534-883000, fax 44-1534-74362

- *Services Offered:* mutual fund manager

Bank of Nova Scotia Trust Company Channel Islands Limited
PO.Box 60, Kensington Chambers, 46/50 Kensington Place
St.Helier, Jersey, Channel Islands, JE4 9PE
tel. 44-1534-89898, fax 44-1534-873327, telex 419-2229

- *Services Offered:* private banking, retail banking, loans and credit, safekeeping services

---

Barclays Private Bank & Trust Limited
PO.Box 82, Barclaytrust House, 39/41 Broad Street
St.Helier, Jersey, Channel Islands, JE4 8WY
tel. 44-1534-73741, fax 44-1534-31676

- *Services Offered:* investment advisor, company formation, trust formation, private banking, loans and credit, deposit backed MC/Visa, safekeeping services

---

Beresford Group
White Lodge, Wellington Road
St.Saviour, Jersey, Channel Islands, JE2 7TH
tel. 44-1534-79502, fax 44-1534-33405

- *Services Offered:* company formation, trust formation, private banking, safekeeping services

---

Blue Chip Capital Management Limited
Hill Street
St.Helier, Jersey, Channel Islands
tel. 888-265-6661, fax 800-560-0645

- *Services Offered:* investment advisor, mutual fund manager, private banking, global investing information, deposit backed MC/Visa, insurance-based investments

---

Centurian Management Services Ltd.
7 Library Place
St.Helier, Jersey, Channel Islands
tel. 44-1534-70152, fax 44-1534-20396

- *Services Offered:* accounting services

Chase Manhattan Bank, N.A.
Chase House, Grenville Street, PO.Box 127
St.Helier, Jersey, Channel Islands, JE4 8QH
tel. 44-1534-25561, fax 44-1534-35301

- *Services Offered:* investment advisor, company formation, trust formation, private banking, retail banking, loans and credit, safekeeping services

---

Coutts & Co. (Jersey) Ltd.
PO.Box 6, 23/25 Broad Street
St.Helier, Jersey, Channel Islands, JE4 8ND
tel. 44-1534-282345, fax 44-1534-282400

- *Services Offered:* investment advisor, company formation, trust formation, private banking, safekeeping services

---

David Morgan, Whitehead & Co., Solicitors
PO.Box 303, Westaway Chambers, 39 Don Street
St.Helier, Jersey, Channel Islands
tel. 44-1534-872766, fax 44-1534-33979

- *Services Offered:* company formation

Flemings (Jersey) Ltd.
Queens House, Don Road
St.Helier, Jersey, Channel Islands, JE2 4QD
tel. 44-1534-73933, fax 44-1534-74576
- *Services Offered:* private banking

Halifax International (Jersey) Limited
PO.Box 664, Halifax House, 31-33 New Street
St.Helier, Jersey, Channel Islands, JE4 8YZ
tel. 44-1534-59840, fax 44-1534-73690
- *Services Offered:* company formation, private banking

Hill Samuel (C.I.) Trust Co. Limited
PO.Box 63, 7 Bond Street
St.Helier, Jersey, Channel Islands, JE4 8PH
tel. 44-1534-604604, fax 44-1534-604606, telex 419-2167
- *Services Offered:* investment advisor, company formation, trust formation, loans and credit, corporate services, safekeeping services

---

HSBC James Capel (Channel Islands) Limited
PO.Box 315, 1 Grenville Street
St.Helier, Jersey, Channel Islands, JE4 8UB
tel. 44-1534-66822, fax 44-1534-58936
- *Services Offered:* investment advisor

HSBC Private Banking (C.I.) Limited
PO.Box 88, 1 Grenville Street
St.Helier, Jersey, Channel Islands, JE4 9PF
tel. 44-1534-606133, fax 44-1534-606504tel. 44-1534-606500
- *Services Offered:* investment advisor, company formation, trust formation, private banking, retail banking, corporate services, safekeeping services

---

ING Bank (Jersery) Trust
Huguenot House, 28a La Motte, 1st Floor
St.Helier, Jersey, Channel Islands, JE2 4SZ
tel. 44-534-78822, fax 44-534-73367
- *Services Offered:* trust formation, private banking

Jordan & Sons (Jersey) Ltd.
PO.Box 578, 17 Bond Street
St.Helier, Jersey, Channel Islands, JE4 8UT
tel. 44-1534-30579, fax 44-1534-26430
- *Services Offered:* company formation, trust formation, corporate services

---

Kleinwort Benson (Jersey) Limited
PO.Box 76, Wests Centre
St.Helier, Jersey, Channel Islands, JE4 8PQ
tel. 44-1534-78866, fax 44-1534-78908

- *Services Offered:* mutual fund manager, company formation, trust formation, private banking, safekeeping services

---

Lloyds Private Banking (Channel Islands) Limited
Waterloo House, Don Street, PO.Box 195
St.Helier, Jersey, Channel Islands, JE4 8RS
tel. 44-1534-284205, fax 44-1534-284333

- *Services Offered:* private banking

Lombard Banking (Jersey) Limited
PO.Box 554, 39 La Motte Street
St.Helier, Jersey, Channel Islands, JE4 8XH
tel. 44-1534-27511, , telex 419-2038

- *Services Offered:* private banking

Midland Bank International Finance Corporation Limited
PO.Box 26, 28/34 Hill Street
St.Helier, Jersey, Channel Islands, JE4 8NR
tel. 44-1534-606501, fax 44-1534-606220

- *Services Offered:* investment advisor, insurance-based investments, company formation, trust formation, private banking, loans and credit, corporate services, estate planning services, deposit backed MC/Visa, safekeeping services

---

Midland Bank PLC Personal Offshore Services
PO.Box 14
St.Helier, Jersey, Channel Islands, JE4 8NJ
tel. 44-1534-606000, fax 44-1534-606145, telex 419-2098

- *Services Offered:* investment advisor, insurance-based investments, company formation, trust formation, private banking, loans and credit, corporate services, deposit backed MC/Visa, safekeeping services

---

Mossack Fonseca & Co. (Jersey) Ltd.
PO.Box 168, 19 Seaton Place
St.Helier, Jersey, Channel Islands, JE2 3QL
tel. 44-1534-67009, fax 44-1534-80673

- *Services Offered:* company formation

Price Waterhouse
Eagle House, Don Road
St.Helier, Jersey, Channel Islands
tel. 44-1534-74222, fax 44-1534-67556

- *Services Offered:* accounting services

Quilter Goodison Channel Islands
5 Britannia Place, Bath Street
St.Helier, Jersey, Channel Islands
tel. 44-1534-506070, fax 44-1534-68108

- *Services Offered:* company formation

Royal Bank of Canada (Jersey) Limited
PO.Box 194, 19/21 Broad Street
St.Helier, Jersey, Channel Islands, JE4 8RR
tel. 44-1534-27441, fax 44-1534-32513, telex 4192351

- *Services Offered:* investment advisor, private banking, loans and credit, deposit backed MC/Visa, safekeeping services

States of Jersey Income Tax Department
Cyril Le Marquand House, PO.Box 56, The Parade
St.Helier, Jersey, Channel Islands, JE4 8PF
tel. 44-1534-603300, fax 44-1534-89142

- *Services Offered:* government services

Swiss Bank Corporation (Jersey) Ltd.
40 Esplanade, PO.Box 34
St.Helier, Jersey, Channel Islands, JE4 8NW
tel. 44-1534-506500, fax 44-1534-506501, telex 4192288 SBCJY

- *Services Offered:* investment advisor, company formation, trust formation, private banking, retail banking, loans and credit, safekeeping services

TSB Bank
25 New Street
St.Helier, Jersey, Channel Islands
fax 44-1534-23058

- *Services Offered:* investment advisor, private banking, retail banking, loans and credit, deposit backed MC/Visa

---

TSB Bank Channel Islands Limited Offshore Centre
8 David Place, PO.Box 597
St.Helier, Jersey, Channel Islands, JE4 8XW
tel. 44-1534-503939, fax 44-1534-503211, telex 4192164 TSBCI G

- *Services Offered:* investment advisor, company formation, trust formation, private banking, retail banking, loans and credit, deposit backed MC/Visa, safekeeping services

---

Warburg Asset Management Jersey Ltd.
Forum House, Grenville Street
St.Helier, Jersey, Channel Islands, JE4 8RL
tel. 44-1534-600600, fax 44-1534-600687

- *Services Offered:* mutual fund manager

Westpac Banking Corporation (Jersey)
PO.Box 393, 7-11 Britannia Place, Bath Street
St.Helier, Jersey, Channel Islands, JE4 8US
tel. 44-1534-504504, fax 44-1534-504575, telex 419-2438

- *Services Offered:* investment advisor, company formation, trust formation, private banking, retail banking, loans and credit, estate planning services, safekeeping services

---

WorldInvest Managers (Jersey) Limited
PO.Box 178, Union House, Union Street
St.Helier, Jersey, Channel Islands
tel. 44-1534-74431, fax 44-1534-74035

- *Services Offered:* mutual fund manager

COOK ISLANDS

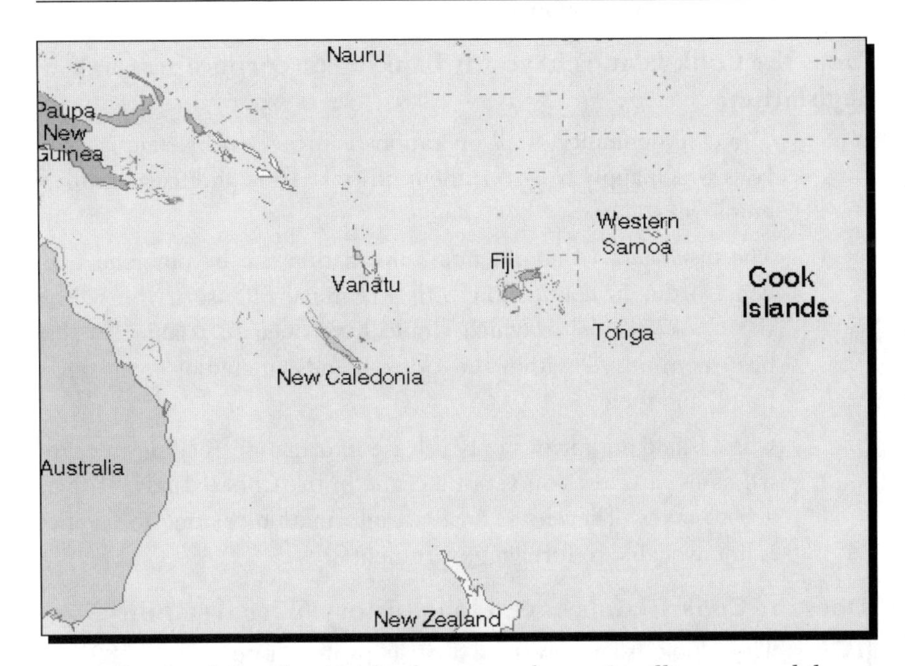

In the South Pacific. 15 islands scattered over 2 million square kilometers of the South Pacific, with a total land mass of less than 250 square kilometers. East of the Samoas, West of French Polynesia. Population is approximately 20,000, with 12,000 living in Rarotonga. Main language is English. Climate is tropical.

The Cook Islands were a protectorate of Great Britain from 1888 to 1891. In 1891 the boundaries of New Zealand were enlarged to include the Cook Islands. New Zealand's Cook Islands Act 1915 declared the common law of England as of January 14, 1840 (the year the colony of New Zealand was established) to apply to the Cook Islands. The Cook Islands became a self governing British colony in 1965. An international airport was opened in Rarotonga in 1974, and in 1977 the Development Investment Act was passed to encourage investment in the Islands.

In 1981, Australian David Lloyd identified the Cook Islands as an ideal location for the establishment of an offshore financial centre. A proposal was presented to the Cook Islands government which included legislation to provide for International Companies and Trusts. This proposed legislation was passed with full support in 1982.

Does the Cook Islands have any banking or corporate secrecy legislation?

YES. The confidentiality of all operations is protected by strict secrecy laws which apply to government officials, bank and trust company employees.

The disclosure of confidential information can be obtained upon court order in connection with a criminal offense triable within the Cook Islands or which would have been so triable if it had been committed within the Cook Islands, including drug trade, fraud, and theft.

Cook Island authorities only release information relating to criminal cases. Tax evasion is not a crime in the Cook Islands, as there are no taxes. Therefore, financial information relating to taxation is not available to foreign governments.

Does the Cook Islands have a long history of legal stability?

YES. The Cook Islands were a British protectorate before 1891. In 1891, the Cook Islands were annexed into New Zealand territory. The islanders hold New Zealand common citizenship to this day. The Cook Islands became self governing under a Westminster model constitution in 1965.

The legal system is based on English common law. New Zealand's Cook Islands Act 1915 declared the common law of England as of January 14, 1840 (the year the colony of New Zealand was established) to apply to the Cook Islands. Appeals are to the Cook Islands Court of Appeal, with the supreme court being represented by the Privy Council in England.

Is there an income tax in the Cook Islands?

NO. There are no taxes in the Cook Islands. International Companies are not liable to pay income tax, capital tax, or withholding tax.

Are there any other taxes in the Cook Islands?

NO. There are no capital gains taxes, gift taxes, estate taxes, capital taxes, or stamp duties in the Cook Islands.

Does the Cook Islands maintain exchange controls?

NO. There are currently no exchange controls in the Cook Islands.

Does the Cook Islands maintain tax treaties with any other countries?

YES. Indirectly there is a tax treaty between the U.S. and the Cook Islands, since the Cook Islands fall under the Income Tax Convention of 1948 between the U.S. and New Zealand.

There is no tax treaty between Canada and the Cook Islands.

Does the Cook Islands allow for the formation of corporate entities?

YES. International Companies (ICs) are governed by the International Companies Act 1981-82. The Act was amended in 1991 to allow for several different types of companies:

- No Liability Companies (shareholders have no capital liability to the company).
- Companies Limited by Guarantee (shareholders have a capital liability limited to the amount stated in their guarantee).
- Companies Limited by both Shares and Guarantee.
- Unlimited Companies (shareholders have unlimited liability for all debts of the company).
- Mutual Companies.

ICs are not liable to pay income tax, capital, estate, or gift tax. The incorporation of an IC must be handled by a licensed Trustee company, who will also provide the registered office. Advantages of Cook Islands companies include:

- Shares may be issued as bearer shares or bearer warrants.
- The holder of a bearer warrant is deemed not a shareholder of the company until the warrant is surrendered.

- Shareholders are not required to have accounts audited, and are not required to hold annual general meetings.
- Shareholders and directors meetings may be held anywhere.
- Only one shareholder is required. Nominee shareholders may be used.
- There is no minimum share capital, and there is no capital duty on share capital. Shares may have no par value.
- Only one director is required. Nominee directors may be used.

It is a requirement that there is a resident secretary.

Does the Cook Islands allow for the formation of Trusts?

YES. Trusts are governed by the International Trusts Act 1984. The requirements are that at least one Settlor or donor is an IC, Trustee company, or registered foreign company, and the Beneficiaries must be non-resident. To form an International Trust, the application to the Registrar of International Trusts must include:

- the name of the Trust and the Trustee;
- the date of the formation of the Trust; and
- the registered office of the Trust.

No other information is disclosed to the Registrar. The Trustee company must certify to the Registrar that the Beneficiaries of the Trust are non-residents. The annual renewal fee is US$100. A term of up to 100 years may be specified. No taxation of any type is applied to an International Trust.

The Cook Islands have passed specific Trust legislation providing protection against matrimonial and other creditors. No foreign judgement affecting an international Trust, the parties to the Trust, nor the Trust property shall be entertained in a court of the Cook Islands if that judgement is based on the application of any law inconsistent with the Cook Islands Trust legislation.

Where a creditor proves beyond a reasonable doubt that an International Trust was formed with the intent of defrauding a creditor, the company or Trust is required to satisfy the claim out of the assets held. The statute of limitations on this type of action is 2 years.

Does the Cook Islands allow for the formation of Captive Insurance Companies?

YES. A Mutual Company may be licensed under the Offshore Insurance Act to issue insurance to both shareholders and outsiders.

Does the Cook Islands allow for the formation of Private Banking Companies?

YES. The Cook Islands allows the formation and management of Banking Companies.

Financial institutions and contacts:

Asiaciti Trust Pacific, Ltd.
CIDB Building, 3rd Floor, PO.Box 822
Avarua, Rarotonga, Cook Islands, 13
tel. 682-23387, fax 682-23385

- *Services Offered:* company formation, trust formation, bank formation, private banking, corporate services, safekeeping services

---

TrustNet (Cook Islands) Limited
PO.Box 208, CIDB Building
Avarua, Rarotonga, Cook Islands
tel. 682-21080, fax 682-21087

- *Services Offered:* company formation, trust formation, captive insurance formation, bank formation, law office, accounting services, corporate services, safekeeping services

---

Westpac Banking Corporation Limited
PO.Box 42, Main Road, Avarua
Avarua, Rarotonga, Cook Islands
tel. 682-20802, fax 682-22014, telex (772) 62014 RG

- *Services Offered:* loans and credit

GIBRALTAR

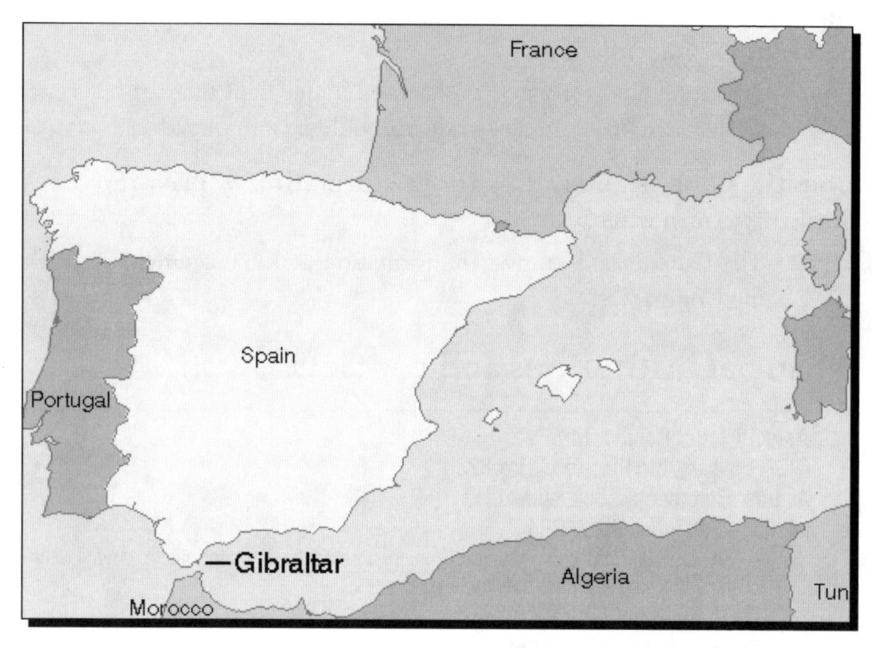

In Europe. "The Rock" is at the opening of the Mediterranean, at the extreme west end of the Mediterranean Sea, covering an area of just over 2.3 square miles. Gibraltar is connected to Spain by an isthmus, and faces North Africa 20 miles across the straits. Population approximately 35,000. Main language is English and Spanish.

The name "Gibraltar" came from the Moorish leader Tariq who used "Gibel Tariq" (Mountain of Tariq) as a base during the 8th century. Gibraltar has been a British Crown Colony since 1704, formally ceded by Spain in the 1713 Treaty of Utrecht. Gibraltar's 1965 constitution granted extensive self governing powers. Gibraltar began its development as a financial centre in 1967 through the Companies (Taxation & Concessions) Ordinance that granted income and estate duty concessions to Gibraltar companies registered as Exempt. Gibraltar was isolated by the Spanish blockade from 1969 to 1985. Stability depends on the Spanish, who would like to again have control of Gibraltar. The Rock itself is made of limestone and is over 1,300 feet high.

Does Gibraltar have any banking or corporate secrecy legislation?

YES. Banks are supervised by the Gibraltarian Banking Authority and subject to restrictive legislation that guarantees anonymity. All clients are guaranteed complete anonymity, therefore ensuring that any transaction will be a matter between the customer and the bank only. The identity of beneficial owners of Exempt companies is protected by law.

The Drug Trafficking Ordinance 1989 allows the release of confidential banking information in matters of drug trafficking and money laundering.

Confidential financial information is not available to foreign governments or tax investigators. Gibraltar tax authorities do not exchange or disclose information with or to any other tax authorities.

Does Gibraltar have a long history of legal stability?

YES. Gibraltar is a self governing British Crown colony, in British possession since 1704. Gibraltar is self governing as a result of the 1965 constitution, and has an autonomous locally elected government which is responsible for local laws. Britain retains control over foreign policy and defense. Spain has made several unsuccessful attempts to claim sovereignty.

The legal system is based on English common law and acts of parliament, and is supplemented by local statutes. There is an independent judiciary with a Supreme Court, Court of First Instance, and lower Courts. The ultimate court of appeal is the Privy Council of England.

Is there an income tax in Gibraltar?

YES. There is an income tax in Gibraltar, although non-residents (other than British nationals) are tax exempt. Qualifying companies are charged a tax rate of 2% to 18%. Resident companies pay income tax at a rate of 35%, and income tax for individuals is 30% to 50%.

Exempt corporations pay no taxes. An Exemption Certificate, once granted, is valid for 25 years, and grants full exemption from income tax, estate duty and stamp duty.

There is no income tax on interest from deposits, no Value Added Tax, and no tax on trade in precious metals.

Are there any other taxes in Gibraltar?

NO. There is no capital gains tax, no tax on gifts or capital movements, and no inheritance tax, although estate duty is levied in Gibraltar.

Ad valorem taxes of 10% were introduced in 1970, applying to most merchandise imported into Gibraltar, with the exception of food, drugs, and building materials.

Does Gibraltar maintain exchange controls?

NO. There are currently no exchange controls in Gibraltar. The currency is the Gibraltar pound, at par with the pound sterling.

Does Gibraltar maintain tax treaties with any other countries?

YES. There is no exchange of information treaty between the U.S. and Gibraltar, although there is a tax treaty between the United Kingdom and Gibraltar.

There is no exchange of information treaty between Canada and Gibraltar.

Does Gibraltar allow for the formation of corporate entities?

YES. Gibraltar offers the Non-resident Company, the Exempt Company and the Qualifying Company, all with special tax advantages. Any Gibraltar company, or a Gibraltar registered branch of a non-Gibraltar company, may apply for registration as an Exempt company under the Gibraltar (Taxation and Concessions) Ordinance.

Non-resident Company - Non-resident Companies are incorporated in Gibraltar but managed and controlled by directors outside Gibraltar's jurisdiction. Gibraltar does not levy flat rate fees such as annual company registration tax or non-resident company duty against a Non-resident Company. Non-resident companies may not derive income from within Gibraltar and should therefore maintain bank accounts outside Gibraltar.

Exempt Company - Exempt companies are entirely exempted from Income Tax, Estate and Stamp Duties and are instead liable for a fixed annual tax of £225 (or £200 if a non-resident Exempt company, £300 if a Gibraltar registered branch of a non-Gibraltar company). The advantage of an Exempt Company over a Non-resident Company is that the Exempt Company is not presumed to be resident elsewhere.

The principal requirements for the granting of Exempt status are that:

- No Gibraltar resident has a beneficial interest in the Exempt company.
- The company does not trade or carry on business in Gibraltar.
- Professional references must be received by the Gibraltar Financial and Development Secretary from a lawyer, banker, or registered accountant.
- An outline of the company's proposed activities must be provided to the Financial and Development secretary.
- Minimum share capital is £100, issued and fully paid.
- The name of the company must end with the word Limited.

As with all Gibraltar companies, the identities of directors and shareholders are a matter of public record, although nominee shareholders may be appointed to protect the identity of beneficial owners. The statutory registers must be held in Gibraltar (usually at the registered office). The identity of beneficial owners of Exempt companies is protected by law. There are no requirements to publish accounts.

A minimum of two shareholders is required. There are no restrictions on the appointment of officers of Exempt companies, although either a director or the secretary must be a Gibraltar resident. There are no restrictions on the location of directors meetings.

When applying for Exempt status it is necessary to provide brief details of the company's proposed activities to the Financial and Development Secretary.

Gibraltar Qualifying Company - A Gibraltar company, or the Gibraltar registered branch of a non-Gibraltar company, may apply for registration as a Qualifying company under the Income Tax (Qualifying Companies) Rules 1983. Qualifying companies are charged a tax rate of 2% to 18%. Qualifying companies require a minimum issued share capital of £1,000, and must deposit £1,000 with the Gibraltar government on account of future income tax liabilities. A one-time fee of £250 is payable on the issue of a Qualifying certificate.

Does Gibraltar allow for the formation of Trusts?

YES. Based on English Common Law, there are two types of Trusts available, the Fixed Trust and the Discretionary Trust. Benefits of a Gibraltar Trust are:

- The assets of a Trust set up by a non-resident of Gibraltar are exempt from Gibraltar tax, provided that any income is derived from outside of Gibraltar (with the exception of bank interest).
- The Trust may remain in force for up to 100 years.
- The Trust is a private arrangement between the Settlor and the Trustee, providing complete anonymity for the Settlor.
- No official register is kept of Trusts, and no requirement exists for the settlement deeds to be made public.
- There are no annual filing fees or audit requirements.

Gibraltar law also allows the formation of an Asset Protection Trust, where if a Settlor (who is solvent at the time and not planning to become insolvent) transfers assets to the Trust and subsequently becomes insolvent, the Trust would not be declared void upon application by a creditor. Under the Bankruptcy (Register of Dispositions) Regulations 1990 an Asset Protection Trust must pay an initial registration fee of £300 and an annual fee of £100.

Fixed Trust - With a Fixed Trust, the Trustee holds assets exclusively for a clearly limited and well-defined group of people. The Trustee cannot change their rights under the Trust.

Discretionary Trust - The standard type of Discretionary Trust is set up for a group of Beneficiaries described in the Trust deed. The Trustee is empowered to distribute Trust funds between all Trust Beneficiaries, or restrict funds to one or several Beneficiaries at his discretion.

Does Gibraltar allow for the formation of Captive Insurance Companies?

YES. Gibraltar is a suitable jurisdiction for the formation of Captive Insurance Companies.

Does Gibraltar allow for the formation of Private Banking Companies?

YES. Gibraltar is a suitable jurisdiction for the formation of Banking Companies.

Financial institutions and contacts:

Abbey National (Gibraltar) Limited
237 Main Street, PO.Box 824
Gibraltar
tel. 350-76090, fax 350-72028

- *Services Offered:* private banking, retail banking

Attias & Levy Barristers-at-Law
Suites 1 & 3, 3 Irish Place, PO.Box 466
Gibraltar
tel. 350-72150, fax 350-74986

- *Services Offered:* law office

Banesto (Gibraltar) Ltd.
114-116 Main Street, PO.Box 630
Gibraltar
tel. 350-77775, fax 350-76333

- *Services Offered:* investment advisor, company formation, trust formation, private banking, retail banking, corporate services, safekeeping services

---

Barclaytrust International Limited
1st Floor, Regal House, 3 Queensway
Gibraltar
tel. 350-78565, fax 350-79987

- *Services Offered:* investment advisor, company formation, trust formation, private banking, loans and credit, deposit backed MC/Visa, safekeeping services

---

BF Continental Services Ltd.
Eurolife Building
Gibraltar
tel. 350-51115, fax 350-51116

- *Services Offered:* company formation, corporate services, safekeeping services, mail forwarding

---

Blue Chip Capital Management Limited
Corral Road
Gibraltar
tel. 888-265-6661, fax 800-560-0645

- *Services Offered:* investment advisor, private banking, global investing information, deposit backed MC/Visa, insurance-based investments

---

Coutts & Co. (Gibraltar) Ltd.
National Westminster House, 57-63 Line Wall Road, PO.Box 709
Gibraltar
tel. 350-72676, fax 350-78874

- *Services Offered:* investment advisor, company formation, trust formation, private banking, safekeeping services

---

CV Management Services Ltd.
PO.Box 453, 3/1a Parliament Lane
Gibraltar
tel. 350-76933, fax 350-76718

- *Services Offered:* company formation

Europa Trust Company Limited
Suite 743, Europort, PO.Box 629
Gibraltar
tel. 350-79013, fax 350-70101

- *Services Offered:* investment advisor, company formation, trust formation, accounting services, corporate services

---

Form-A-Co (Gibraltar) Limited
PO.Box 563, 25 Turnbull's Lane
Gibraltar
tel. 350-79959, fax 350-79894
Services Offered: company formation, corporate services, mail forwarding

---

Gibraltar Financial Services Handbook
PO.Box 555
Gibraltar
tel. 350-79385

- *Services Offered:* books or newsletters

J.A. Hassan & Partners
57-63 Line Wall Road, PO.Box 199
Gibraltar
tel. 350-79000, fax 350-71966

- *Services Offered:* law office

Jordan & Sons (Gibraltar) Ltd.
Suite 2A, Eurolife Building, 1 Corrall Road, PO.Box 569
Gibraltar
tel. 350-75446, fax 350-42701

- *Services Offered:* company formation, trust formation, corporate services

---

KPMG Peat Marwick
Regal House, Queensway, PO.Box 191
Gibraltar
tel. 350-74015, fax 350-74016, telex 2248 KPMGIB GK

- *Services Offered:* company formation, trust formation, accounting services, corporate services, safekeeping services

---

M & M Management Services Limited
117 Main Street, PO.Box 213
Gibraltar
tel. 350-40888, fax 350-40999

- *Services Offered:* company formation, trust formation, corporate services

---

Massias & Partners
117 Main Street, PO.Box 213
Gibraltar
tel. 350-40888, fax 350-40999

- *Services Offered:* law office

Riggs Valmet Finsbury
PO.Box 472, 50 Town Range
Gibraltar
tel. 350-40000, fax 350-40404, telex 2103 RV GK

- *Services Offered:* company formation, corporate services

Royal Bank of Scotland (Gibraltar) Limited
1 Corral Road, PO.Box 766
Gibraltar

- *Services Offered:* retail banking

Rutherford Associates (International) Ltd.
Eurotowers Bl., 1/303 GBZ
Gibraltar
tel. 350-52750, fax 350-50647

- *Services Offered:* company formation, corporate services, mail forwarding

---

Triay & Triay Barristers at Law; Solicitors
28 Irish Town
Gibraltar
tel. 350-72020, fax 350-72270

- *Services Offered:* law office

HONG KONG

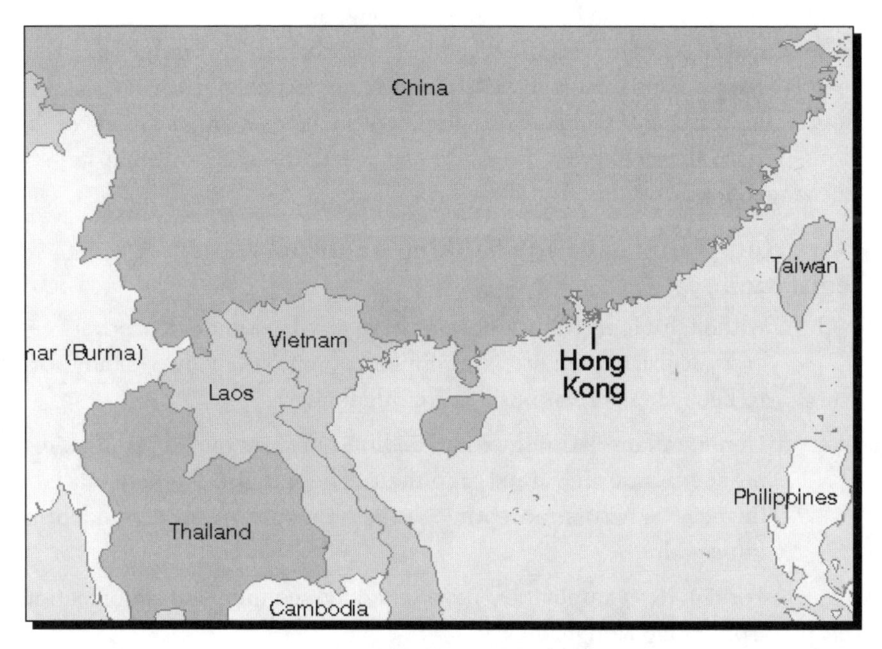

In southeast Asia. It has only 1,071 square kilometers of land, including 235 islands, and a population of approximately 6 million. Main language is Cantonese and English. Climate is moderate sub-tropical with a long, humid summer and a mild winter. Average temperatures are 31°C in summer and 15°C in winter.

The British officially arrived in Hong Kong early in 1841. Possession of the island of Hong Kong was taken on January 26, 1841 and it was proclaimed a Crown Colony by Royal Letters Patent dated April 25, 1843. The island had been ceded to Britain by the Ching government of China as a result of the Convention of Chuenpi, signed January 20,1841 and ratified by the Treaty of Nanking on August 29, 1842. Twenty years later, a small area on the Kowloon peninsula was also ceded to Britain. In 1898 the New Territories were leased for a 99-year term. Hong Kong continued under British rule from 1841 to 1941 when it was occupied by the Japanese. The British returned in 1945 at the end of World War II. In 1949 a Communist government came to power, following the nationalist republican government which had over-thrown the Ching dynasty in 1912. The colonial status of Hong Kong was not disturbed.

Negotiations on the future of Hong Kong, after the expiry of the 1898 lease on July 1, 1997, were finalized in December 1984. Under an agreement between China and the UK, Hong Kong has changed hands, and is now in the control of China. The agreement includes many detailed conditions, where the economy, life-style and freedoms will continue largely unchanged for 50 years.

Does Hong Kong have any banking or corporate secrecy legislation?

NO. Although Hong Kong does not have any banking or corporate secrecy legislation, there is an implied common law duty of advisors to keep clients relationships confidential.

Confidential relationships can be lifted in cases of drug trafficking, money laundering, fraud, and theft. There is also the possibility of financial advisors accepting bribes in return for confidential information.

Foreign tax authorities have obtained confidential information from Hong Kong banks.

Does Hong Kong have a long history of legal stability?

NO. The British signed a 99 year lease with China in 1898 on an area called the New Territories, which was to become Hong Kong. The impending expiry of the New Territories lease prompted negotiations that led in 1984 to the signing of the Sino-British Joint Declaration. In July 1997, all of Hong Kong changed hands to Chinese sovereignty. Hong Kong has become a Special Administrative Region within the People's Republic of China, with a high degree of autonomy, its own Basic Law, and a promise that its way of life will be maintained for 50 years.

An extensive localization policy has ensured that the Hong Kong Government is now administered largely by Hong Kong Chinese.

Is there an income tax in Hong Kong?

YES. Income is taxed at a rate of 17.5% for corporations and 15% for individuals, partnerships, and sole proprietorships. Certain income is not taxable, including:

- Dividend income.
- Profits or income from the sale of capital assets.
- Interest and profits from certain Hong Kong dollar denominated debt instruments.

Stamp duty is levied on the sale or purchase of any Hong Kong stock at a rate of 0.3% of share value.

Capital duty is levied on the authorized share capital of a company at a rate of 0.6% of share value. Any subsequent increase in share capital is subject to this Capital duty tax.

Are there any other taxes in Hong Kong?

YES. Estate taxes range from 6% where the total Hong Kong assets exceed HK$5 million to 18% where those assets exceed HK$7 million. Estate taxes do not apply to assets outside Hong Kong, even if the deceased was resident in Hong Kong.

There is no capital gains tax or gift tax in Hong Kong.

Does Hong Kong maintain exchange controls?

NO. There are currently no exchange controls in Hong Kong. The currency is the Hong Kong dollar which is freely exchangeable.

Does Hong Kong maintain tax treaties with any other countries?

YES. Hong Kong and the U.S. signed a treaty in 1989 that provides a mutual tax exemption applicable only to shipping profits. Hong Kong maintains no other tax treaties with any other countries.

There is no tax treaty between Canada and Hong Kong.

Does Hong Kong allow for the formation of corporate entities?

YES. There are three types of Limited Companies in Hong Kong, a Private Limited Company, a Public Limited Company, and a branch office of a foreign company incorporated outside Hong Kong. Requirements are:

- At least two shareholders, who need not be residents of Hong Kong and can be corporate entities.
- At least two directors who have attained the age 18.
- A secretary who must be a resident of Hong Kong if an individual, or have its registered office in Hong Kong if the secretary is corporate.

Additionally, every business established in Hong Kong is required to obtain a Business Registration Certificate, currently HK$160 annually.

Private Limited Company - Most businesses in Hong Kong are private limited companies whose articles of association:

- Restrict the right to transfer the company's shares.
- Limit the number of members to 50.
- Prohibit the offering of shares to the public.

There are no restrictions on foreign ownership of companies in Hong Kong and no residency requirements for directors or shareholders.

Public Limited Company - Companies intending to issue shares to the general public must provide a prospectus giving full details of the proposed share value, capitalization, and details of current and future business prospects. Corporations are not permitted to act as a director or secretary of a Public Limited Company.

Branch Office - Companies operating in Hong Kong and incorporated elsewhere must register with the Registrar of Companies under Part XI of the Hong Kong Companies Ordinance. This requires:

- Certified copy of the companies documents of incorporation.
- Background information on the Directors.
- Background information on the company secretary.
- Power of Attorney or other document appointing a person to accept notices in Hong Kong.

- Details of the address of the registered office in Hong Kong.
- Details of the principal place of business in the companies country of incorporation.

Does Hong Kong allow for the formation of Trusts?

YES. Although Hong Kong is a suitable jurisdiction for forming Trusts (low tax, English common law, excellent infrastructure), questions raised by the transfer of power to China in 1997 makes Hong Kong a poor choice compared to other excellent offshore centres.

Does Hong Kong allow for the formation of Captive Insurance Companies?

YES. Although Hong Kong allows the formation of Captive Insurance Companies, questions raised by the transfer of power to China in 1997 makes Hong Kong a poor choice compared to other excellent offshore centres.

Does Hong Kong allow for the formation of Private Banking Companies?

YES. Although Hong Kong allows the formation of Banking Companies, the strict requirements make them impractical for tax planning purposes. Questions raised by the transfer of power to China in 1997 makes Hong Kong a poor choice compared to other excellent offshore centres.

Financial institutions and contacts:

Bank in Liechtenstein AG (Hong Kong)
Suite 1001, One Exchange Square, 8 Connaught Place, Central
Hong Kong
tel. 852-523-6180, fax 852-868-0059

- *Services Offered:* private banking

Bank Julius Baer
2101 Jardine House, 1 Connaught Place
Hong Kong
tel. 852-2877-3328, fax 852-2845-9272, telex 8-9439

- *Services Offered:* investment advisor, private banking, retail banking, safekeeping services

---

Bank of N.T. Butterfield & Son Ltd.
26/F Bank of China Tower, 1 Garden Road
Central, Hong Kong
tel. 852-2868-1010, fax 852-2845-0336, telex 82370 BNTB HX

- *Services Offered:* investment advisor, company formation, trust formation, private banking, retail banking, safekeeping services

---

Banque Generale du Luxembourg S.A.
1 Connaught Place,Suite 2310, Jardine House
Central, Hong Kong
tel. 852-2810-7266, fax 852-2845-0201

- *Services Offered:* investment advisor, private banking, retail banking, loans and credit, safekeeping services

---

Chase Manhattan Private Bank
1 Exchange Square, 41st Floor
Central, Hong Kong
tel. 852-5841-4770, fax 852-5845-5900

- *Services Offered:* investment advisor, company formation, trust formation, private banking, retail banking, loans and credit, safekeeping services

---

Deloitte Touche Tohmatsu
26th Floor, Wing On Centre, 111 Connaught Road
Central, Hong Kong
tel. 852-2545-0303, fax 852-2541-1911

- *Services Offered:* company formation, accounting services, corporate services

---

Hill Samuel Investment Services (Asia)
35th Floor, Bank of America Tower, 12 Harcourt Road
Hong Kong
tel. 852-2847-3000, fax 852-2868-4733

- *Services Offered:* investment advisor, company formation, trust formation, private banking, loans and credit, safekeeping services

Hong Kong Federation of Industries
Hankow Centre, 4th Floor, 5-15 Hankow Road, Tsimshatsui
Kowloon, Hong Kong
tel. 852-2723-0818, fax 852-2721-3797

- *Services Offered:* government services

Hong Kong General Chamber of Commerce
22nd Floor, United Centre, 95 Queensway
Hong Kong
tel. 852-2525-6385, fax 852-2845-2610

- *Services Offered:* government services

Hong Kong Industries Department
14th Floor, Ocean Centre, 5 Canton Road, Tsimshatsui
Kowloon, Hong Kong
tel. 852-2737-2573, fax 852-2730-4633

- *Services Offered:* government services

HSBC HongkongBank
PO.Box 80208, Cheung Sha Wan
Kowloon, Hong Kong
tel. 852-2748-3322, fax 852-2729-8398

- *Services Offered:* private banking, retail banking, loans and credit

---

KPMG Peat Marwick
8th Floor, Prince's Building
Central, Hong Kong
tel. 852-2522-6022, fax 852-2845-2588, telex 74391 PMMHK HX

- *Services Offered:* company formation, accounting services, corporate services, safekeeping services

---

Mossack Fonseca & Co. (Hong Kong) Ltd.
Suite 1504, 15F, Tower 1, 33 Canton Road
Kowloon, Hong Kong
tel. 852-2376-1998, fax 852-2376-0308

- *Services Offered:* company formation

Regent Financial Services Ltd.
904-906 Asia Pacific Finance Tower, 3 Garden Road
Central, Hong Kong
tel. 852-514-6111, fax 852-810-6346

- *Services Offered:* mutual fund manager

Standard Chartered Bank
8/F Edinburgh Tower, The Landmark
Central, Hong Kong
tel. 852-5842-2822, fax 852-5810-0651

- *Services Offered:* retail banking

TrustNet Group
Central, Hong Kong
tel. 852-2525-9991, fax 852-2877-6852

- *Services Offered:* company formation, trust formation, law office, accounting services, corporate services

Wardley Investment Services Limited
12th Floor, BA Tower, 12 Harcourt Road
Central, Hong Kong
tel. 852-2847-9099, fax 852-2845-2024

- *Services Offered:* mutual fund manager

Westpac Banking Corporation (Jersey)
Level 20, Exchange Square III, 8 Connaught Place
Central, Hong Kong
tel. 852-2842-9811, fax 852-2842-9868

- *Services Offered:* retail banking

Yorkwo Consultancy Services
Leader Industrial Centre, Room 311, 57-59 Au Pui Wan Street, Fo Tan
Shatin, Hong Kong, NT
tel. 852-2684-1098, fax 852-2601-6935

- *Services Offered:* private banking

ISLE OF MAN

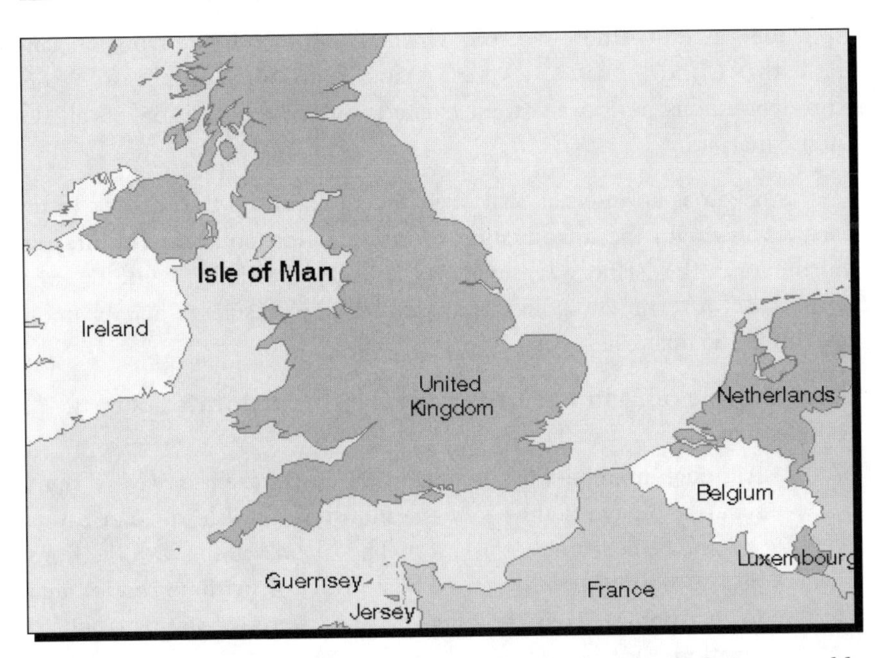

Off the British coast. A 227 square mile island in the Irish Sea, roughly equidistant from England, Wales, Scotland and Ireland. Population is approximately 70,000. Cold summers and mild winters, often humid and overcast, with strong westerly winds. Main language is English and Gaelic. No visa is required for stays up to six months.

The Isle of Man is an ancient Norse/Gaelic Kingdom that was the principal island of the Kingdom of the Sudreyjar. The Kingdom of the Sudreyjar came to be called the Kingdom of Mann and the Isles, part of an independent Norse Kingdom which disintegrated in the 13th century. This lead to a dispute between the Kingdoms of Scotland and England, with the King of Scotland seizing the Hebrides, and attempting to seize Mann also. Near the end of the 14th century, the Anglo-Scots wars ended, with the Scots abandoning their claim to Mann. England agreed not to claim Mann, with the island instead continuing as an independent sovereign kingdom with its own parliament and king. The Manx parliament, called Tynwald, was founded by the early Vikings and boasts the longest continuous history of any legislature in the world (celebrating 1,000 years of continuous parliamentary rule in 1979). The ruler of the Isle of Man was known as the Lord of Man, with the Lordship being purchased by the British Crown from the Duke of Atholl in 1765. This led to indirect rule from England until the Island's finances were separated from England's in 1866. Throughout this period Tynwald existed, enacting legislation on all domestic matters.

Its origin as an international finance centre can be traced back to the early 1960's with the introduction of low taxation policies. The first investments in the Island were made by British expatriates, while the present Manx government policy is to attract new residents and promote growth in the financial sector.

Does the Isle of Man have any banking or corporate secrecy legislation?

NO. Although members of the financial industry are required to sign a security pledge if they join the industry, the Isle of Man has no specific bank secrecy legislation. The Island's status with the European Community is governed by a Protocol, with no requirement to harmonize laws relating to disclosure of information or taxation.

There is an implied contractual duty for advisors to keep their client information confidential, and it should be noted that confidentiality is a bank license condition.

The Isle of Man followed the UK by introducing Drug Trafficking Offenses legislation to prevent criminals from using the Island's financial industry facilities. Client confidentiality is not available where a banker has reason to suspect drug trafficking, insider trading, or the finance of terrorism. Confidential information can be released if there is a suspected criminal activity such as illegal drug activities, theft, or fraud.

Confidential financial information is not released to foreign governments for tax investigations.

Does the Isle of Man have a long history of legal stability?

YES. Although the British Government purchased the regalities of the Isle of Man on behalf of the crown, the Isle of Man is not, and never has been, part of the United Kingdom. The Isle of Man's parliament, Tynwald, is over 1000 years old and legislates on all domestic matters. The United Kingdom assumes responsibility for foreign affairs and external defense. In 1961 the Isle of Man Constitution Act was adopted, providing for a crown appointed governor, an appointed executive council, partially elected legislative council, and an elected lower house (House of Keys).

The Isle of Man is not a member of the European Economic Community, although it has a special relationship with the EEC, set out under Protocol 3 of the UK's Treaty of Accession to the European Community, which guarantees free movement of goods. The UK is responsible for external affairs and defense, receiving an annual contribution for this service.

The Island has its own legal system, Anglo Saxon in origin. Most Manx legislation, Company and Trust law in particular, has been modeled on English law, and the rules of English Common Law and Equity are generally followed by the Manx courts. The Island has its own courts, with the heads of the judicial system known as "Deemsters." The supreme court is the English Privy Council.

Is there an Income Tax on the Isle of Man?

YES. Income derived from the Isle of Man is taxable. The standard rate of personal income tax is 15%. Residents are liable to pay income tax on their world-wide income. Non-residents are taxed only on income derived from the Isle of Man.

Resident Companies are subject to Manx Income Tax which is a flat rate of 20% on taxable profit. Exempt Companies require an annual payment (Exempt Fee) of £300 made in lieu of tax. Non-Resident Companies pay a duty of £600 annually in lieu of tax. Interest on bank accounts maintained in the Isle of Man in the names of exempt companies is not taxed. There is no income tax for non-resident activities.

Insurance companies are subject to a tax of 20% on underwriting and investment profits derived from the Isle of Man. However, insurance companies licensed under the Exempt Insurance Companies Act of 1981 are exempt from all income taxes.

Are there any other taxes in the Isle of Man?

NO. There is no capital gains or capital transfer tax, no gift tax, and no estate or succession tax in the Isle of Man. There is no stamp duty, no capital transfer tax, no wealth tax, and no death duty.

Value added tax is collected by the Isle of Man Customs & Excise at standard UK rates.

Does the Isle of Man maintain exchange controls?

NO. There are currently no exchange controls in the Isle of Man. The Isle of Man issues its own currency, the Manx pound, which is interchangeable with the pound sterling.

Does the Isle of Man maintain tax treaties with any other countries?

YES. There is no double-taxation agreement between the U.S. and the Isle of Man, although there is a double-taxation agreement between the UK and the Isle of Man.

There is no double-taxation agreement between Canada and the Isle of Man.

Does the Isle of Man allow for the formation of corporate entities?

YES. Company law is based on The Companies Acts 1931-1992 and subsequent amendments. The three types of Isle of Man companies are Resident Company, Exempt Company, and Non-Resident Company.

All three types of companies have the same minimum statutory requirements, requiring:

- At least two shareholders (need not be residents of the Isle of Man).

- A minimum two directors and one secretary. Alternate directors are permitted, corporate directors are not permitted. Exempt companies must appoint at least one Isle of Man resident director.
- A registered office on the Isle of Man.
- Maintain a register of members, directors and secretary, register of charges, and minutes of shareholders meetings.
- At least two shares must be issued. Shares must be issued at par value.
- Bearer share warrants may be issued.
- Companies must hold an annual general meeting.
- Annual general meeting may be held in any jurisdiction.

Each year the company must prepare audited accounts to be placed before the members of the company, although these are not filed at the companies registry and not available to the public (in the Manx Budget of April 1993, the Treasury Minister stated that he was to allow Private Exempt and Non-Resident companies to dispense with the need to provide audited accounts).

Since June 1988, companies governed by the Companies Act 1986 have the capacity, rights, powers, and privileges of an individual. A Manx company can undertake different types of activity, such as holding investments, holding intellectual property rights, trade, re-invoice, and any other activity an individual can undertake. Advantages of Isle of Man companies include:

- Directors meetings may be held in any jurisdiction.
- Bearer shares are permitted.
- No minimum authorized share capital is required.

Resident Company - A resident company is required to pay a flat income tax of 20%.

Exempt Company - Any company may apply for and obtain exemption from Isle of Man corporation taxes provided that ownership of the company is non-resident and that income is earned from sources outside the Isle of Man. An Exempt Company is only required to pay an annual registration tax which is currently £300. The company must have a resident director and a resident qualified secretary. The company is required to keep proper books of account but has no filing requirements unless requested to do so.

Non-Resident Company - A non-resident company is only required to pay an annual registration tax which is currently £600. Beneficial ownership, trading, management, and control must be outside of the Isle of Man. A majority of directors must be resident outside the Isle of Man, and their meetings should not be held on the Island. Other than bank interest, there should be no Isle of Man source of income. Non-Resident companies may be administered in, but not directed from the Isle of Man.

International Company - The International Business Act 1994 was introduced following close consultation with the Isle of Man's finance community. The legislation provides for a minimum 1% rate of taxation on a sliding scale to a maximum of 35%, subject to a minimum income tax charge of £300, based upon the specific requirements of the International Company. Applications must be made to the Assessor of Income Tax who will determine the appropriate rate based on the nature of the company's application.

Does the Isle of Man allow for the formation of Trusts?

YES. Trust law is based on the Trustee Act 1961, The Perpetuities & Accumulation Act 1968, Variation of Trusts Act 1961 and Recognition of Trusts Act 1988. They are based on normal common law precedents.

A Manx resident Trust and any distributions of income are exempt from tax, providing:

- the Settlor and Beneficiaries are non-resident,
- the funds did not originate in the Isle of Man, and
- there is no local income apart from bank deposit interest.

No registration is required for Trusts In fact, there is no registere of Trusts in the Isle of Man, althouth Trustees do have the option of lodging Trust instruments in the Isle of Man Deeds Registry. All Manx Trust documents and accounts are confidential. No registration fees or duties are payable on the formation of an Isle of Man Trust. There is no restriction on the accumulation of income within the perpetuity period which is 80 years. It is possible to provide for the transfer of such Trusts to another jurisdiction if needed. Types of Trusts available in the Isle of Man include the Fixed Trust, Discretionary Trust, and Protective Trust.

Fixed Trust - The interest of the Beneficiaries are so defined as to leave the Trustee with no discretion as to how to benefit them.

Discretionary Trust - The disposal of the Trust assets is at the sole discretion of the Trustee, who may receive recommendations from the Settlor.

Protective Trust - This is a form of Trust where the object of the Trust is to provide for a Beneficiary with some form of disability.

Does the Isle of Man allow for the formation of Captive Insurance Companies?

YES. The Isle of Man is a tax-free international insurance centre with high standards. Throughout the 1980's, the Isle of Man has emerged as a stable offshore financial centre with hundreds of captive insurance companies. The Parliament (Tynwald) has full autonomy on internal affairs, and is firmly committed to developing a secure, tax efficient international insurance centre, with:

- No tax on underwriting profits.
- No tax on investment income.
- No withholding tax on dividends.
- No capital gains tax.
- No currency exchange controls.

Captive Insurance Companies are governed by the Insurance Act of 1986 (and supporting regulations), defining:

- Minimum requirements for paid-up share capital.
- Minimum solvency margins to be maintained.
- The financial credentials of companies involved.
- Specific requirements enacting "fit and proper" officers of insurance companies.
- Government licensing and tax exemption fees.
- Statutory reporting requirements.

The regulatory and tax exemption legislation of the Isle of Man applies to captive insurance companies, general insurance companies, life assurance companies, and reinsurance companies. Annual fees are £2,000 payable to the Manx government.

Does the Isle of Man allow for the formation of Private Banking Companies?

YES. Isle of Man Companies based on The Companies Act 1931-1992 may apply for a banking license governed by the Banking Acts 1975-1986. International Companies may not apply.

Financial institutions and contacts:

Abchurch Corporate Services Limited
PO.Box 204, 20 North Quay
Douglas, Isle of Man, IM99 1QZ
tel. 44-1624-662262, fax 44-1624-662272

- *Services Offered:* company formation, trust formation, captive insurance formation, corporate services, estate planning services, safekeeping services

---

Allied Dunbar International Fund Managers Ltd.
Allied Dunbar International Centre, Lord Street
Douglas, Isle of Man, IM99 1ET
tel. 44-1624-661551, fax 44-1624-662183

- *Services Offered:* mutual fund manager

Anglo Irish Bankcorp
69 Athol Street
Douglas, Isle of Man, IMI 1ME
tel. 44-1624-625508, fax 44-1624-625497

- *Services Offered:* investment advisor, private banking

Ansbacher (Isle Of Man) Limited
Suite 1, 11 Myrtle Street
Douglas, Isle of Man, 1M1 1ED
tel. 44-1624-674657, fax 44-1624-623861

- *Services Offered:* investment advisor, company formation, trust formation, private banking, safekeeping services

---

Aston Corporate Trustees Ltd.
19 Peel Road
Douglas, Isle of Man, IM1 4LS
tel. 44-1624-626591, fax 44-1624-625126, telex 627691 ASTON G

- *Services Offered:* company formation, trust formation, captive insurance formation, bank formation, accounting services, corporate services, estate planning services, safekeeping services

---

Bank of Bermuda (Isle of Man) Limited
PO.Box 34, 12/13 Hill Street
Douglas, Isle of Man, IM99 1BW
tel. 44-1624-637777, fax 44-1624-637778

- *Services Offered:* investment advisor, company formation, trust formation, private banking, retail banking, corporate services, deposit backed MC/Visa, safekeeping services

---

Barclays Isle of Man Offshore Banking Centre
PO.Box 213, Asgard House, Ridgeway Street
Douglas, Isle of Man, 1M99 1RH

- *Services Offered:* investment advisor, private banking, estate planning services

---

Barclays Private Bank & Trust Limited
PO.Box 48, 4th floor, Queen Victoria House, Victoria Street
Douglas, Isle of Man, IM99 1DF
tel. 44-1624-673514, fax 44-1624-620905, telex 629587 BARTRTG

- *Services Offered:* investment advisor, company formation, trust formation, private banking, loans and credit, deposit backed MC/Visa, safekeeping services

---

Blue Chip Capital Management Limited
Victory House, Prospect Hill
Douglas, Isle of Man
tel. 888-265-6661, fax 800-560-0645

- *Services Offered:* investment advisor, mutual fund manager, private banking, global investing information, deposit backed MC/Visa, insurance-based investments

---

Britannia International Limited
Britannia House, Victoria Street
Douglas, Isle of Man, IM99 1SD
tel. 44-1624-628512, fax 44-1624-661015

- *Services Offered:* mutual fund manager

City Trust Limited
3rd Floor, Murdoch House, South Quay
Douglas, Isle of Man, IM1 5AS
tel. 44-1624-661881, fax 44-1624-611423

- *Services Offered:* company formation, trust formation, corporate services

---

Czerlau & Associates Limited
Victory House, Prospect Hill
Douglas, Isle of Man
tel. 800-226-5703, fax 242-356-0223

- *Services Offered:* company formation, trust formation, corporate services, estate planning services, deposit backed MC/Visa

---

Hansard International Limited
Anglo International House, PO.Box 192, Bank Hill, North Quay
Douglas, Isle of Man, IM99 1QL
tel. 44-1624-688000, fax 44-1624-629144

- *Services Offered:* mutual fund manager

IBI Global Funds Ltd.
4 Christian Road
Douglas, Isle of Man, IM1 2FD
tel. 44-1624-622676, fax 44-1624-662776

- *Services Offered:* mutual fund manager

IFG International Limited
International House, Castle Hill, Victoria Road
Douglas, Isle of Man, IM2 4RB
tel. 44-1624-626931, fax 44-1624-624469

- *Services Offered:* company formation, trust formation, corporate services, estate planning services, safekeeping services

---

ILS Corporate Services
Salisbury House, 15 Victoria Street
Douglas, Isle of Man
tel. 44-1624-624400, fax 44-1624-628488

- *Services Offered:* company formation

International Company Services Limited
Sovereign House, Station Road
St.Johns, Isle of Man, IM4 3AJ
tel. 44-1624-801801, fax 44-1624-801800

- *Services Offered:* company formation, trust formation

International Law Systems Ltd.
Salisbury House, 15 Victoria Street
Douglas, Isle of Man, 1M1 2SQ
tel. 44-1624-624400, fax 44-1624-628488
- *Services Offered:* law office

Irish Permanent (IOM) Ltd.
St.James's Chambers, 64a Athol Street
Douglas, Isle of Man, IM1 1JE
tel. 44-1624-676726, fax 44-1624-676795
- *Services Offered:* private banking, retail banking

Island Resources Limited
National House
Stanton, Isle of Man, IM4 1HA
tel. 44-1624-824555, fax 44-1624-823949
- *Services Offered:* company formation, trust formation, corporate services

---

Isle of Man Assurance Company
PO.Box 179, IOMA House
Douglas, Isle of Man
tel. 44-1624-624141, fax 44-1624-622500
- *Services Offered:* captive insurance management

Isle of Man Financial Services Commission
PO.Box 58, 1-4 Goldie Terrace
Douglas, Isle of Man
tel. 44-1624-624487, fax 44-1624-629342
- *Services Offered:* government services

Isle of Man Financial Trust Limited
IOMA House, Prospect Hill
Douglas, Isle of Man, IM99 1HA
tel. 44-1624-663466, fax 44-1624-663467, telex 627924 IOMINS
- *Services Offered:* investment advisor, company formation, trust formation, captive insurance formation, corporate services, estate planning services, safekeeping services

---

Isle of Man Government Insurance Authority
S&F House, 12-14 Ridgeway Street
Douglas, Isle of Man
tel. 44-1624-685695, fax 44-1624-663346
- *Services Offered:* government services

Isle of Man Government-Commercial Development Division
1-4 Goldie Terrace, Meghraj Centre, 2nd Floor, Dept 262
Douglas, Isle of Man, 1M1 1PG
tel. 44-1624-671737, fax 44-1624-615038

- *Services Offered:* government services

John C. Sturgeon & Company
8 Prospect Hill
Douglas, Isle of Man, 1M1 1ES
tel. 44-1624-617050, fax 44-1624-617051

- *Services Offered:* company formation, trust formation, law office, corporate services, estate planning services

Jordan & Sons (Isle of Man) Ltd.
24 Ridgeway Street
Douglas, Isle of Man, IM1 1QA
tel. 44-1624-624298, fax 44-1624-626719

- *Services Offered:* company formation, trust formation, corporate services

Lloyds Bank PLC
Isle of Man Expatriate Centre, Box 12, Peveril Buildings, Peveril Square
Douglas, Isle of Man, IM99 1SS
tel. 44-1624-638100, fax 44-1624-638181

- *Services Offered:* private banking, retail banking

Lloyds Private Banking (Isle of Man) Limited
PO.Box 111, Peveril Building, Peveril Square
Douglas, Isle of Man, IM99 1JJ
tel. 44-1624-638100, fax 44-1624-676289

- *Services Offered:* private banking

Lorne House Trust Limited
Lorne House
Castletown, Isle of Man, IM9 1AZ
tel. 44-1624-823579, fax 44-1624-822952, telex 629265 LORNHO G

- *Services Offered:* investment advisor, company formation, trust formation, bank formation, corporate services

Manx Corporate Services Limited
10/12 Prospect Hill, 3rd Floor
Douglas, Isle of Man, IM1 1EJ
tel. 44-1624-662727, fax 44-1624-662332

- *Services Offered:* company formation, trust formation, corporate services

---

MeesPierson (Isle of Man) Limited
Pierson House, PO.Box 156, 18-20 North Quay
Douglas, Isle of Man, IM99 1NR
tel. 44-1624-688300, fax 44-1624-688334, telex 626159 MEESPN G

- *Services Offered:* investment advisor, company formation, trust formation, private banking, corporate services, deposit backed MC/Visa, safekeeping services

---

Mercury Fund Managers (IOM) Limited
12-13 Hill Street
Douglas, Isle of Man
tel. 44-1624-662255, fax 44-1624-662850

- *Services Offered:* mutual fund manager

Meridian Management Limited
PO.Box 66, Suite 1, Empress House, Empress Drive
Douglas, Isle of Man, IM99 1EE
tel. 44-1624-625935, fax 44-1624-671848

- *Services Offered:* corporate services

Midland Bank International Finance Corporation Limited
Celtic House, Victoria Street
Douglas, Isle of Man, IM99 1BU
tel. 44-1624-684953, fax 44-1624-684869

- *Services Offered:* private banking

Midland Bank Trust (Isle of Man) Ltd.
PO.Box 39 Heritage Court, 39 Athol Street
Douglas, Isle of Man
tel. 44-1624-623118, fax 44-1624-623202, telex 62-8037

- *Services Offered:* private banking

N & P Overseas Limited
PO.Box 150, 56 Strand Street
Douglas, Isle of Man, 1M99 1NH
tel. 44-1624-662244, fax 44-1624-662482

- *Services Offered:* private banking

Riggs Valmet Isle of Man Limited
4 Finch Road
Douglas, Isle of Man
tel. 44-1624-677522, fax 44-1624-677523

- *Services Offered:* company formation

Royal Bank of Scotland (IOM) Limited
PO.Box 151, Victory House, Prospect Hill
Douglas, Isle of Man, IM99 INJ
tel. 44-1624-629111, fax 44-1624-672685

- *Services Offered:* investment advisor, company formation, trust formation, captive insurance formation, private banking, retail banking, corporate services, safekeeping services

---

The Associated Trust Company Ltd.
Barrantagh House, Bucks Road
Douglas, Isle of Man, IM1 3DD
tel. 44-1624-624211, fax 44-1624-625469

- *Services Offered:* company formation, private banking

Touche Ross & Company
PO.Box 250, Bank of Scotland House, Prospect Hill
Douglas, Isle of Man, IM99 1XJ
tel. 44-1624-672332, fax 44-1624-672334

- *Services Offered:* accounting services

Tyndall Bank International Limited
PO.Box 62, Tyndall House, Kensington Road
Douglas, Isle of Man, IM99 1DZ
tel. 44-1624-29201, fax 44-1624-20200, telex 62-8732

- *Services Offered:* investment advisor, private banking, retail banking, safekeeping services

---

William's & Glyn's Bank (Isle of Man)
Victory House, Prospect Hill
Douglas, Isle of Man

- *Services Offered:* retail banking

LIECHTENSTEIN

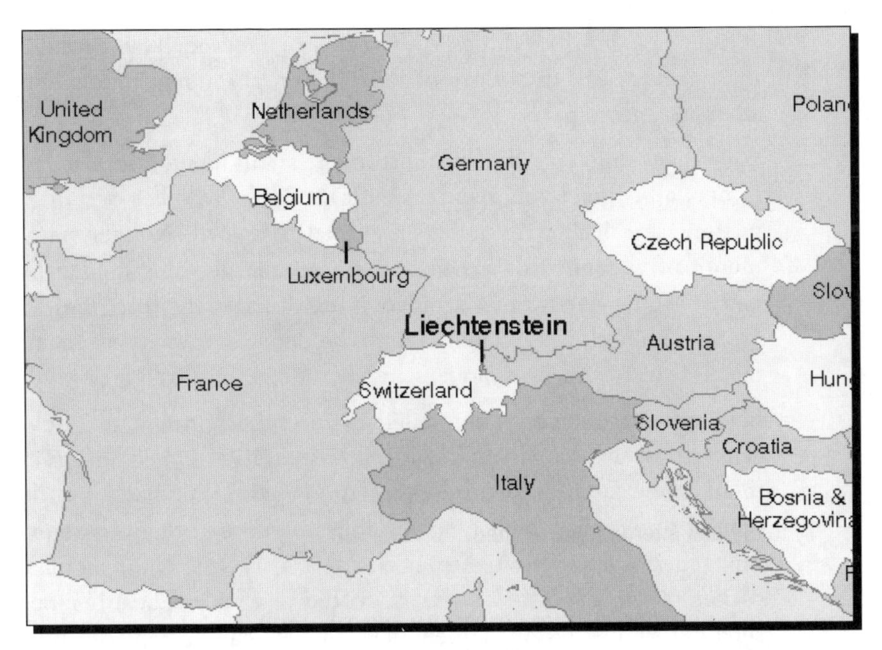

In Europe. Borders Switzerland and Austria. A sliver on the eastern border of Switzerland, only 150 square km in area, with approximately 30,000 citizens. Zurich is one hour's drive away. Main language is German and Alemanni, although English is widely spoken. Climate is cold with snow in winter and mild in summer.

The Principality of Liechtenstein includes the former territories of the County of Vaduz and the Lordship of Schellenberg. These territories were united by inheritance in 1434 with the status of fiefs of the Holy Roman Empire. In 1712 the two territories were purchased separately by Prince John Adam Andrew of Liechtenstein, whose name was taken from Liechtenstein's Castle, a family possession in Vienna. In 1719, the two territories were formally united as the Principality of Liechtenstein, becoming a sovereign state in 1806. In 1923 Liechtenstein joined Switzerland in a customs and currency union. Today Prince Franz Joseph II is the head of state. His Gutenberg castle overlooks the capital city, Vaduz. The royal family is also the majority shareholder of BIL (Bank in Liechtenstein).

Does Liechtenstein have any banking or corporate secrecy legislation?

YES. Revealing bank-account information is a criminal offense punishable by jail time. Liechtenstein's very strict secrecy laws prohibit the unauthorized disclosure of information pertaining to a clients affairs to a third party.

Some banks offer a "discreet customer" status. As a discreet customer, all contact you maintain with the bank, whether oral or in writing, are dealt with under an agreed password. Neither statements of account nor receipts mention the account holder by name. Thus, a customer's name is disclosed only to a limited group of employees. The account holder's anonymity is maintained toward other employees and unauthorized third parties.

Banking establishments domiciled in Liechtenstein and the Government of the Principality of Liechtenstein have signed an agreement on establishing business relations with the bank in the receipt of money. The banking establishments are bound to determine their customers identities and to clarify who the beneficial owner of the deposited assets is. In the case of juridical persons such determination of the beneficial owner may be replaced by a declaration submitted by a Liechtenstein official in charge of professional secrets. An appropriate form has to be signed upon establishing an account relationship.

In case of criminal offenses committed by an account holder, the bank is not permitted to rely on banking secrecy. The banks have also instituted precautionary measures intended to curb money laundering and insider trading.

A typical Bank or Trust Company "Information Waiver" reads as follows:

The undersigned (hereinafter called the "Customer") hereby confirms that he will not carry out any transaction concerning his securities account with (This Bank) which is considered as insider trading not allowed by law or other regulations in that country in which the transaction is carried out ("Insider Trading").

If proceedings against the bank are by the authorities having jurisdiction for investigations in insider trading in the respective countries

("Authorities"), the Bank will inform the customer ("Information") immediately after receipt of a request for information.
The Bank reserves the right to take any steps which it may deem appropriate after due consideration and the expiration of 30 days since the forwarding of the information to the Customer. In such case the Customer authorized the Bank to reveal to the Authorities his name and details of any alleged insider trading.
This authorization shall be effective only if proceedings are initiated against the Bank because of insider trading.

In 1970, the Principality of Liechtenstein joined the European Agreement on Mutual Judicial Assistance in Criminal Matters. This agreement allows for bank secrecy to be lifted only if the underlying act is liable to prosecution in the State requesting judicial assistance as well as in accordance with Liechtenstein law.

Liechtenstein does not have any exchange of information agreements that would allow foreign tax authorities to obtain banking information. Liechtenstein banking and government officials consider their strict secrecy laws to be an important advantage, and the foundation of their success.

Does Liechtenstein have a long history of legal stability?

YES. Liechtenstein gained independence on July 12, 1806, after being part of the Holy Roman Empire for nearly 100 years. Directed by the constitution of 1921, the Principality of Liechtenstein is a hereditary constitutional monarchy, with the last ruling Hapsburg, Prince Franz Josef III. The Customs Treaty with Switzerland, signed in 1923, is the basis of the strong economic ties between the two countries. It was followed by the Currency Treaty after the introduction in 1924 of the Swiss Franc as Liechtenstein's legal tender.

The legal system has Austrian influence (criminal and civil law), Swiss influence (contract and property law), and German influence (commercial law). The present constitution, formed in 1921, calls for a 15 member legislature that is elected every 4 years, with the Prince sanctioning all law passed by the legislature.

Is there an income tax in Liechtenstein?

NO. There is no income tax in Liechtenstein on income or profits derived from outside Liechtenstein. There is, however, a net worth, or capital tax of 0.1% of total capital resources, subject to a minimum tax of SFr1,000, applying to Domiciliary and Holding Companies.

Dividends are subject to a withholding tax of 4%. Interest payments on loans exceeding SFr50,000 with a term longer than two years, and interest from bank deposits having a term longer than one year are subject to a withholding tax of 4%.

There are no local income taxes on corporations. Corporations pay an annual capital tax of 0.1% of capital and reserves, with a minimum annual capital tax of SFr1,000. Non-resident corporations and individuals are liable to tax only on income derived from a permanent establishment in Liechtenstein.

Are there any other taxes in Liechtenstein?

YES. Capital gains realized from the sale of real property located in Liechtenstein are subject to a real estate profits tax ranging from 3.6% to 35.6%. There is no capital gains tax in Liechtenstein on capital gains derived from outside Liechtenstein. Please note the net worth tax of 0.01% of total capital, with a minimum tax of SFr1,000.

Estate taxes of up to 5%, gift taxes of up to 27%, and succession taxes of up to 27% apply to Liechtenstein residents only.

There is no gift tax in Liechtenstein.

Does Liechtenstein maintain exchange controls?

NO. There are currently no exchange controls in the Liechtenstein. The official currency is the Swiss Franc.

Does Liechtenstein maintain tax treaties with any other countries?

YES. There is no double-taxation agreement between the U.S. and Liechtenstein, although there is a double-taxation agreement between Liechtenstein and Austria and between Liechtenstein and the Swiss Cantons of Graubuenden and St.Gallen.

There is no double-taxation agreement between Canada and Liechtenstein.

Does Liechtenstein allow for the formation of corporate entities?

YES. Limited companies registered in Liechtenstein are governed by the regulations outlined in the Persons and Companies Act (Personen und Gesellschaftsrecht or PGR).

Forms of legal entities acknowledged by the Liechtenstein Persons and Companies Act are:

- Aktiengesellschaft (company limited by shares).
- Kommanditaktiengesellschaft (partnership limited by shares).
- Verein (association).
- Gesellschaft mit beschrankter Haftung (private company limited by shares).
- Genossenschaft (registered co-operative society).
- Versicherungsverein auf Gegenseitigkeit/Hilfskassen (registered mutual insurance association / registered relief fund).
- Anstalt (establishment).
- Stiftung (foundation).

Taxes and Revenue Duty for Domiciliary and Holding Enterprises are as follows:

- **Limited Company** - formation fee (stamp duty) 3% of capital. Capital tax 0.1% of net assets, minimum SFr1,000. No profits tax. Coupon tax 4% of monetary value remittance (eg. dividends, liquidation surplus, etc.).
- **Establishment** - formation fee (stamp duty) 3% of capital. Capital tax 0.1% of net assets, minimum SFr1,000. No profits tax. No coupon tax.
- **Foundation** (Assets Administration) - formation fee (stamp duty) 0.2% of capital (minimum SFr200). Capital tax 0.1% of net assets, minimum SFr1,000. No profits tax. No coupon tax.

Companies may be classified as either a Domestic Operating Company, Domiciliary Company, or Holding Company:

Domestic Operating Company - A Domestic Operating Company is allowed to trade and conduct commercial activities in Liechtenstein.

Domiciliary Company - A Domiciliary Company will have its registered office in Liechtenstein, but will now be allowed to trade or conduct commercial activities in Liechtenstein.

Holding Company - A Holding Company is a company that has been incorporated for the purpose of administering or managing assets and investments.

Companies are required to provide certain information to be entered in the Public Register. Third parties may obtain information from the Public Register without providing any evidence of direct interest. The following information is subject to registration:

- Company name, domicile, and object.
- Statutory capital.
- Date of the articles of association.
- Administration body (number, names, addresses).
- Legal representative.
- Signature rights.
- Form in which official announcements are made.

The entry of a company in the Public Register must be published in the journal provided for official announcements (Amtsblatt). In the case of Domiciliary Companies and Holding Companies, the relevant information is displayed on the court notice board. The identity of company owners can be kept discreet through bearer shares held anonymously or by nominees.

The registration documents (formation deed, articles, etc.) may be inspected by third parties with the Registrar's consent, provided that they can submit evidence of a justified interest in doing so.

At least one member of the administration authorized to manage and represent the company must fulfill the following requirements, pursuant to Article 180a of the Persons and Companies Act:

- Member must be a Liechtenstein citizen with residence in the Principality of Liechtenstein or a foreigner with permission to settle in the Principality of Liechtenstein.
- Member must posses a professional license to act as lawyer, legal agent, auditor or Trustee, or alternately a government recognized business qualification, or he must exercise the authority to manage and represent the company within the framework of a fixed, main employment with a lawyer, legal agent, fiduciary enterprise, auditor or bank.

The above requirements are not applicable to:

- Legal entities which pursuant to the trade law have a qualified manager.
- Legal entities pursuing activities in Liechtenstein which do not fall within the scope of application of the trade law.

The administration body is liable only for damages caused intentionally or by neglect.

Companies limited by shares, establishments and Trust enterprises must comply with accounting and disclosure requirements, and are under obligation to:

- Keep orderly books of account.
- Submit within six months of the close of each business year the annual balance sheet and the profit and loss account drawn up according to recognized business rules.
- Preserve the accounting books for a period of at least ten years.

The PGR Code provides for the following types of shares:

- Bearer shares and registered shares.
- Preference shares and ordinary shares.
- Quota shares.

Does Liechtenstein allow for the formation of Trusts?

YES. Forms of Trusts acknowledged by the Liechtenstein Persons and Companies Act (PGR) are:

- Treuhandschaft (Trust settlement).
- Treuunternehmen (Trust enterprise).

Taxes and Revenue Duty for Trusts are as follows:

- **Trust** (reg.932a PGR) - formation fee (stamp duty) 3% of capital. Capital tax 0.1% of net assets, minimum SFr1,000. No profits tax. No coupon tax.
- **Trust** (reg.897 PGR) - no formation fee (stamp duty). Capital tax 0.1% of net assets, minimum SFr1,000. No profits tax. No coupon tax.

A Trust enterprise is set up by means of a formation deed with the attached notarized signature of the Settlor. The Trust articles must contain at least the following:

- Declaration of the settlor's intent to form a Trust enterprise.
- Trust articles.
- Amount of the Trust fund.
- Appointment of the board of trustees.
- Appointment of the legal representative.

The Trust enterprise acquires its legal personality only upon registration. Settlors of a Trust enterprise may be persons with residence in Liechtenstein or abroad. More than one Settlor is not required. The object must clearly indicate whether the Trust enterprise may engage in commercial activities. The minimum capital of the Trust enterprise is SFr30,000 which may be provided by payment in cash or contributions in kind.

Only the Trust assets are liable for the debts of the Trust enterprise. The governing bodies and the Settlor are not under obligation to make further contributions.

The legal representative is the permanent local agent appointed to represent the Trust enterprise. The legal representative is able to receive documents of all kinds from the local authorities, and may act on other matters only if the legal representative has power of attorney.

Does Liechtenstein allow for the formation of Captive Insurance Companies?

YES. A form of Insurance Company acknowledged by the Liechtenstein Persons and Companies Act (PGR) is:

- Konzessionierte Versicherungsunternehmen (licensed insurance company).

It is not practical to use Liechtenstein as a base for a Captive Insurance Company, as there are other jurisdictions with lower costs and friendlier legislation.

Does Liechtenstein allow for the formation of Private Banking Companies?

YES. A form of Banking Company acknowledged by the Liechtenstein Persons and Companies Act (PGR) is:

- Hypothekarinstitute (mortgage lending institution).

Liechtenstein banking licenses are very restricted and not practical for investment purposes.

Financial institutions and contacts:

Advokaturburo
Vaduz, Liechtenstein
tel. 41-75-232-06-30, fax 41-75-232-06-30

- *Services Offered:* company formation

Agentia Treuunternehmen Reg.
Landstrasse 36, Postfach 1608
Vaduz, Liechtenstein, FL-9490
tel. 41-75-232-83-32, fax 41-75-232-00-64

- *Services Offered:* company formation, trust formation, accounting services, corporate services, estate planning services

---

Allgemeines Treuunternehmen
Aeulestrasse 5
Vaduz, Liechtenstein, FL-9490
tel. 41-75-237-34-34, fax 41-75-237-34-60

- *Services Offered:* company formation, trust formation, law office, estate planning services

---

Bank in Liechtenstein AG
Postfach 85, Herrengasse 12, Furstentum
Vaduz, Liechtenstein, FL-9490
tel. 41-75-235-11-22, fax 41-75-235-15-22, telex 889 222

- *Services Offered:* company formation, trust formation, private banking, retail banking, loans and credit, deposit backed MC/Visa, safekeeping services

---

BIL Treuhand Aktiengesellschaft
Stadtle 18, PO.Box 683
Vaduz, Liechtenstein, FL-9490
tel. 41-75-235-27-27, fax 41-75-235-27-15

- *Services Offered:* private banking

Bilfinanz Aktiengesellschaft
Pflugstrasse 28
Vaduz, Liechtenstein, FL-9490
tel. 41-75-232-77-55, fax 41-75-232-77-01

- *Services Offered:* private banking, retail banking

BILTRUST Management Aktiengesellschaft
Stadtle 18, PO.Box 683
Vaduz, Liechtenstein, FL-9490
tel. 41-75-235-27-35, fax 41-75-235-27-15

- *Services Offered:* private banking

Centrum Bank AG
Heiligkreuz 8
Vaduz, Liechtenstein, FL-9490
tel. 41-75-235-85-85, fax 41-75-235-86-86

- *Services Offered:* private banking

CorTrust Aktiengesellschaft fur Trenhandschaften
Pflugstrasse 10
Vaduz, Liechtenstein, FL-9490
tel. 41-75-236-52-52, fax 41-75-236-54-95

- *Services Offered:* investment advisor, company formation, trust formation

---

Fiduciana Verwaltungsanstalt
Egon Kaiser, Iratell 1005, Egreta 53, POB 2
Balzers, Liechtenstein, FL-9496
tel. 41-75-388-02-02, fax 41-75-388-02-19

- *Services Offered:* company formation, trust formation

Liechtensteinische Landesbank AG
Stadtle 44, Postfach 384
Vaduz, Liechtenstein, FL-9490
tel. 41-75-236-88-11, fax 41-75-236-88-22

- *Services Offered:* investment advisor, private banking, retail banking, loans and credit, safekeeping services

---

Private Trust Bank Corporation
Im Zentrum
Vaduz, Liechtenstein, FL-9490
tel. 41-75-235-66-55, fax 41-75-235-65-00

- *Services Offered:* private banking

Sercor Treuhand Anstalt
Postfach 749
Vaduz, Liechtenstein, FL-9490
tel. 41-75-232-15-11, fax 41-75-233-36-23

- *Services Offered:* company formation, trust formation

Verwaltungs- und Privat-Bank AG
Postfach 885
Vaduz, Liechtenstein, FL-9490
tel. 41-75-235-66-55, fax 41-75-235-65-00, telex 889 200

- *Services Offered:* investment advisor, private banking, retail banking, loans and credit, safekeeping services

LUXEMBOURG

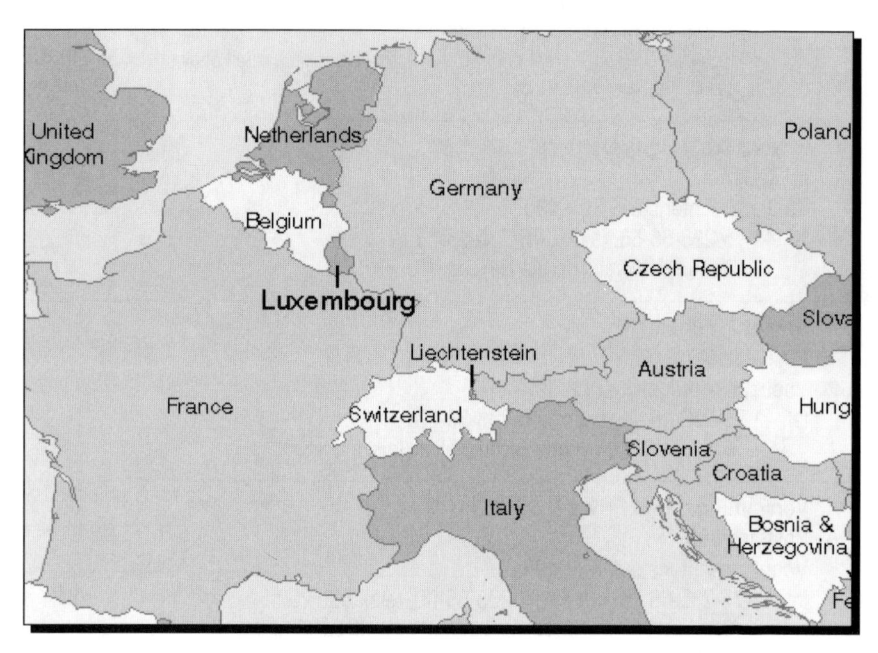

In Europe. Borders Belgium, France, and Germany. Main language is French, German, Luxembourgeois, and English.

The tiny state of Luxembourg enjoyed varying degrees of self-government until being conquered by France in 1795. In 1815 the current Grand Duchy came into being under the Dutch monarchy, and in 1890 full independence came when a junior branch of the Dutch royal family inherited Luxembourg. The Grand Duke is closely involved in administration with the democratically elected parliament. Luxembourg is considered a constitutional monarchy in the form of a Grand Duchy.

Luxembourg bank secrecy was compromised in 1995 by a blackmailing thief. The thief stole computer files from Luxembourg's Commerzbank with information on two thousand customers. He then threatened to publicize the contents of the stolen files unless his demands were met. Unfortunately, he was traced, and the file was recovered. The file was then illegally turned over to the German tax office, instead of being rightfully returned to the Luxembourg bank.

Does Luxembourg have any banking or corporate secrecy legislation?

YES. Luxembourg's secrecy laws prohibit the unauthorized disclosure of information pertaining to a clients affairs to a third party. Revealing bank-account information is punishable by jail time, however, violation of secrecy laws is only a civil offense, not a criminal offense.

Although Luxembourg's secrecy law prohibits the unauthorized disclosure of information, the law does not apply to activities that are considered crimes in Luxembourg, such as illegal drug activities, theft, or fraud. Furthermore, activities such as money laundering are criminal offenses, effectively canceling bank secrecy. Luxembourg's participation in the EC may further reduce bank secrecy. The collapse of the Bank of Credit and Commerce International (BCCI) based in Luxembourg has also further compromised bank secrecy.

Confidential information can only be released if there is a suspected criminal activity such as illegal drug activities, theft, or fraud. Luxembourg banks will not release information for tax investigations.

Does Luxembourg have a long history of legal stability?

YES. Luxembourg gained independence in 1839.

The legal system is based on a combination of Belgian, French, and German systems supplemented by local statutes. The courts in Luxembourg deal in Civil Law and Civil Code. The Supreme Court is the highest legal authority.

Is there an income tax in Luxembourg?

NO. Holding companies pay no income taxes, though there are modest levies on their capital.

Are there any other taxes in Luxembourg?

N/A.

Does Luxembourg maintain exchange controls?

NO. There are currently no exchange controls in Luxembourg. The official currency is the Luxembourg Franc.

Does Luxembourg maintain tax treaties with any other countries?

YES. There is a double-taxation agreement between the U.S. and Luxembourg. Luxembourg also maintains double-taxation agreements with Belgium, Brazil, Denmark, Finland, France, Germany, Iceland, Ireland, Italy, Korea, Morocco, the Netherlands, Norway, Spain, Sweden, and the United Kingdom.

There is no double-taxation agreement between Canada and Luxembourg.

Does Luxembourg allow for the formation of corporate entities?

YES. Although Limited Companies can be formed in Luxembourg, there are other jurisdictions with lower costs and friendlier legislation.

Does Luxembourg allow for the formation of Trusts?

NO. Civil law does not readily support the formation of International Trusts.

Does Luxembourg allow for the formation of Captive Insurance Companies?

YES. Although Captive Insurance Companies can be formed in Luxembourg, there are other jurisdictions with lower costs and friendlier legislation.

Does Luxembourg allow for the formation of Private Banking Companies?

YES. Although Banking Companies can be formed in Luxembourg, there are other jurisdictions with lower costs and friendlier legislation.

Financial institutions and contacts:

ABN AMRO Bank (Luxembourg) S.A.
4, rue Jean Monnet, PO.Box 581
Luxembourg-Kirchberg, Luxembourg, L-2015
tel. 352-42-49-49-42, fax 352-42-49-49-499
- *Services Offered:* private banking

American Express Bank (Luxembourg) S.A.
34, avenue de la Porte-Neuve, PO.Box 919
Luxembourg, Luxembourg, L-2019
tel. 352-4-18-91, fax 352-47-24-19
- *Services Offered:* private banking

Bank of Bermuda (Luxembourg) S.A.
13, rue Goethe, PO.Box 413
Luxembourg, Luxembourg, L-2014
tel. 352-40-46-46-1, fax 352-40-46-74tel. 352-40-46-66
- *Services Offered:* private banking

Banque Ferrier Lullin (Luxembourg) S. A.
26, avenue Monterey, PO.Box 547
Luxembourg, Luxembourg, L-2163
tel. 352-25-47-47, fax 352-44-95-67
- *Services Offered:* private banking

Banque Generale du Luxembourg S.A.
27, avenue Monterey
Luxembourg, Luxembourg, L-2951
tel. 352-4799-1, fax 352-47-99-25-79, telex 3401 BGL LU
- *Services Offered:* private banking, retail banking

Banque Internationale a Luxembourg S.A.
69, route d'Esch, 2, boulevard Royal
Luxembourg, Luxembourg, L-2953
tel. 352-4590-1, fax 352-4590-2010, telex 3626 BIL LU
- *Services Offered:* private banking, retail banking

Banque Leu (Luxembourg) S.A.
16, rue Jean-Pierre Brasseur, PO.Box 718
Luxembourg, Luxembourg, L-2017
tel. 352-45-32-22-1, fax 352-45-31-77
- *Services Offered:* private banking

Banque Privee Edmond de Rothschild S.A.
20, boulevard Emmanuel Servais, PO.Box 474
Luxembourg, Luxembourg, L-2014
tel. 352-47-93-46-1, fax 352-46-11-52

- *Services Offered:* private banking

Brown Brothers Harriman (Luxembourg)S.A.
33, boulevard du Prince Henri, PO.Box 403
Luxembourg, Luxembourg, L-2014
tel. 352-47-40-66-1, fax 352-47-05-80

- *Services Offered:* investment advisor, mutual fund manager

---

Chase Manhattan Bank Luxembourg, S.A.
5, rue Plaetis, PO.Box 240
Luxembourg, Luxembourg, L-2012
tel. 352-462-6851, fax 352-224-590

- *Services Offered:* investment advisor, company formation, trust formation, private banking, retail banking, loans and credit, safekeeping services

---

Commercial Union (Luxembourg) S.A.
Centre Mercure, 41 Avenue de la Gare
Luxembourg, Luxembourg, L-1611
tel. 352-4028-20261, fax 352-4028-20221

- *Services Offered:* mutual fund manager

Credit Lyonnais Luxembourg S.A.
26a, boulevard Royal
Luxembourg, Luxembourg, L-2094
tel. 352-47-68-31-1, fax 352-22-38-68

- *Services Offered:* private banking, retail banking

Credit Suisse (Luxembourg) S.A.
56, Grand-Rue, PO.Box 40
Luxembourg, Luxembourg, L-2010
tel. 352-46-00-11-1, fax 352-47-55-41

- *Services Offered:* private banking

Fidelity Investments Intl. (Luxembourg)
3rd Floor, Kansallis House, Place de L'Etoile, BP 2174
Luxembourg, Luxembourg, L-1021
tel. 352-250-4041, fax 352-250-340

- *Services Offered:* mutual fund manager

Fleming Fund Management (Luxembourg) S.A.
45 Rue des Scillas, Howald
Luxembourg, Luxembourg, L-2529
tel. 352-405040, fax 352-492392

- *Services Offered:* mutual fund manager

GT Management PLC (Luxembourg)
Bank in Liechtenstein Representative, 9A Boulevard Prince Henri
Luxembourg, Luxembourg, L-1724
tel. 352-462-844, fax 352-465-701

- *Services Offered:* mutual fund manager, private banking, retail banking

HSBC Global Investment Funds Luxembourg S.A.
7 rue du Marche-aux-Herbes, PO.Box 889
Luxembourg, Luxembourg, L-1728
tel. 352-4768121, fax 352-475569

- *Services Offered:* mutual fund manager

IMI Bank (Lux) S.A.
8, avenue de la Liberte, PO.Box 1022
Luxembourg, Luxembourg, L-1010
tel. 352-40-45-75-1, fax 352-49-36-22

- *Services Offered:* private banking

ING Bank (Luxembourg) Trust
8, Boulevard Joseph 2, PO.Box 2383
Luxembourg, Luxembourg, L-1023
tel. 352-250440, fax 352-250448

- *Services Offered:* trust formation, private banking

Kredietbank S.A. Luxembourgeoise
43, Boulevard Royal
Luxembourg, Luxembourg, L-2955
tel. 352-47-97-20-20, fax 352-47-2667, telex 3418 KBLUX LU

- *Services Offered:* investment advisor, insurance-based investments, private banking, retail banking, loans and credit, safekeeping services

Lloyds Bank Plc (Luxembourg)
1, rue Schiller, PO.Box 1643
Luxembourg, Luxembourg, L-1016
tel. 352-40-22-12-1, fax 352-40-21-67

- *Services Offered:* private banking

Luxembourg Chamber of Commerce
7, rue Alcide de Gasperi
Kirchbar, Luxembourg, L-1615
tel. 352-423-939-210

- *Services Offered:* government services

Prudential-Bache International Bank S.A.
9, rue Schiller, PO.Box 821
Luxembourg, Luxembourg, L-2018
tel. 352-40-17-17-1, fax 352-40-70-19

- *Services Offered:* private banking

Republic National Bank of New York (Luxembourg) S.A.
32, boulevard Royal, PO.Box 733
Luxembourg, Luxembourg, L-2017
tel. 352-47-93-31-1, fax 352-47-93-31-226

- *Services Offered:* private banking

United Overseas Bank (Luxembourg) S.A.
3B,boulevard du Prince Henri, PO.Box 830
Luxembourg, Luxembourg, L-2018
tel. 352-47-54-76, fax 352-22-84-28

- *Services Offered:* private banking

VP Bank (Luxembourg) S.A.
23, avenue de la Liberte, B.P. 923
Luxembourg, Luxembourg, L-2019
tel. 352-404-7771, fax 352-401-117

- *Services Offered:* private banking, retail banking

Wardley Investment Services S.A.
Maison Gilly, 7 Rue du Marche-aux-Herbes
Luxembourg, Luxembourg, L-1728
tel. 352-476-8121, fax 352-475-569

- *Services Offered:* mutual fund manager

MALTA

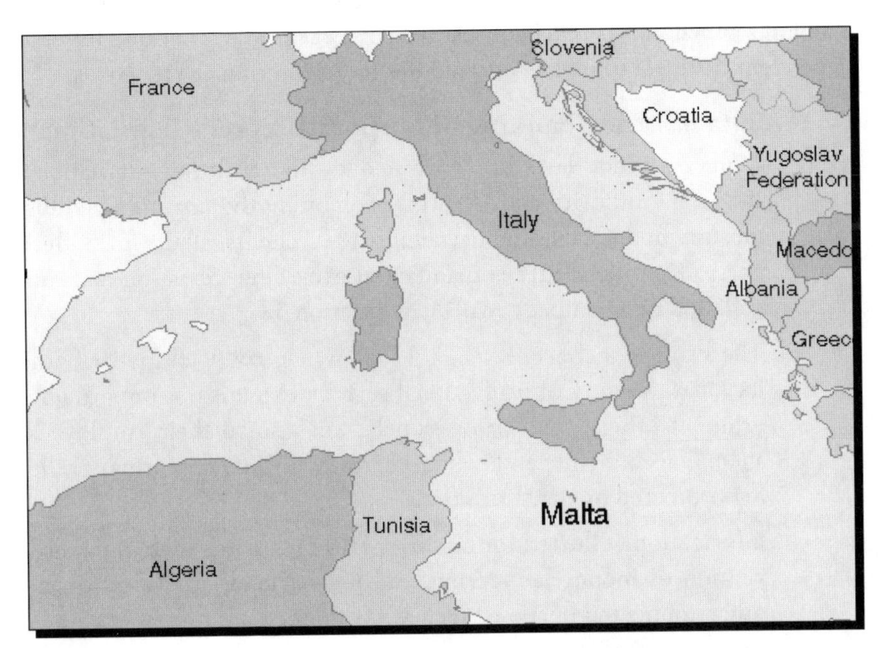

In the centre of the Mediterranean. Five islands positioned between Gibraltar and Suez. Italy is to the north, North Africa to the south. Main language is English, Italian, French, and Maltese (of Semitic origin and related to Arabic, although written in the Roman alphabet). Population is approximately 350,000. Climate is subtropical with relatively low humidity.

Malta's cultural heritage dates back to some time before 4,000 B.C. The Phoenicians, Carthaginians and the Romans; the Byzantines, Arabs and the Normans; the Knights of St.John; the French and the British; all have played a notable part in Malta's history. The arrival of the Knights of St.John marks what may be the most impressive point in the island's history. After a victory over the Turks in the Great Siege of 1565, the Knights built on the island some of the finest examples of fortifications and architecture in Europe. The period of the Knights in Malta lasted nearly 270 years from 1530 to 1798, until the islands fell to Napoleon Bonaparte. This short period of unrest came to an end with the arrival of British rule in Malta. During World War II Malta was a vital British naval base and came under massive attack by German and Italian forces. In 1942 King George VI awarded the George Cross for Bravery to Malta, the only time a nation as a whole has received this type of award. Malta became fully independent in 1964, though economic ties to Britain remain strong.

Does Malta have any banking or corporate secrecy legislation?

YES. Malta's secrecy laws are governed by the Maltese International Business Authority (MIBA) Act, prohibiting the unauthorized disclosure of information pertaining to a clients affairs to a third party. Confidentiality is maintained even after cessation and cancellation of a company (MIBA Act section 38).

The Professional Secrecy Bill, 1994, was introduced to clarify the fact that the duty of professional secrecy extends not only to government officials and professionals, but also to their employees, agents, accountants and solicitors, with all secret information being protected by penal sanctions.

Information collected for one regulatory purpose, such as the prevention of money laundering, can not be made available for another connected purpose, such as taxation.

The supervisory authorities of the financial sector are obliged to report any evidence of money laundering to the Commissioner of Police. The financial sector does not have the power to communicate directly with authorities in other countries.

The MIBA Act provides investigation regulations to safeguard against abuse of offshore status in cases of criminal activity.

Tax evasion is not a criminal activity in Malta, with no requirement for the disclosure of financial information in tax cases.

Does Malta have a long history of legal stability?

YES. Malta is a sovereign European state with a democratic parliamentary system based on the British model. It is a member of the commonwealth with its first self-governing constitution dating back to 1921. Malta became an independent sovereignty with its own constitution on September 21, 1964. In 1974 the constitution was revised and Malta became a republic within the British Commonwealth.

Malta's legal system is based on Roman Law and the Napoleonic Codes, while more recent fiscal, company, shipping and Trust laws are based on a model of English Common Law and statutes.

Is there an income tax in Malta?

YES. There is a domestic income tax of 15% deducted at source. An outright 10 year corporate tax holiday is guaranteed for any export-oriented project.

The following companies are exempt from income tax:

- General Trading Offshore Companies.
- Non-trading Offshore Companies.
- Banking Offshore Companies.
- Insurance Offshore Companies.
- Insurance Broking Offshore Companies.
- Shipping Companies.

Trusts pay a small fixed annual tax in lieu of a registration fee.

Are there any other taxes in Malta?

NO. No tax is chargeable on any capital-gain, dividend or interest paid by an Offshore Trading or Non-Trading company to a non-resident.

There is no gift tax or customs duty on company property or on expatriate employees' personal belongings being imported into Malta. Property held under a Trust is likewise exempt from Customs Duty if imported into Malta. There are no municipal or local taxes.

No death, donation or stamp duties are levied in relation to offshore companies or Trusts. No duty is chargeable under the Death and Donation Duty Act, 1973, in respect of any asset held under an Offshore Trust.

Does Malta maintain exchange controls?

NO. No exchange control restrictions apply to offshore companies. The same applies to Trusts.

Does Malta maintain tax treaties with any other countries?

YES. There is a double-taxation agreement between the U.S. and Malta. There are also double-taxation treaties with all the major European countries, Australia, and others.

There is a double-taxation agreement between Canada and Malta.

Does Malta allow for the formation of corporate entities?

YES. The Maltese government set up a specific Ministry, in May 1987, with responsibility to develop the offshore sector, resulting in the Malta International Business Activities Act, 1988, the Offshore Trusts Act, 1988, and various amendments to revise and update the Merchant Shipping Act, 1973.

Trading Offshore Companies - Trading Offshore Companies are divided into four categories:

- Banking Offshore Companies.
- Insurance Offshore Companies.
- Insurance Broking Offshore Companies.
- General Trading Offshore Companies.

Trading offshore companies will be expected to have a physical and functional presence on the Island, following Malta's determination to establish itself as a reputable international financial and business centre. A general trading offshore company is an offshore company which has as its object any trade or business other than the business of banking, insurance and insurance broking.

Non-Trading Offshore Companies - Non-Trading offshore companies are totally exempt from tax and may opt for non-disclosure of shareholders and directors, registration being possible in the name of local nominees. The law provides for protection of this privacy in legal proceedings and includes special provisions to facilitate the transfer of shares in a non-trading company after death. Non-Trading companies do not require that their accounts be audited, nor are they required to file an annual return or copy of their accounts with the Registrar of Partnerships or with the MIBA. Non-Trading companies include:

- Corporate and personal holding companies.

- Other companies which limit their activities to the ownership, management and administration of their own property of any kind, including patents, copyrights, trademarks and similar property (fund and financial management operations are regarded as a trading activity and require classification as a Trading Company).

An offshore activity is defined as any business activity carried on from Malta:

- In a convertible foreign currency.
- By persons not resident in Malta, with persons not resident in Malta.

An offshore company may use a bank in Malta for the purposes of any transaction in foreign currency which it could lawfully carry out with any other bank.

Does Malta allow for the formation of Trusts?

YES. Offshore Trusts are regulated by the Offshore Trusts Act, 1988, and by certain provisions of the Malta International Business Activities Act, 1988. A Trust is an Offshore Trust if:

- The Settlor is not resident in Malta at the time the Trust is created.
- The Trust property does not include any immovable property situated in Malta; or shares, stock or debentures in a company whose assets include immovable property situated in Malta; or a company, other than an offshore company, registered in Malta.
- All the Beneficiaries under the Trust are not resident in Malta at the time the Trust is created.

A Trust may continue until the 100th anniversary of the date on which it was created, and will then terminate (unless terminated sooner). This provision does not apply to charitable Trusts.

As Malta does not have a long history of Trust law, unit Trusts will have the option of being governed by a foreign Trust law, while being managed from Malta, under the Recognition of Trusts Bill, 1994, and amendments to the Offshore Trusts Act, 1988.

Does Malta allow for the formation of Captive Insurance Companies?

YES. Insurance Offshore Companies are subject to The Insurance Business Act (IBA), 1981, and The Banking Act, 1970. An Insurance Offshore Company may be:

- An insurance offshore Oversea company.
- An insurance offshore Subsidiary company.
- An insurance offshore Local company.
- Any other offshore company which expressly restricts its objects to the business of insurance. Such a company may be a captive insurance offshore company, which is defined as "*an insurance offshore company which restricts its business of insurance to risks originating with companies being members of a group of companies, of which it is itself a member, and having one parent or holding company.*"

The IBA, 1981, states that "*a company shall not be registered as an insurance offshore company unless the Authority is satisfied that the company is capable of properly conducting and supporting the business to be carried on, that it has the expertise and the financial resources for such purpose and that it will keep such resources in such assets and maintain where appropriate margins of solvency, as may be required by the Authority to be kept or maintained.*" Note that the IBA does not apply to an insurance broking offshore company or to a company whose business is exclusively the management of Insurance Offshore Companies.

Exemptions and amendments applicable to all Insurance Offshore Companies include:

- In order to carry on business as principals, insurance offshore companies (other than Oversea and captive companies) must have a minimum paid-up share capital of US$750,000.
- In the case of captive companies, the paid-up capital must amount to at least US$250,000.

- Insurance Offshore Oversea Companies are exempted from the requirement of keeping within Malta, and out of their own funds, paid-up capital assets.
- Insurance Offshore Companies are exempted from the requirement of transferring at least 25% of their net annual profits (before dividends) to a reserve fund, until the fund reaches the amount of the company's paid-up share capital (Insurance Offshore Oversea Companies are not required by the IBA to keep such a reserve fund).

Does Malta allow for the formation of Private Banking Companies?

YES. Banking Offshore Companies are subject to The Banking Act, 1970, and amendments. A Banking Offshore Company may be:

- An offshore Oversea company, where a bank (which is recognized by the MIBA as being of international standing and repute) establishes a branch in Malta exclusively for offshore activities.
- An offshore Subsidiary company, where a bank forms and registers in Malta a private Subsidiary company exclusively for the business of offshore banking.
- An offshore local company, where a bank (which is licensed under the Banking Act, 1970 to carry on business in Malta) forms and registers in Malta a private subsidiary company exclusively for the business of offshore banking.
- Any other offshore company which expressly restricts its objects to the business of banking.

Requirements, exemptions and amendments applicable to all Banking Offshore Companies include:

- Must have a minimum paid-up share capital of US$1.5 million.
- Exempted from the requirement of transferring at least 25% of their net annual profits (before dividends) to a reserve fund, until the fund reaches the amount of the Bank's paid-up share capital.

- Banking Offshore Companies are exempted from the prohibition on commercial banks of the payment of dividends in certain circumstances.
- Banking Offshore Companies need not obtain Ministerial approval to use the word "bank" in the description or title under which they carry on business.
- Section 12 of the Banking Act prohibits commercial banks from carrying out certain transactions, such as the granting of credit facilities to any person to a value exceeding 25% of the Bank's paid-up capital and reserves.

Does Malta allow the formation of Shipping Companies?

YES. Non-Trading companies may operate as Shipping Companies which own or operate ships registered under any flag. The benefit of tax exemption applies equally to a Holding Company and to its subsidiaries, each of which may own or operate one or more ships. Malta encourages owners of all types of vessels, from pleasure yachts to oil rigs, to register their ships under the Maltese Flag.

The registration and operation of Maltese ships is regulated by a Merchant Shipping Act which is based mainly on United Kingdom legislation. There are no restrictions regarding the nationality of the crew, or the trading, sale or mortgaging of Maltese registered ships.

Financial institutions and contacts:

Bank of Valletta International Ltd.
86 South Street
Valletta, Malta, VLT 11
tel. 356-249970, fax 356-222132

- *Services Offered:* investment advisor, private banking, retail banking, loans and credit

---

Finac Nominee Limited
105 S. Psaila Street
Birkirkara, Malta, BKR 02
tel. 356-483707, fax 356-491136

- *Services Offered:* company formation, corporate services

Malta Development Corporation
House of Catalunya, Marsamxetto Road
Valletta, Malta
tel. 356-221431, fax 356-606407

- *Services Offered:* government services

Malta International Business Authority
Palazzo Spinola, PO.Box St.Julians 29
Valletta, Malta, STJ 01
tel. 356-344230, fax 356-344334, telex 1692 MIBA MW

- *Services Offered:* government services

Mid-Med Bank (Overseas) Ltd.
15, Republic Street
Valletta, Malta, VLT 04
tel. 356-249801, fax 356-249805

- *Services Offered:* private banking

MSD Tax & Corporate Services Ltd.
Lower Ground Floor, Valletta Buildings, South Street, PO.Box 472
Valletta, Malta, CMR 01
tel. 356-243258, fax 356-225528

- *Services Offered:* company formation

MONACO

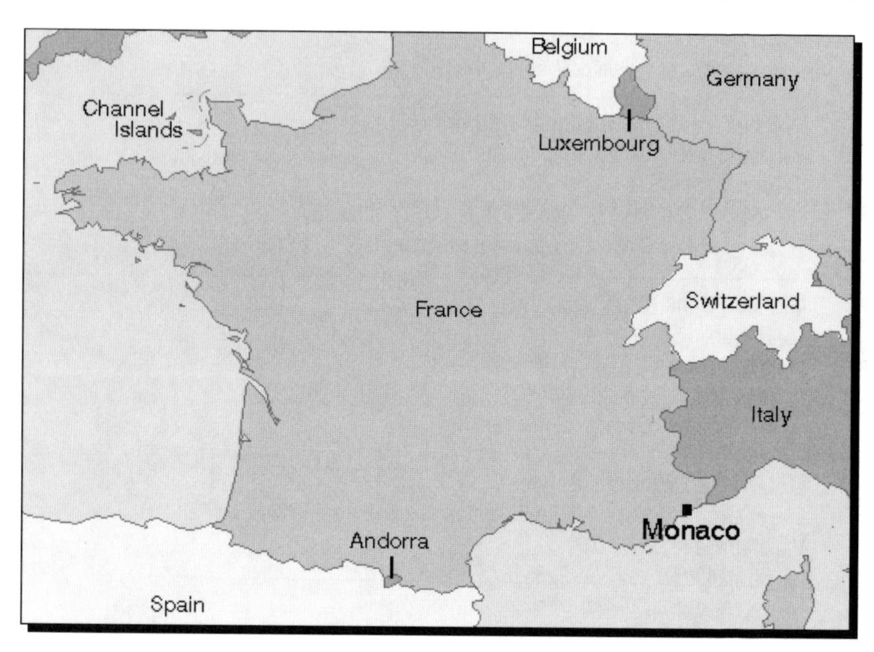

In Europe. In the heart of the French Riviera. At 0.073 square miles in size (465 acres) Monaco is the second smallest country in the world. Population is approximately 30,000. Main languages are French, English, Italian, and Monegasque. Climate is sub-tropical with relatively low humidity.

The Principality of Monaco has been the domain of the Grimaldi family since 1297, placing itself under French protection in 1861. During the 1800's, Prince Charles III saved the economy by introducing gambling. The government is a hereditary constitutional monarchy led by Prince Rainier III.

Cost of living is high. Connections to the rest of the world are excellent.

Does Monaco have any banking or corporate secrecy legislation?

N/A.

Does Monaco have a long history of legal stability?

YES. Monaco is a stable, independent sovereignty that initially gained independence in 1489. The government is a hereditary constitutional monarchy led by Prince Rainier III.

The legal system is based on Monegasque law (similar to civil law) and is supplemented by French civil code.

Is there an income tax in Monaco?

YES. Companies pay a 35% income tax if more than 25% of their income is derived from Monaco. Companies that derive income from passive sources such as patents, licenses, or intellectual property rights pay profit taxes. There is no income tax for citizens of Monaco.

Are there any other taxes in Monaco?

YES. There are registration and stamp duties on the transfer of real estate.

There is no capital gains tax, gift tax, stamp duty, withholding tax, or estate tax for non-residents.

Does Monaco maintain exchange controls?

NO. There are currently no exchange controls in Monaco. The official currency is the French Franc.

Does Monaco maintain tax treaties with any other countries?

YES. There is no double-taxation agreement between the U.S. and Monaco, although there is a tax treaty between France and Monaco.

There is no double-taxation agreement between Canada and Monaco.

Does Monaco allow for the formation of corporate entities?

YES. Although Monaco supports the formation of a limited company known as the Société Anonyme Monegasque, in practice it is very difficult and time consuming. Incorporation can take up to 4 months, and requires prior government approval. If establishing a branch of a foreign corporation, audited financial statements must be filed for the previous 3 years. Minimum requirements include:

- Two shareholders and two directors. One director must be a legal resident.
- Minimum capitalization is FF500,000.
- Shares issued in kind are restricted from trade for two years.
- A registered chartered accountant must be appointed as auditor.

Does Monaco allow for the formation of Trusts?

NO. Civil law does not readily support the formation of International Trusts.

Does Monaco allow for the formation of Captive Insurance Companies?

YES. Although Captive Insurance Companies can be formed in Monaco, there are other jurisdictions with lower costs and friendlier legislation.

Does Monaco allow for the formation of Private Banking Companies?

YES. Although Banking Companies can be formed in Monaco, there are other jurisdictions with lower costs and friendlier legislation.

Financial institutions and contacts:

Ansbacher (Monaco) SAM
24 Boulevard Princesse Charlotte
Monte Carlo, Monaco, 98000
tel. 33-9350-9686, fax 33-9350-5344

- *Services Offered:* investment advisor, company formation, trust formation, private banking, safekeeping services

---

Banque de Placements et de Credit
Av. de Grande-Bretagne 2
Monte Carlo, Monaco
tel. 33-9315-5815, , telex 469 955

- *Services Offered:* retail banking

Banque du Gothard (Monaco)
Le Monte-Carlo Palace, 9, boulevard de Boulin
Monte Carlo, Monaco, MC-98000
tel. 33-9350-6070, fax 33-9350-6071, telex 469 606

- *Services Offered:* investment advisor, company formation, trust formation, private banking, retail banking, safekeeping services

Gordon S. Blair Law Offices
3, rue Louis Aureglia, B.P. 449
Monte Carlo, Monaco, MC 98011
tel. 33-9325-8525, fax 33-9325-7958

- *Services Offered:* law office

Hoogewerf & Co. SAM
2 Avenue de Monte Carlo, PO.Box 343
Monte Carlo, Monaco, MC 98006
tel. 33-9350-0820, fax 33-9350-2412

- *Services Offered:* retail banking

United Overseas Bank Geneve
26, boulevard d'Italie, B.P. 319
Monte Carlo, Monaco, MC 98007
tel. 33-9315-7474, fax 33-9350-1537, telex 479464 MC

- *Services Offered:* investment advisor, private banking, retail banking, loans and credit

NAURU

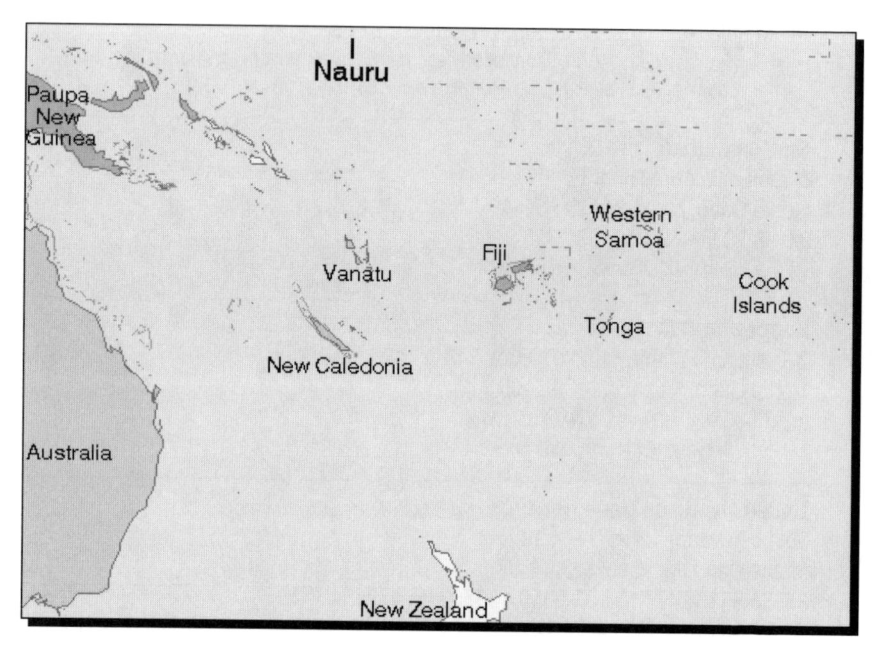

In the South Pacific. One of the smallest countries in the world, a 21 square km island 41 km south of the equator. Nauru is reachable only through Fiji and the Marshal Islands. Population is approximately 9,000. Main language is Nauruan and English. Climate is tropical with high humidity, average temperature 84°F.

The population is a mix of Polynesian and Melanesians that have been on Nauru for many generations. The island fell under German control in 1881, passing to Australia in 1914, and finally becoming independent in 1968.

Phosphate is the single natural resource, and is expected to be depleted early in the next century. Currently, every citizen receives over $20,000 annually in royalties from the production and export of phosphates. To ensure the continuation of the Nauruan race, the government has established Trusts with the Nauruan people as Beneficiaries. The

Trusts have over 4 billion dollars invested in Australian, Hawaiian, and other south Pacific real estate. Immigration is discouraged.

Does Nauru have any banking or corporate secrecy legislation?

YES. Nauru's secrecy laws prohibit the unauthorized disclosure of information pertaining to a clients affairs to a third party, although the interpretation of the law depends on the attitude of the Nauruan court officials at that particular time. Exercise caution.

It appears that in the past, bank secrecy has been absolute. In the late 1980's, the New Zealand Serious Frauds Office claimed that Nauruan banks were being used for money laundering, although the New Zealand government could never obtain the information to prove their case.

Nauru will not cooperate with foreign governments when dealing with tax investigations. Generally, confidential information will remain confidential, although the interpretation of statutes is always at the discretion of the Nauruan court.

Does Nauru have a long history of legal stability?

NO. Nauru became an independent sovereign state on January 31, 1968 and is an associate member of the British Commonwealth. The present constitution was adopted in 1968 and the Government is operated as a parliamentary democracy.

Modern company and Trust statutes have been enacted together with legislation to control the activities of banks, trust companies and insurance business, although the "interpretation" of the law may be at some times different than the "letter" of the law. Modern legislation, including the preservation of secrecy, has been specifically designed to meet the needs of tax planners.

Is there an income tax in Nauru?

NO. There is no income tax in Nauru.

Are there any other taxes in Nauru?

NO. There is no capital gains tax, gift tax, or estate tax in Nauru.

Does Nauru maintain exchange controls?

NO. There are currently no exchange controls in Nauru. The official currency is the Australian Dollar.

Does Nauru maintain tax treaties with any other countries?

NO. There is no double-taxation agreement between the U.S. and Nauru.

There is no double-taxation agreement between Canada and Nauru.

Does Nauru allow for the formation of corporate entities?

YES. Companies are governed by the Nauru Corporation Act 1972. Commercial law in Nauru recognizes the concept of "trading" and "holding" corporations with limited liabilities. Corporations are entitled to apply for licenses for establishment of trusts, banks and insurance companies.

Any individual or corporation may be a shareholder, secretary or director of a holding or trading corporation incorporated in Nauru. Every corporation must have a registered resident secretary. Nauru Secretaries Incorporated acts as the registered resident secretary for all corporations in Nauru. Presently any one of the following corporations may act as Registered Director:

- Nauru Nominee Corporation, PO.Box 300, Aiwo, Nauru
- Nauru Secretaries Incorporated, PO.Box 300, Aiwo, Nauru
- Buada Corporation, PO.Box 300, Aiwo, Nauru

Applications for incorporation must be routed through Registered Corporation Agents. Nauru Agency Corporation and Central Pacific Agency Corporation have been appointed as agents for this purpose.

Holding Corporation - A holding corporation is not authorized to trade, factor, broker, manufacture, or deal in goods. Certain exemptions and privileges apply to holding corporations as follows:

- A minimum of only one shareholder and one director are required.

- Corporations may be formed by the Nauru Government commercial authority on request by a person who would like to remain anonymous.
- May have any amount of share capital with no minimum or maximum limits prescribed by law.
- The identity of company owners can be kept discreet through bearer shares held anonymously or by nominees.
- May convert itself into a trading corporation.
- May not have more than 20 shareholders.
- May issue shares by way of gift without receiving any valuable consideration up to a par value of A$10.
- May not offer or issue debentures to the public.
- Need not have the accounts audited by a Registered Corporation Auditor.
- May have management and control anywhere in the world.

Trading Corporation - A trading corporation may trade, factor, broker, manufacture, or deal in goods, as long as these activities conform to the laws of Nauru or the laws of the country in which it operates. Certain exemptions and privileges apply to trading corporations as follows:

- A minimum of only two shareholders and two directors are required.
- May have any amount of share capital with no minimum or maximum limits prescribed by law.
- May issue bearer shares (with amended Articles of Association).
- May not convert itself into a holding corporation.
- Is not restricted to the number of shareholders.
- Is permitted to offer and issue debentures to the public.
- Is subject to public inspection of documents filed with the Registrar of Corporations; however, the records maintained by the Nauru Agency Corporation are not accessible to a third party without the permission of the sponsors of the corporation.

- May have management and control anywhere in the world.

The filing of an annual return is required for the renewal of incorporation at the end of each year, detailing changes in registered office, directors and secretaries, allotment of shares, and change in share capital.

Does Nauru allow for the formation of Trusts?

YES. Trusts are governed by the Nauru Trustee Corporation Act 1972, closely following the Trust laws of Britain, except where modified by the Foreign Trusts, Estates, and Wills Act 1972:

- The rule against perpetuities does not apply.
- There are no restrictions on directions for accumulation of income.
- Trusts may be of perpetual duration.
- Trusts established in Nauru are not required to be registered under Nauruan laws.

The Nauru Trustee Corporation Act 1972 established a Trustee corporation called the Nauru Trustee Corporation (NTC) with a statutory charter. It is permitted to act as Trustee for all types of Trusts, including purpose Trusts under the Foreign Trusts, Estates, and Wills Act 1972. No taxes or duties are payable in respect to any will admitted to probate in Nauru. At least one of the executors or administrators appointed by a foreign will must be a Nauruan Trustee Corporation, which is required to hold a Trustee license.

Does Nauru allow for the formation of Captive Insurance Companies?

YES. Insurance companies are governed by the Insurance Act 1974. Captive Insurance Companies are required to conform to the same requirements as Banking Companies, as noted above.

Does Nauru allow for the formation of Private Banking Companies?

YES. Banking Companies are governed by the Banking Act 1975. Banking licenses are granted only to "*persons who have a sound financial standing, are well reputed in commercial and financial circles, and have acquired sufficient expertise in banking, trade, and industry*." To obtain a banking license, the bank must comply with the following conditions:

- The bank must have a minimum paid-up capital of US$100,000 within a period of two years from the date of issue of the license.
- The bank must furnish to the Registrar audited balance sheets and profit and loss accounts of each year within six months of year end.
- All the operations of the bank should be "in house" and should not accept deposits from the public.

The low capitalization, non-interference in operations, minimum administrative expenses and simplicity of the banking laws, rules and regulations are designed to provide incentive for entrepreneurs to seek banking licenses under the laws of Nauru.

Financial institutions and contacts:

Nauru Agency Corporation
PO.Box 300
Aiwo, Nauru
tel. 674-555-4011, fax 674-444-3730, telex 775-33090

- *Services Offered:* company formation, trust formation, captive insurance formation, bank formation

NIUE

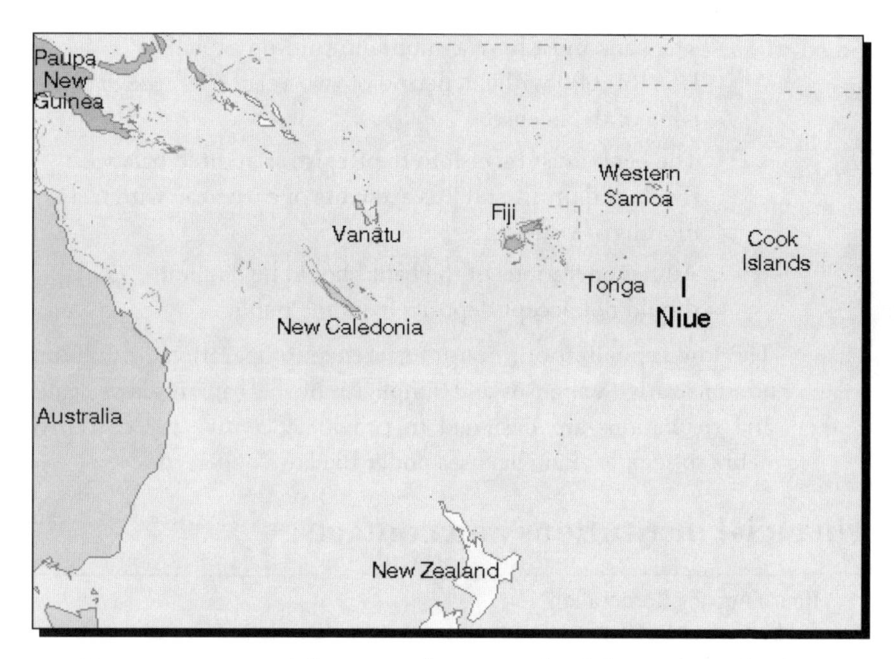

Niue (pronounced "new way") is an island located in the heart of Polynesia, north-east of New Zealand. The official commercial language is English and legal tender the New Zealand Dollar. Due to their unique relationship with New Zealand, Niueans are also British subjects and New Zealand citizens. A self-governing nation with an elected assembly, and a British Commonwealth Associate Member protected by the British Crown, the island enjoys political stability.

Telecommunications and other services are good. Niue's tourism industry, bolstered by the island's natural beauty and the clarity of its surrounding waters with visibility averaging 150 feet, is developing steadily.

In a forceful move to boost its economic development, Niue has become a full-fledged tax haven with a complete package of newly enacted tax-effective financial, commercial and investment facilities, including an international business companies registry and offshore banking and trust services.

Niue has received financial assistance from New Zealand which was given responsibility for the island by the British Crown in 1901. In 1974, Niue chose self-government in free association with New Zealand, as opposed to full independence or political integration. Since then, the funds from New Zealand have been steadily decreasing.

In order to turn the tide against these cutbacks, the Niue government introduced a legislative package in 1994 creating the statutory framework to establish tax-exempt International Business Companies, as well as comprehensive supporting statutes and regulations regarding trust and trustee companies, and offshore banking and insurance matters. In addition, Niue has no tax treaties, mutual legal assistance treaties or information exchange agreements with any country. Niue has thus established itself as a viable offshore financial centre which is chosen by clients seeking a secure and tax-effective base in the Australasia region.

Does Niue have a secrecy law?

YES. The Offshore Centre (Miscellaneous Provisions) Act 1994 provides that any person who divulges any information in respect of an IBC formed in Niue is liable to imprisonment of up to two years and a fine of up to NZ$250,000.

In addition, the Offshore Banking Act 1994 provides that any person who divulges information concerning any offshore banking business, bank account or transfer of funds in Niue is liable to imprisonment of up to one year and a fine of up to NZ$10,000.

The Offshore Centre (Miscellaneous Provisions) Act 1994 allows the High Court of Niue to require information about an IBC to be divulged for the purposes of an investigation or prosecution in relation to drug trafficking or money laundering of drug trafficking, or any "serious criminal activity" (defined as a criminal conviction for at least three years' imprisonment, provided the offence carries a similar penalty in Niue).

Niue will only release information relating to criminal cases. There is no treaty or agreement between Niue and foreign countries which would authorize disclosure of information for tax purposes. As well, the Offshore Centre (Miscellaneous Provisions) Act 1994, prohibits disclosure of information by an officer of an

IBC to a foreign government or court which will result in the payment of tax, penalty or fine by the IBC.

Does Niue have a long history of legal stability?

YES. Niue was annexed by New Zealand in 1901, which administered Niue until 1974 when it opted for self-government in free association with New Zealand. In that year, it enacted its constitution, and was recognized by the United Nations. Niueans are British subjects and New Zealand citizens. New Zealand's Ministry of Foreign Affairs may deal with certain items of Niuean defence and external relations, after consultation with the Premier of Niue. There is a democratically-elected legislative assembly, which elects the Premier, who in turn chooses the cabinet.

Niuean law is based on English Common Law and statutes, as well as New Zealand and Niuean legislation. The superior court of Niue is the High Court, from which appeals lie to the New Zealand Supreme Court and then to the Privy Council in London, England.

Is there an income tax in Niue?

YES. However, IBC's are exempt from income tax pursuant to the International Business Companies Act 1994, which also exempts dividends, interest, rents, royalties, capital gains, compensations and other amounts paid to people who are not residents of Niue. Similar exemptions apply to offshore banks, insurance companies and trusts.

Are there any other taxes in Niue?

YES. However, no estate, inheritance, succession or gift tax is payable on securities of an IBC held by people not resident in Niue. Similar exemptions apply to offshore banks, insurance companies and trusts.

Does Niue maintain exchange controls?

NO. There are no exchange controls in Niue.

Does Niue maintain tax treaties with any other countries?

NO. Niue has no treaty with the U.S. It is also excluded from the Income Tax Convention of 1984 between New Zealand and the U.S.

Niue has no treaty with Canada. It is also excluded from the tax treaties which New Zealand has signed with Canada, the United Kingdom and Sweden.

Does Niue allow for the formation of corporate entities?

YES. The International Business Companies Act 1994 embodies all the desirable elements of contemporary IBC law enacted during recent years in the Caribbean jurisdictions, and adds a number of unique features:

- Confidentiality - no requirements to disclose beneficial owners, file annual returns or financial statements, or hold annual general meetings of shareholders or directors; strict secrecy imposed by the Offshore Centre (Miscellaneous Provisions) Act
- Full Tax Exemption - on any business activity carried on outside Niue; no taxes levied on offshore and banking transactions; no exchange controls
- Speedy Incorporation - via Regional Registry offices in key worldwide locations; documents may be in English or any other language (with an English translation); no corporate seal is required
- Low Costs - competitive formation and maintenance charges, minimum registration fees on capital
- Flexible Capital Requirements - no minimum or maximum; shares may be issued in any one or more currencies; bearer, nominative or no par value shares permitted; register of mortgages and charges is optional, which can be registered if desired
- Wide Objects - IBC's may engage in any lawful business in any country and in whatever currencies they choose

- Directors and Shareholders - may be any nationality and may be residents of any country; only one director is required; directors and officers may be corporate entities; no requirement to register initial or ongoing change in directors or officers; register of directors is optional and may be kept anywhere in the world
- Meetings - may be held in any country and may be attended by proxy
- Accounts and Records - books, records and register of members may be kept anywhere in the world
- Company Names - broad selection of name endings permitted; may be in any language, including Chinese characters, Cyrillic script and other accepted language forms; wide choice currently available; with prior approval, names can also include the words "Trust", "Insurance" or a word conveying a similar meaning if the company will not carry on trust or insurance business, be the trustee of one trust only or be used solely for captive insurance activities
- Continuation - foreign companies can continue as Niue IBC's (notwithstanding prior jurisdiction permission)

Niue has no domestic company law. Companies which are controlled by Niueans and do business in Niue must register under New Zealand's company legislation; nevertheless, the New Zealand income tax statute exempts such companies from New Zealand taxation. In addition, Niue permits the formation of general, special and limited liability partnerships by the Partnership Amendment Act 1994.

Does Niue allow for the formation of Trusts?

YES. Trusts are governed by the Trusts Act 1994, and Trustee Companies Act 1994. Each trust is registered with the Registrar of the Court, who records the name of the trust and either names of the settlor and beneficiaries, or the trust's purpose. This information is not available to a foreign government or court without an order of the High Court, which is only granted in criminal matters.

The Niuean Court will not set aside a trust in respect of matrimonial property, succession rights, or creditors' claims in an insolvency, and unlike other well-known trust jurisdictions there is no waiting period for this asset protection. However, a trust is invalid if established by duress, fraud, mistake, undue influence or misrepresentation.

Trustee companies initially register for a term of two years, after which they may apply for permanent registration. They are required to have a minimum paid-up capital of at least NZ$250,000, maintain liability insurance or a reserve fund of NZ$500,000, and file annual audited financial statements. Registration as a trustee company involves stringent requirements of expertise, competence and integrity.

Does Niue allow for the formation of Captive Insurance Companies?

YES. The Offshore Insurance Act 1994 permits IBC's to obtain offshore insurance licences. Applications to the Monetary Board require information on the nature and character of the business, financial standing, shareholders, management, and financial statements showing a $500,000 surplus of tangible assets over liabilities. The licensee must file annual audited financial statements, and there is an inspector who can review the licensee's books and records. Officers and directors who violate confidentiality or other legal provisions are liable to imprisonment of up to two years and a fine of up to NZ$20,000.

Does Niue allow the formation of Banking Companies?

YES. The Offshore Banking Act 1994 establishes three classes of offshore banking licences:

- Class A - requires the licensee have a permanent establishment in Niue. If it is not an IBC, it must have a surplus of tangible assets over liabilities of NZ$2.5 Million; if it is an IBC, it must either have paid-up capital of NZ$2.5 Million or a bank guarantee for this amount. A Class "A" licensee may call itself a bank.

- Class B - requires all business be transacted through a Niuean trustee company unless it receives permission to maintain a permanent establishment in Niue. The licence must specify the number of currencies in which the banking business will be conducted. The asset requirement is reduced to NZ$500,000. A Class "B" licensee may not call itself a bank.
- Class C - requires the licensee be a Niue IBC, and may not issue a cheque or draft drawn on the licensee. The asset requirement is reduced to NZ$50,000, with $5,000 being deposited with the Government. A Class "C" licensee may not call itself a bank.

Offshore banking licences are granted for one year. The licensee must file annual audited financial statements, and there is an inspector who can review the licensee's books and records. Registration as an offshore banking company involves stringent requirements of expertise, competence and integrity. Domestic banking in Niue is regulated by the Banking Act 1986 which does not apply to offshore banking business.

Special thanks to Mr. Thomas C. Sharp of Mossack & Fonseca & Co. (Canada), telephone 604-688-3934, for his assistance in the preparation of this section.

Financial institutions and contacts:

Mossack Fonseca & Co. (Niue) Ltd.
No.2 Commercial Centre Square, PO.Box 71
Alofi, Niue
tel. 683-4228, fax 683-4357

- *Services Offered:* company formation

PANAMA

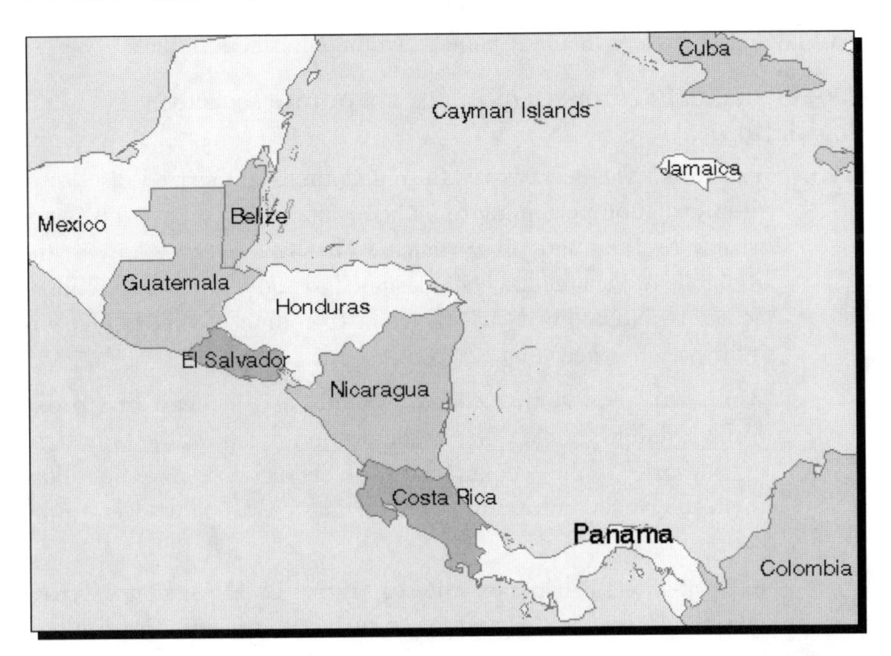

In Central America. Borders both the Pacific Ocean and the Caribbean Sea, between Costa Rica and Colombia. Population approximately 2.4 million. Main language is Spanish and English.

The province of Panama declared itself independent from Colombia in 1903 because the Colombian government had refused to sanction the construction of the Panama Canal, which was eventually completed in 1914. The U.S. held land flanking the Canal, but returned the land to Panama in 1979.

Panama developed a sound reputation as a tax exempt offshore jurisdiction over a number of yeas following the introduction of its first Fiscal Code in 1916, which exempted all persons carrying out commercial transactions abroad from paying taxes. Since then, Panama has established itself as a primary offshore centre.

Once regarded as one of the premier tax havens, Panama's status diminished temporarily in the late 1980s, culminating with the removal of

General Manual Noriega. By 1993, Panama's economy had fully recovered, with most of the funds which left having returned and its exchange reserves restored. The democratically elected government continues to pass laws aimed at enhancing Panama's favorable business climate.

Does Panama have any banking or corporate secrecy legislation?

YES. Panama's strict secrecy laws prohibit the unauthorized disclosure of information pertaining to a clients affairs to a third party, punishable by fines and jail sentences. The Bank Secrecy Law of the Republic of Panama has been designed to allow numbered (coded) accounts. No authority has the right to compel a bank to give any information concerning a coded account.

Banks will request that coded accounts have at least one proxy named, due to the fact that in the event of death of the only signing authority of the account, the Bank Secrecy Law does not allow them to give any information concerning the account, even to the courts.

In April 1991, Panama executed a Mutual Legal Assistance Treaty with the United States, relating to such criminal activities as illegal narcotics, theft, crime or violence, fraud or use of fraud, or violation of a law of one of the contracting states relating to currency or other financial transactions contributing to the crime. It remains to be seen whether this treaty will allow the release of information in a situation involving a failure to report a currency transaction out of the U.S. that would require filing of IRS form 4789, the Currency Transaction Report.

The Treaty does not allow for exchanging information in matters relating to taxation.

Does Panama have a long history of legal stability?

YES. The Republic of Panama is an independent country with elections held every five years. The three levels of government are executive, legislative, and judicial.

The legal system is based on Civil Law.

Is there an income tax in Panama?

NO. There is no income tax in Panama on income earned outside of Panama. Bank interest is not subject to taxation at source. Interest paid by Panamanian banks is exempt from Panamanian income tax.

Are there any other taxes in Panama?

NO. Income and capital gains from activities outside of Panama are not taxed. There is no gift tax or estate tax in Panama.

Does Panama maintain exchange controls?

NO. There are currently no exchange controls in Panama, with complete freedom in the movement of funds. Official currency is the U.S. dollar.

Does Panama maintain tax treaties with any other countries?

YES. There is a double-taxation agreement between the U.S. and Panama covering shipping income.

There is no double-taxation agreement between Canada and Panama.

Does Panama allow for the formation of corporate entities?

YES. Companies limited by shares are governed by Law Number 32 of 1927 on Corporations, an adaptation of 1927 Delaware company law. Panamanian companies have the following features, benefits, and restrictions:

- beneficial owners are not required to be disclosed to the government;
- registered shareholders are not required to be disclosed to the public;
- financial statements are not required to be filed with the government authorities;
- legislation provides for the use of 20 bearer or nominative shares;
- the minimum number of shareholders required is 1;
- shareholders may be corporate;
- shareholders are required to be resident in Panama;

- the minimum number of directors is 3;
- directors may be corporate;
- directors are not required to be resident in Panama;
- the corporate secretary may be corporate;
- accounting records are not required to be kept;
- meetings of shareholders and directors may be held in any country;
- meetings of shareholders and directors may be by proxy, telephone, fax, internet, or any other electronic media; and
- company names must end with the following words or their abbreviations: Limited, Corporation, Incorporated, Société Anonyme, or Sociedad Anonima.

Unless a company does business in Panama, no tax returns are required. Incorporation is accomplished simply and quickly at the fully computerized registry.

Does Panama allow for the formation of Trusts?

YES. Law Number 1 of 1984 enacted international trusts in Panama. The trustee, together with public servants and private sector employees with knowledge of the trust's affairs, are required by Panamanian law to maintain strict secrecy. Failure to do so is punishable by up to six months imprisonment and a fine of up to US$50,000, plus exposure to damages if the trust brings up a civil suit.

In 1995, Panama enacted legislation to create Private Foundations, improving on the Liechtenstein foundation (or "Stiftung" in German). Both Panama and Liechtenstein are civil law jurisdictions, and as such have had decades to observe the benefits and pitfalls of modern trusts as they have developed in common law countries. In contrast, the Panama Foundation is a "hybrid" entity which combines the strengths of both companies and trusts.

Like a company, the Panama foundation is a judicial person, and its assets (initially transferred by the founder) constitute a separate legal estate. Foundations are registered at the Panama Public Registry with a minimum US$10,000 assets (which need not be deposited in advance) and pay a minimal annual registration tax similar to international business companies. Unlike a company, it may not be profit-oriented. It may however engage in commercial activities on a non-habitual basis or exercise rights accruing to shares of business companies held as part of the Foundation assets, provided the earnings are used exclusively towards its goals.

Many characteristics of the Panama Foundation are similar to a trust:

- assets are transferred to the Foundation;
- there are beneficiaries;
- it may have a protector to ensure the founder's wishes are fulfilled; and
- it may be revocable.

Unlike a trust, the Foundation owns its assets like a company, and has a Foundation council with combined functions of both directors and trustees. The Panama Foundation is thus a unique legal entity with many key attributes for financial and tax planning:

- it offers complete secrecy and anonymity, with no requirements to disclose beneficiaries, or file annual returns or financial statements;
- it enjoys full exemption form taxation on any business activity or transaction carried on outside Panama;
- it may transact its affairs in any currency;
- its founder, foundation council and protector may have any nationality and be residents of any country;
- its accounts may be kept anywhere;
- in no case may its assets be used to satisfy obligations of the founder or beneficiaries; and
- the inheritance law in the domicile of the founder or beneficiaries is expressly prohibited from affecting its validity or preventing the fulfilment of its objectives.

The Panama Private Foundations Law protects the Foundation's assets by specifying they constitute a separate estate from the founder's personal assets for all legal purposes. This means they may not be seized, attached or be the object of any action or preventative measures, save for obligations incurred or damages caused upon fulfilment of the foundation's aims, or the legitimate rights of the beneficiaries. Moreover, the founder's creditors have three years from the transfer date in which to object to a fraudulent transfer of assets to a Foundation, after which they lose their claim. Confidentiality of information regarding Foundations is protected on the same basis as trusts, described above.

Does Panama allow for the formation of Captive Insurance Companies?

YES. Law Number 60 of 1966 governs Captive Insurance Companies, and is designed to attract foreigners to create a Panamanian company to insure or reinsure foreign risks. "Rent-a-captive" services are also available.

Does Panama allow for the formation of Private Banking Companies?

YES. However, Panama is an "operation" as opposed to a "registration" banking centre. In other words, banks are required to have a permanent establishment in Panama which carries on actual banking operations.

Special thanks to Mr. Jurgen Mossack and Mr. Ramon Fonseca of Mossack & Fonseca & Co. (Panama), telephone (507) 263-8899, for their assistance in the preparation of this section.

Financial institutions and contacts:

Bank of Nova Scotia
PO.Box 7437, Edificio Bonanza, Calle Manuel Maria Lcaza
Campo Alegre, Panama, 5
tel. (507) 263-6255, fax (507) 263-8636, telex 2073/3266

- *Services Offered:* retail banking

Chase Manhattan Bank, N.A.
Plaza Chase, Urbanizacion Marbella, 8th Floor
Marbella, Panama, 9A
tel. (507) 263-5319

- *Services Offered:* investment advisor, company formation, trust formation, private banking, retail banking, loans and credit, safekeeping services

---

Euro-American Trust and Management Services Limited
Elvira Mendez Street, Vallarino Building, 1st Floor
Panama City, Panama
tel. (507) 269-1806, fax (507) 269-2714

- *Services Offered:* company formation, trust formation

First Incorporating Business
PO.Box 550142
Paitilla, Panama
tel. (507) 269-1677, fax (507) 269-1037

- *Services Offered:* company formation

Francis & Francis
PO.Box 8807N 7283, Eastern Building, 12th Floor
Panama, 5
tel. (507) 263-8555

- *Services Offered:* law office

Hutchinson y Asociados
PO.Box 1290
Panama, 9A
tel. (507) 227-5256

- *Services Offered:* law office

International Management & Trust Corp.
PO.Box 7440
Panama, Panama, 5
tel. (507) 263-6300, fax (507) 263-6392

- *Services Offered:* company formation, mail forwarding

Mata & Pitti, Attorneys-at-Law
PO.Box 87-1319, Calle Ricardo Acias, Banco Aliado Building
Panama, 7
tel. (507) 264-5570, fax (507) 264-6127

- *Services Offered:* company formation

Morgan y Morgan
Bancosur Building, 53rd Street, PO.Box 1824
Panama City, Panama

- *Services Offered:* law office

Mossack Fonseca & Co., Attorneys at Law
Arango-Orillac Building, 54th Street, PO.Box 8320
Panama City, Panama, 7
tel. (507) 263-8899, fax (507) 263-9218

- *Services Offered:* company formation, trust formation, law office

---

Mossack Fonseca & Co., Attorneys at Law
Arango-Orillac Building, 54th Street, PO.Box 8320
Panama City, Panama, 7
tel. (507) 263-8899, fax (507) 263-9218

- *Services Offered:*

Offshore Management International, Inc.
34-44 Cuba Avenue, Dontin Building, 4th Floor, Suite 18, PO.Box 6-9879
El Dorado, Panama, 6A
tel. (507) 227-2658, fax (507) 227-1358, fax (507) 233-3459

- *Services Offered:* company formation, trust formation, corporate services

---

Swiss Bank Corporation (Overseas) S.A.
Torre Swiss Bank, Calle 53 Este
Marbella, Panama, 9A
tel. (507) 263-7181, fax (507) 269-5995, telex 3166

- *Services Offered:* investment advisor, private banking, retail banking, deposit backed MC/Visa, safekeeping services

ST.KITTS & NEVIS

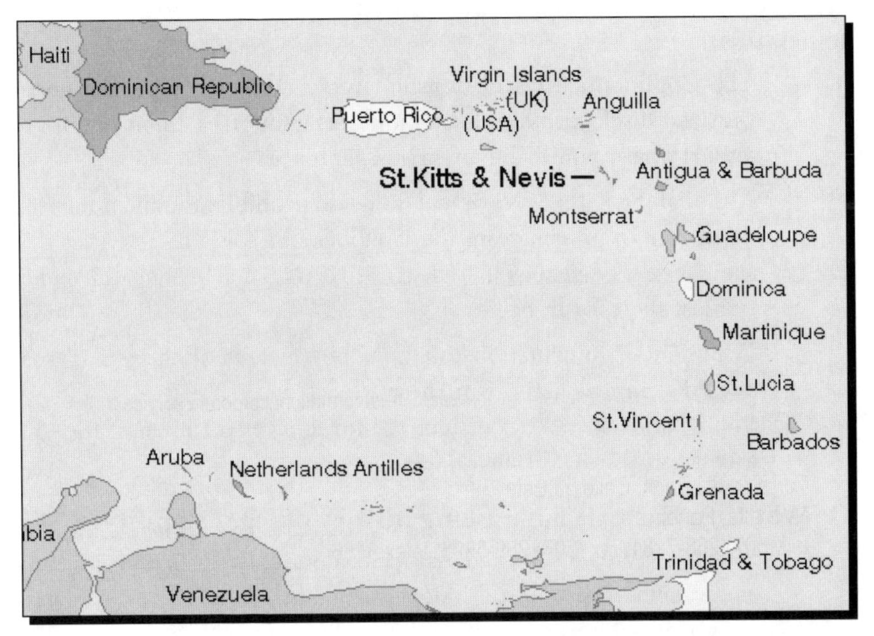

In the Caribbean (Lesser Antilles). St.Kitts & Nevis is located 1,200 miles southeast of Miami, 200 miles east of Puerto Rico. St.Kitts covers a land area of 68 square miles, while Nevis covers a land area of 36 square miles. They are separated by a channel two miles wide. Population is approximately 44,000. Main language is English. Climate is tropical with average humidity, average temperature is 79°F.

St.Kitts & Nevis (officially known as St.Christopher Nevis) was discovered by Columbus in 1493 and was colonized by Sir Thomas Warner in 1623, becoming the Mother Colony of the West Indies. St.Kitts & Nevis achieved Associated Status with Britain in 1967 and attained full political independence in 1983. The twin island destination enjoys a democratic government and is a member of the United Nations.

The government has recently upgraded their offshore financial centre in St.Kitts, fully computerizing the registration of companies and trusts.

This continues the attempt to make St.Kitts & Nevis into one of the premiere tax haven countries in the world.

Does St.Kitts & Nevis have any banking or corporate secrecy legislation?

YES. The Confidentiality Relationship Act of 1985 prohibit the unauthorized disclosure of information pertaining to a clients affairs to a third party, punishable by prison sentence.

Although St.Kitts & Nevis' secrecy law prohibits the unauthorized disclosure of information, the law does not apply to activities that are considered crimes in St.Kitts & Nevis, such as illegal drug activities, theft, or fraud.

Confidential information can only be released if there is a suspected criminal activity such as illegal drug activities, theft, or fraud, and is not available to foreign governments for tax investigations.

Does St.Kitts & Nevis have a long history of legal stability?

YES. St.Kitts & Nevis achieved Associated Status with Britain in 1967 and attained full political independence in 1983. The twin islands are governed by a stable democracy. St.Kitts & Nevis is a member of the British Commonwealth and the United Nations.

The legal system is based on English Common Law and is supplemented by local statutes. The Island is served by the High Court of Justice and the Court of Appeal.

Is there an income tax in St.Kitts & Nevis?

YES. Local companies are liable to pay tax at a rate of up to 40% of net annual profits, paid annually. This tax does not apply to the profits of an approved enterprise which has been granted benefits under the Fiscal Incentives Act. Offshore companies doing business outside St.Kitts & Nevis are exempt from all forms of taxation.

Are there any other taxes in St.Kitts & Nevis?

NO. There is no capital gains tax, gift tax, or estate tax in St.Kitts & Nevis.

Does St.Kitts & Nevis maintain exchange controls?

NO. There are currently no exchange controls in St.Kitts & Nevis. The official currency is the East Caribbean Dollar.

Does St.Kitts & Nevis maintain tax treaties with any other countries?

YES. There is no double-taxation agreement between the U.S. and St.Kitts & Nevis, although double-taxation agreements are maintained with Denmark, New Zealand, Norway, Sweden, Switzerland, and the United Kingdom.

There is no double-taxation agreement between Canada and St.Kitts & Nevis.

Does St.Kitts & Nevis allow for the formation of corporate entities?

YES. Non-resident domestic companies are governed by the Business Corporation Ordinance 1984, which has been modeled after Delaware and New York company law. St.Kitts & Nevis corporations offer the following advantages and benefits:

- Bearer shares or registered shares may be issued.
- Share capital may have a par value or no par value.
- Only one director and one shareholder is required.
- Directors and secretary may be corporate, and may be of any nationality.
- There are no nationality restrictions on beneficial owners.
- Shareholders and directors meetings may be held in any jurisdiction.
- Filing of annual returns is not required.
- It is not necessary to file the names of the directors, officers, or shareholders.
- Company records and principal office may be located in any jurisdiction.

Does St.Kitts & Nevis allow for the formation of Trusts?

YES. In April 1994 St.Kitts & Nevis introduced new Asset Protection Trust (APT) legislation. Unique features include a requirement that anyone starting an action against a St.Kitts & Nevis Trust must first post a bond of US$25,000.

Does St.Kitts & Nevis allow for the formation of Captive Insurance Companies?

YES. St.Kitts & Nevis is a suitable jurisdiction for the formation of Captive Insurance Companies.

Does St.Kitts & Nevis allow for the formation of Private Banking Companies?

YES. St.Kitts & Nevis is a suitable jurisdiction for the formation of Banking Companies.

Financial institutions and contacts:

Bank of Nevis Ltd.
Main Street, PO.Box 450
Charlestown, Nevis, W.I.
tel. 869-469-5564, fax 869-469-5798

- *Services Offered:* retail banking

First Fidelity Trust Ltd.
National Bank Building, West Square St., PO.Box 605
Charlestown, Nevis, W.I.
tel. 869-469-0278, fax 869-469-0225

- *Services Offered:* investment advisor, company formation, trust formation, corporate services, estate planning services

---

Morning Star Holdings Limited
Main Street, PO.Box 556
Charlestown, Nevis, W.I.
tel. 869-469-1817, fax 869-469-1794

- *Services Offered:* company formation, corporate services

Myrna R. Walwyn & Associates
Main Street, PO.BOx 84
Charlestown, Nevis, W.I.
tel. 869-469-5645, fax 869-469-1161

- *Services Offered:* company formation, law office

Nevis Ministry of Finance
Administration Building
Charlestown, Nevis, W.I.
tel. 869-469-5521, fax 869-469-1081

- *Services Offered:* government services

Nevis Trust Limited International
Springate, Suite 100 West, Government Road
Charlestown, Nevis, W.I.
tel. 869-469-1017, fax 869-469-1603

- *Services Offered:* company formation, trust formation, corporate services, estate planning services

---

Offshore Business Center
PO.Box 407
Fortlands, Nevis, W.I.
tel. 869-465-2610, fax 869-469-4346

- *Services Offered:* company formation, trust formation, bank formation, corporate services, estate planning services, safekeeping services

---

Reginald L. Kawaja & Associates
Bank of Nevis Building
Charlestown, Nevis, W.I.
tel. 869-469-0625, fax 869-469-5446

- *Services Offered:* law office

St.Kitts-Nevis-Anguilla National Bank Ltd.
West Square Street
Charlestown, Nevis, W.I.
tel. 869-469-5244

- *Services Offered:* retail banking

A.M.S. Financial Services
PO.Box 535
Basseterre, St.Kitts, W.I.
tel. 869-465-2801, fax 869-465-1421

- *Services Offered:* company formation, accounting services, corporate services

---

International Sales Management & Associates
Herbert Office Complex, Bay & Bird Rock Roads, Box 398
Basseterre, St.Kitts, W.I.
tel. 869-465-8385, fax 869-465-6191

- *Services Offered:* company formation, private banking, accounting services, corporate services

---

Lee L. Moore & Associates
Central College Street
Basseterre, St.Kitts, W.I.
tel. 869-465-2276, fax 869-465-5867

- *Services Offered:* law office

Royal Bank of Canada (St.Kitts)
Corner Bay & Fort Streets, PO.Box 91
Basseterre, St.Kitts, W.I.
tel. 869-465-2389, fax 869-465-1040

- *Services Offered:* retail banking

St.Kitts-Nevis Chamber of Industry and Commerce
South Square Street
Basseterre, St.Kitts, W.I.
tel. 869-465-2980

- *Services Offered:* government services

St.Kitts-Nevis-Anguilla National Bank Ltd.
Basseterre, St.Kitts, W.I.
tel. 869-465-2204

- *Services Offered:* retail banking

SWITZERLAND

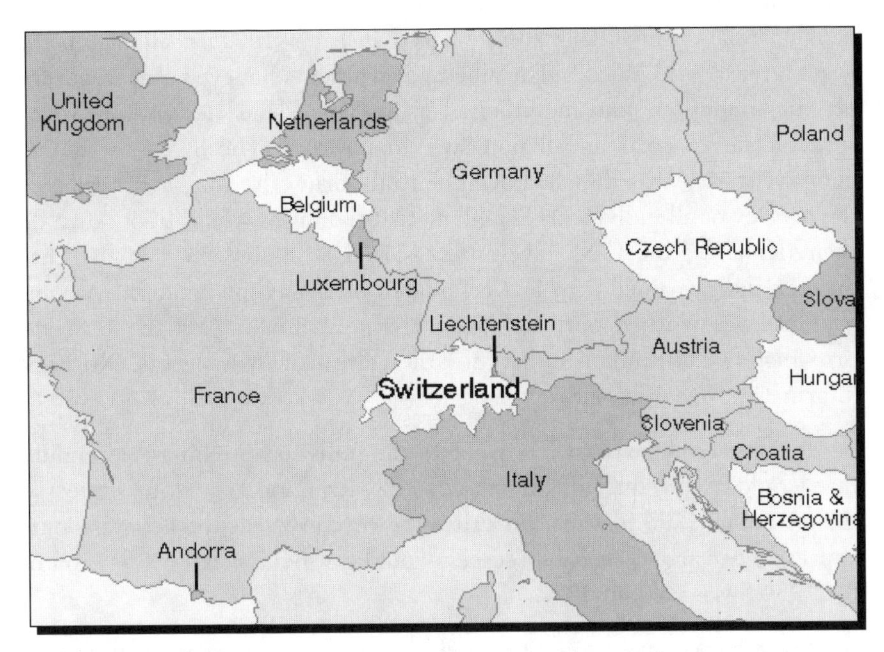

In Western Europe. Borders Austria, France, Germany, Italy, and Liechtenstein, and covers a total area of 15,940 square miles. Population is approximately 7 million. Main language is German, French, Italian, and Romansh.

The state of Switzerland traces its origins to a defensive alliance between Uli Schwyz and Unterwalden in 1291, and saw many wars in the early centuries of its existence. Since 1815 Switzerland has been neutral, with the European rulers deciding in Vienna on the recognition and protection of a lasting neutrality in Switzerland. The Swiss constitution of 1874 outlines the founding principles of federalism and democracy. In 1991 Switzerland proudly celebrated the 700th anniversary of its founding. Switzerland's currency has remained unchanged since the beginning of the century; a Swiss franc from 1900 is still accepted as legal tender today. Historically, the country has always enjoyed complete freedom in the import and export of capital.

The Swiss wrote their own banking laws to protect refugees fleeing Hitler and made it a serious offense, subject to heavy fine and imprisonment, for any bank or bank employee to reveal even the existence of a banking relationship. Bank secrecy faced an even greater challenge in the years after World War II. The allied governments believed that Nazi officials had deposited gold and other assets in Switzerland, demanding disclosure of bank records of all non-Swiss depositors. The Swiss refused to comply, stating that they had been neutral during the war, and respected the privacy of all individuals. Thinking that the Swiss would back down on their demands, the U.S. government seized all Swiss assets in the U.S. Switzerland remained firm and refused to offer any information. A compromise was worked out, and the Swiss government paid the U.S. approximately $60 million dollars for the return of Swiss assets. No bank information was ever released.

In May 1984 Swiss voters went to the polls to vote on a referendum that would have reduced bank secrecy in Switzerland. The voters rejected the proposal by a 3 to 1 margin. After the vote in 1984, the Federal Court expressly declared that bank secrecy would not be affected by revision of the 1934 Swiss Banking Law.

Swiss banks have agreed to provide U.S. investigators with the names of persons doing certain kinds of insider stock transactions through their facilities.

Does Switzerland have any banking or corporate secrecy legislation?

YES. Swiss bank secrecy is fixed in article 47 of the Swiss Federal Law Relating to Banks and Savings Institutions of November 8, 1934, as amended in 1970. It applies not only to everyone working within the bank, but also to members of its external auditors, even if the holders of private information are no longer working with the bank. Switzerland's bank secrecy law makes it a criminal offense for a bank or any of the bank's employees to divulge information of any kind to any individual, institution, public or private, with respect to any bank customer. Any infringement of the law can lead to criminal prosecution. The penalty for breaking bank secrecy is a minimum fine of SFr50,000 or six months in jail.

If the act has been committed by negligence, the penalty shall be a fine not exceeding SFr30,000. The violation of professional secrecy remains punishable even after termination of the employment relationship.

Bank secrecy can be lifted in cases of criminal activity. However, there must be a violation of Swiss *criminal law* (in Switzerland tax evasion is not a criminal offense, it is an administrative offense). A Swiss judge must sign a court order stating that there was a violation of Swiss law before bank secrecy can be lifted.

If a request for information is made by foreign authorities, they must be approved by the Federal Department of Justice, who will examine whether the request should be passed on to the judge in the bank's jurisdiction. Bank secrecy can also be lifted in favor of an heir in the event of a depositors death.

Since tax evasion is not a crime in Switzerland, an inquiry by any foreign government would not be in accord with Swiss law, and therefore would not provide adequate grounds to have bank secrecy lifted (because tax evasion is not a crime in Switzerland). However, there is a test to determine if a banking transaction has been constructed to avoid taxes, and in certain extreme circumstances, bank secrecy may be compromised.

Does Switzerland have a long history of legal stability?

YES. Switzerland is a stable, politically neutral country that proudly celebrated the 700th anniversary of its founding in 1991. The government consists of the Federal Council, the Federal Assembly, and the Federal Tribunal.

Swiss law is based on over 700 years of civil and commercial law. Switzerland's highest court is the Federal Tribunal, made up of 26 judges and 12 alternatives.

Is there an income tax in Switzerland?

YES. A corporation will pay less than 10% income tax, although corporations and banks are required to retain a 35% withholding tax on interest and dividends from Swiss sources. Swiss investment insurance products are completely exempt from Swiss taxes for non-residents.

Are there any other taxes in Switzerland?

YES. Swiss corporations are liable to pay a 3% stamp duty on capital stock upon incorporation. Each of Switzerland's 26 Cantons impose a different tax system on local residents.

Due to tax treaties, there are no taxes of any kind owed to the Swiss government by foreigners. If a non-resident purchases a Swiss life insurance policy, the insurance policy is protected by Swiss law against any collection procedures initiated by the creditors of the insured person.

Does Switzerland maintain exchange controls?

NO. There are currently no exchange controls in Switzerland. The official currency, the Swiss Franc, is by law 40% backed by gold.

Does Switzerland maintain tax treaties with any other countries?

YES. There is double-taxation agreement between the U.S. and Switzerland. There are also double-taxation agreements with Australia, Austria, Belgium, Brazil, Canada, Denmark, Egypt, Finland, France, Germany, Greece, Hungary, Iceland, Indonesia, Ireland, Italy, Japan, Malaysia, Netherlands, New Zealand, Norway, Pakistan, Portugal, Singapore, South Africa, South Korea, Spain, Sri Lanka, Sweden, Trinidad and Tobago, and the United Kingdom.

There is a double-taxation agreement between Canada and Switzerland.

Does Switzerland allow for the formation of corporate entities?

YES. Switzerland's Laws of Obligation allow the formation of three types of companies; two types of Aktiengesellschaft (Private Company Limited by Shares or Public Limited Company), and the Gesellschaft mit beschrankter Haftung (Private Limited Company Without Shares).

Aktiengesellschaft (AG) - Private Companies Limited by Shares have the following statutory requirements:

- Issued shares may be either registered shares or bearer shares.
- A minimum of three shareholders are required.

- The incorporators may be nominees (to provide anonymity) and may be either individuals or corporations.
- Only one director is required, who must be a Swiss resident. The majority of directors (if more than one) must be Swiss residents.
- The directors of the AG must be stockholders, and directors and incorporators may be the same person or company.
- The minimum share capital is currently SFr50,000. Minimum par value is SFr100 per share.
- An annual audit is a statutory requirement.
- A withholding tax of 35% is imposed on dividends.

The memorandum must give details of the company's objectives. Upon incorporation a capital duty of 3% is payable.

Public Limited Companies are able to offer shares to the public after meeting the requirements of Swiss authorities and the Stock Exchange.

Gesellschaft mit beschrankter Haftung (GmbH) - A Private Limited Company Without Shares lists ownership in the Commercial Register instead of issuing shares. The incorporators may be nominees and may be either individuals or corporations. Only one director is required, who must be a Swiss resident. The majority of directors (if more than one) must be Swiss residents.

Does Switzerland allow for the formation of Trusts?

YES. Where a creditor proves beyond a reasonable doubt that an International Company or Trust was formed with the intent of defrauding a creditor, the Company or Trust is required to satisfy the claim out of the assets held. The statute of limitations on this type of action is 2 years.

Does Switzerland allow for the formation of Captive Insurance Companies?

YES. Although Switzerland allows the formation of Captive Insurance Companies, other jurisdictions offer much friendlier legislation and lower formation costs.

Does Switzerland allow for the formation of Private Banking Companies?

YES. Although Switzerland allows the formation of Banking Companies, the strict requirements make them impractical for tax planning purposes.

Financial institutions and contacts:

ASN - Advisory Services Network
Todistr. 38
Zurich, Switzerland, CH-8002
tel. 411-284-37-86, fax 411-284-37-46

- *Services Offered:* estate planning services, global investing information, expat health insurance

---

Bank Julius Baer
Bahnhofstrasse 36
Zurich, Switzerland, CH-8010
tel. 01-228-5111, fax 01-211-2560, telex 823 865

- *Services Offered:* investment advisor, private banking, retail banking, estate planning services, safekeeping services

---

Bank Leu Ltd.
Bahnhofstrasse 32
Zurich, Switzerland, CH-8022
tel. 41-1-219-2863, fax 41-1-219-2456

- *Services Offered:* private banking

Bank vonErnst & Cie AG
63-65 Marktgasse, 3001
Berne, Switzerland
tel. 44-31-329-1111, fax 41-31-311-6391

- *Services Offered:* mutual fund manager, retail banking

Banque Generale du Luxembourg (Suisse) S.A.
Rennweg 57
Zurich, Switzerland, CH-8023
tel. 41-1-225-67-67, fax 41-1-225-68-68, telex 813 003 BGL CH

- *Services Offered:* investment advisor, private banking, retail banking, loans and credit, safekeeping services

---

Banque SCS Alliance
11, route de Florissant, Case Postale 3733
Geneva, Switzerland, CH-1211
tel. 41-22-839-0100, fax 41-22-346-1530, telex 422 058 SCS CH

- *Services Offered:* investment advisor, company formation, trust formation, private banking, safekeeping services

---

Barclays Bank (Schweiz) AG
Schuetzengasse 21
Zurich, Switzerland, CH-8001
tel. 1-221-13-35, fax 1-211-54-26

- *Services Offered:* investment advisor, company formation, trust formation, private banking, loans and credit, deposit backed MC/Visa, safekeeping services

---

Barclays Bank (Suisse) S.A.
10 rue d'Italie
Geneva, Switzerland, CH-1204
tel. 22-310-65-50, fax 22-310-64-60

- *Services Offered:* investment advisor, company formation, trust formation, private banking, loans and credit, deposit backed MC/Visa, safekeeping services

---

Bilfinanz und Verwaltung AG
Gladbachstrasse 105, PO.Box 832
Zurich, Switzerland, CH-8044
tel. 01-250-81-81, fax 01-252-51-78

- *Services Offered:* private banking, retail banking

Bilfinanz und Verwaltung AG Rappresentanza di Lugano
Via Serafino Balestra 12
Lugano, Switzerland, CH-6901
tel. 091-23-62-81, fax 091-23-90-48

- *Services Offered:* private banking

Blue Chip Capital Management Limited
Talstrasse
Zurich, Switzerland
tel. 888-265-6661, fax 800-560-0645

- *Services Offered:* investment advisor, mutual fund manager, private banking, global investing information, deposit backed MC/Visa, insurance-based investments

Business Advisory Services SA
7 Rue Muzy, 1207
Geneva, Switzerland
tel. 41-22-030540, fax 41-22-7860644

- *Services Offered:* company formation

Chase Manhattan Bank (Switzerland) S.A.
63, rue du Rhone
Geneva, Switzerland, CH-1204
tel. 41-22-787-9111

- *Services Offered:* investment advisor, company formation, trust formation, private banking, retail banking, loans and credit, safekeeping services

Credit Suisse
8180 Bulach
Bulach, Switzerland
tel. 41-1-872-2111, fax 41-1-872-2112

- *Services Offered:* investment advisor, company formation, trust formation, private banking, retail banking, estate planning services, safekeeping services

GMF Finanz AG
Henric-Petre-Str 19
Basel, Switzerland, CH-4051
tel. 41-61-279-92-96, fax 350-50647

- *Services Offered:* company formation, trust formation, corporate services

ING Bank (Switzerland) Trust
Glarnischstrasse 36
Zurich, Switzerland, CH-8002
tel. 41-1-2074111, fax 41-1-2074260

- *Services Offered:* trust formation, private banking

Investment Forum Ltd.
Sonneggstrasse 84
Zurich, Switzerland, CH-8006
tel. 41-1-363-18-10, fax 41-1-363-18-14

- *Services Offered:* insurance-based investments

Jawer
20 route de Pre-Bois, I.C.C. Building, PO.Box 1918
Geneva, Switzerland, 1215
tel. 41-22-798-51-55, fax 41-22-798-54-39

- *Services Offered:* investment advisor, trust formation, accounting services, corporate services

Kreditbank (Suisse) S.A., Basle Branch
Steinenring 60, PO.Box CH-4002
Basel, Switzerland
tel. 61-281-33-07, fax 61-281-33-77

- *Services Offered:* investment advisor, insurance-based investments, private banking, retail banking, loans and credit, safekeeping services

---

Louis Oehri & Partner Ltd.
PO.Box 335, Poststrasse 403
Ruggell, Switzerland, FL-9491
tel. 41-75-373-21-30, fax 41-75-373-21-31

- *Services Offered:* company formation, trust formation

Megevand, Grosjean, Revaz & Associes
1, rue Etienne, Dumont, CP 3487
Geneva 3, Switzerland, 1211
tel. 41-22-312-1161, fax 41-22-312-1163

- *Services Offered:* law office

PAX Swiss Life Insurance Company
PO.Box, Aeschenplatz 13
Basle, Switzerland, CH-4002
tel. 41-61-277-6666, fax 41-61-277-6456

- *Services Offered:* insurance-based investments

Riggs Valmet S.A.
14 Chemin Rieu
Geneva, Switzerland, CH-1211
tel. 41-22-477575, fax 41-22-467241, telex 427 729 RVLCH

- *Services Offered:* company formation

Trade Administration Services AG
PO.Box 4818, Baarerstrasse 23, 4
Zug, Switzerland, CH-6304

- *Services Offered:* company formation

Uptrend Treuhand Managementberatung
Schauenbergstrasse 12
Zurich, Switzerland, 8046
tel. 41-13-711110, fax 41-13-711211

- *Services Offered:* company formation

Volcon SA
PO.Box 649
Basel, Switzerland, CH-4010
tel. 41-61-271-2100, fax 41-61-271-2144

- *Services Offered:* insurance-based investments

VPB Finanz AG
Talstrasse 83
Zurich, Switzerland, CH-8001
tel. 01-212-21-41, fax 01-212-00-31

- *Services Offered:* retail banking

TURKS & CAICOS

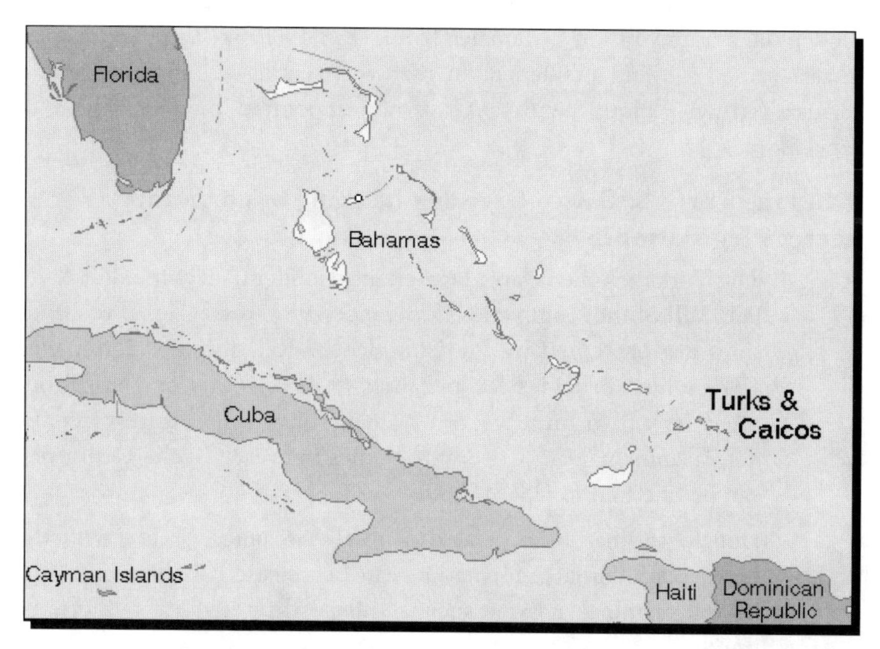

In the Caribbean. An archipelago of 40 islands and cays located 575 miles south east of Miami, 30 miles south east of the Bahamas and midway between Miami and Puerto Rico, north of the Dominican Republic and Haiti. The islands cover a land area of 193 square miles. The islands are each surrounded by a continuous coral reef. Population approximately 15,000. Main language is English. Climate is tropical with relatively low humidity, average temperature 83°F in summer and 77°F in winter.

The Arawak Indians were the first people to inhabit the Turks & Caicos Islands which were discovered in 1512 by Spanish explorer Juan Ponce del Leon, although the local belief is that the Islands were first discovered by Columbus on his first voyage in 1492. In 1678, Bermudian immigrants settled on the islands of Salt Cay, Grand Turk and South Caicos where they established and developed a salt industry. The Bahamas tried unsuccessfully to annex the islands in 1700. During the next century the Turks & Caicos were invaded first by the Spanish and then by the French. British loyalists tried to establish cotton plantations in 1780. The Bahamas gained administrative control of the islands and governed them from 1799 to 1848, when the Turks & Caicos separated from the Bahamas, and were governed by their own council for over 20 years. The islands were placed under the administration of Jamaica from 1873 to 1962, the year that Jamaica gained her independence. In that year Turks & Caicos became a British Crown Colony, with a Governor appointed by the Queen of England.

Does the Turks & Caicos have any banking or corporate secrecy legislation?

YES. The Turks & Caicos have high client confidentiality. In addition to Part VIII of the Companies Ordinance 1981, professional relationships are protected by the Confidential Relationships Ordinance 1979 which provides for penalties of US$10,000 and imprisonment for up to three years for unauthorized disclosure of confidential information. Corporate bodies in breach of the Ordinance can be fined up to US$50,000.

Due to the narcotics related Mutual Assistance Treaty with the U.S., confidential information can be released if there is a suspected criminal activity such as illegal drug activities, theft, or fraud.

Confidential financial information is not available to foreign governments conducting tax investigations. Specific legislation states that judgements and requests for information in foreign tax cases are not enforceable in the Turks & Caicos.

Does the Turks & Caicos have a long history of legal stability?

YES. The Turks & Caicos is a self governing British Crown colony, governed by an Executive Council of ministers appointed from the Legislative Council of elected members. A Governor appointed by Britain presides over the Legislative Council and Britain maintains responsibility for defense and foreign affairs. There is no desire for independence and the Islands are considered politically, economically, and racially stable.

The legal system is based on English Common Law and is supplemented by local ordinances. Commercial laws have been specifically designed to encourage offshore business.

Is there an income tax in the Turks & Caicos?

NO. There is no income tax in the Turks & Caicos. IBCs are guaranteed tax exempt status for 20 years from date of incorporation. It is unlikely that any taxes will be introduced in the foreseeable future as the prosperity of the Turks & Caicos depends on the success of the financial industry.

The Turks & Caicos government receives income from import duties of 30% and stamp duties, such as an 8% stamp duty on real estate transactions over US$50,000. Other sources of government income are hotel taxes, license fees, and a $15 departure tax.

Are there any other taxes in the Turks & Caicos?

NO. There are no direct taxes in the Turks & Caicos, no capital gains tax, no gift tax, no estate tax, and no death duties.

Does the Turks & Caicos maintain exchange controls?

NO. There are no exchange controls in the Turks & Caicos. The official currency is the U.S. dollar.

Does the Turks & Caicos maintain tax treaties with any other countries?

NO. There is no double-taxation agreement between the U.S. and the Turks & Caicos. In fact, there is no tax treaty with any country.

There is no double-taxation agreement between Canada and the Turks & Caicos.

Does the Turks & Caicos allow for the formation of corporate entities?

YES. The Turks & Caicos Companies Ordinance of 1981 and subsequent amendments provide for the formation of the Ordinary Company, Exempted Company, Limited Life Company, and Foreign Company.

Minimum statutory conditions require that each company must have a registered office in the Turks & Caicos. An exempted company must have a local resident representative.

Ordinary Company - An ordinary company is used for conducting business within the Turks & Caicos. All information is a matter of public record, including names of shareholders, directors, and officers.

Exempted Company - An exempted company, which must carry on its business outside the Turks & Caicos, is free from the necessity to report to the Registrar changes in its shareholders and directors. Whereas an ordinary company files a detailed annual return, exempted companies file a simple form declaring that certain requirements of the Ordinance have been met and that the operations of the company continue mainly outside the Turks & Caicos.

Advantages and benefits of exempted companies include:

- Shares can be issued in bearer form.
- Shares may have no par value.
- There is no requirement to hold annual or general meetings.
- An exempted company requires only one shareholder and one director. Typically the owners of an exempted company would act as directors and shareholders.
- Directors and officers have no nationality restrictions and can be nominee corporations.
- Exempted companies require one secretary, who may also be a director.
- The register of shareholders is not required to be available for public inspection.
- No local auditors are required.
- The name need not contain the words Limited, Incorporated, Public Limited Company, Société Anonyme, or their abbreviations.

The Registrar's stated target is to incorporate companies on the day that documents are received. Providing that the Registrar approves the name, the necessary papers can be prepared and presented the same day, with the Certificate of Incorporation and Articles of Association being issued by the Registrar on the following day.

The annual government filing fee is US$250 for Ordinary Companies and US$300 for Exempted Companies. The Companies (Amendment) Ordinance 1993 allows the option of pre-paying annual Turks & Caicos government fees for a period of 5, 10 or 15 years at a substantial discount. For instance, by pre-paying for 15 years at a cost of US$2,000, you save US$2,500 in fees. This ensures the good standing of the company with a simple declaration each year. In addition, and as a further incentive, new IBCs incorporated between July 1 and December 31 will be excused from payment of the annual fee the following January.

Another provision in the 1993 Ordinance made it possible for Turks & Caicos IBCs to be limited by shares, limited by guarantee, have members with unlimited liability, or to have any combination of these three options. IBCs are guaranteed from any new taxation introduced during the 20 year period following incorporation.

Limited Life Company - The Companies (Amendment) Ordinance 1993 introduced the concept of a Limited Life Company. Minimum statutory conditions require that:

- The company has a minimum of two subscribers.
- The memorandum of association must limit the life of the company to less than 50 years.
- The company name must end with LLC or Limited Life Company.

Foreign Company - Foreign companies wishing to trade within the Turks & Caicos must submit to the Registrar of Companies the following:

- Memorandum of incorporation from the foreign company's home jurisdiction.
- Complete details on directors including name, address, and nationality.
- Name and address of local resident representative.

Does the Turks & Caicos allow for the formation of Trusts?

YES. Trusts are governed by the Trusts Ordinance 1990, which is similar to Jersey Trust law, with some refinements. The Trusts

Ordinance recognizes Trusts formed in other jurisdictions. Advantages of Turks & Caicos Trust law include:

- No time restrictions - Trusts can continue indefinitely and are not limited to any set time period.
- The instrument creating the Trust can be executed in any jurisdiction.
- The Trust can specify that the laws of another jurisdiction are to apply to the interpretation and settlement of the Trust.
- The Trust is a private document and there is no requirement for it to be registered (unless the Trust holds Turks & Caicos land titles).
- Trustee Corporations are not required to be licensed under the Trustees (Licensing) Ordinance 1992 if the Trustee Corporation is acting for only one Trust, and is wholly owned by the Settlor or Beneficiary.

A Trustee is not required to reveal to any person, other than the Beneficiary of the Trust, any information regarding the forming or operating of the Trust, allowing for complete secrecy. A Turks & Caicos Trust can:

- Allow for the addition of future Beneficiaries.
- Exclude a Beneficiary from certain Trust assets.
- Require certain terms & conditions to be met before distributing Trust assets.

The Turks & Caicos Trusts Ordinance 1990 also allows the formation of an Asset Protection Trust, where if a Settlor (who is solvent at the time and not about to become insolvent) transfers assets to the Trust and subsequently becomes insolvent, the Trust would not be declared void upon application by a creditor. An advantage of the Ordinance is that the intent of the Settlor in establishing the Asset Protection Trust is irrelevant to any attack against Trust assets.

Does the Turks & Caicos allow for the formation of Captive Insurance Companies?

YES. Captive Insurance Companies are permitted in the Turks & Caicos Islands.

Does the Turks & Caicos allow for the formation of Private Banking Companies?

YES. Banking Companies are permitted in the Turks & Caicos Islands.

Special thanks to Mr. Paul R. LeBreux and Mr. Gregory H. Harris of Harris & Harris Barristers & Solicitors, telephone 416-798-2722, for their assistance in the preparation of this section.

Financial institutions and contacts:

Bank of Nova Scotia
Providenciales, Turks and Caicos Islands, B.W.I.
tel. 649-946-4750

- *Services Offered:* retail banking

Barclays Bank PLC
Butterfield Square, PO.Box 236
Providenciales, Turks and Caicos Islands, B.W.I.
tel. 649-946-4245, fax 649-946-4573, telex 8418 BARPRO

- *Services Offered:* retail banking, deposit backed MC/Visa, safekeeping services

---

Barclays Bank PLC
PO.Box 61, Cockburn Town
Grand Turk, Turks and Caicos Islands, B.W.I.
tel. 649-946-2831, fax 649-946-2965

- *Services Offered:* investment advisor, company formation, trust formation, private banking, retail banking, loans and credit, safekeeping services

---

Blue Chip Capital Management Limited
Providenciales, Turks and Caicos Islands, B.W.I.
tel. 888-265-6661, fax 800-560-0645

- *Services Offered:* investment advisor, mutual fund manager, private banking, global investing information, deposit backed MC/Visa, insurance-based investments

---

Caribbean Management Services Limited
PO.Box 127, Town Centre Mall
Providenciales, Turks and Caicos Islands, B.W.I.
tel. 649-946-4732, fax 649-946-4734

- *Services Offered:* company formation

Czerlau & Associates Limited
Providenciales, Turks and Caicos Islands, B.W.I.
tel. 800-226-5703, fax 242-356-0223

- *Services Offered:* company formation, trust formation, corporate services, estate planning services, deposit backed MC/Visa, safekeeping services

---

Depository Services International Ltd.
PO.Box 193, Times Square
Providenciales, Turks and Caicos Islands, B.W.I.
tel. 649-946-4967, fax 649-946-4928

- *Services Offered:* investment advisor, mutual fund manager, company formation, trust formation, corporate services, deposit backed MC/Visa, safekeeping services

---

Grand Turk International Trust Co.
PO.Box 61
Grand Turk, Turks and Caicos Islands, B.W.I.
tel. 649-946-2047

- *Services Offered:* company formation

Morris Cottingham Assoc. Ltd.
Hibiscus Square, PO.Box 156
Grand Turk, Turks and Caicos Islands, B.W.I.
tel. 649-946-2504, fax 649-946-2503

- *Services Offered:* company formation

Northcote & Co.
PO.Box 164
Grand Turk, Turks and Caicos Islands, B.W.I.

- *Services Offered:* law office

Private Sector Development Office
Saber House, Front Street
Grand Turk, Turks and Caicos Islands, B.W.I.
tel. 649-946-2732, fax 649-946-2556

- *Services Offered:* government services

Registrar of Companies
Grand Turk, Turks and Caicos Islands, B.W.I.
tel. 649-946-2550
- *Services Offered:* government services

Savoy & Co.
Harbor House, Queen Street, PO.Box 157
Grand Turk, Turks and Caicos Islands, B.W.I.
tel. 649-946-2601
- *Services Offered:* law office

Standard Private Trust Ltd.
PO.Box 193, Times Square
Providenciales, Turks and Caicos Islands, B.W.I.
tel. 649-946-4387, fax 649-946-4928
- *Services Offered:* investment advisor, mutual fund manager, company formation, trust formation, corporate services, deposit backed MC/Visa, safekeeping services

Superintendent of Offshore Finance
Finance Department
Grand Turk, Turks and Caicos Islands, B.W.I.
tel. 649-946-2937, fax 649-946-2557
- *Services Offered:* government services

MARGINAL TAX HAVENS

The following countries, although not perceived as major tax havens, do offer certain attributes commonly found in tax haven jurisdictions.

Andorra

In Europe. A tiny haven in the eastern Pyrenees between France and Spain. Population is approximately 52,000. Alpine climate. Main languages are Spanish and Catalan, the official language. French is also spoken.

The independent state of Andorra has been independent since 1278, when rival powers of the region agreed on a compromise. Under the 700 year old agreement the state is ruled jointly between the Bishop of Urgel and the Count of Foix. As the estates of Foix have since passed to France, the present joint rulers are the Bishop of Urgel and the President of France.

Andorra's secrecy laws prohibit the unauthorized disclosure of information pertaining to a clients affairs to a third party, providing for criminal penalties or prison terms.

The legal system is based on Spanish Law. There is no income tax, capital gains tax, gift tax, or estate tax in Andorra. There are no exchange controls. Andorra has no currency of its own and instead uses the French franc. There is no exchange of information agreement between the Andorra and the U.S. or Canada.

Foreigners are not permitted to start a business, therefore incorporation is impractical.

Consult S.L.
Carrer Dr., Nequi No.7, 3 er A
Andorra la Vella, Andorra
tel. 33-628-29-190, fax 33-628-29-783, telex 391 CONSULT

- *Services Offered:* law office

March & Partners Ltd.
PO.Box 2.222
Andorra La Vella, Andorra
tel. 376-837595, fax 376-835008

- *Services Offered:* company formation, law office, accounting services, corporate services, mail forwarding

Aruba

In The Southern Caribbean. 12 miles north of Venezuela. Main language is Papiamento, English, Dutch, and Spanish.

Aruba's citizens are descendants of the peace-loving Arawak Indians, Dutch, Spanish and a blend of people from all corners of the world who came to the island in the twentieth century. Today there are over 40 nationalities living on the island.

No specific laws enforce bank secrecy, although according to Mr. E.J. Brion at Aruba Bank Ltd., "*the Bank Secrecy Act in Aruba provides that no information of the bank relationship can be given to third parties unless mandated by court order.*" No specific laws enforce bank secrecy, therefore bank accounts may be open to government inspection.

Aruba became independent on January 1, 1986, although Aruba is still a member of the United Kingdom of the Netherlands. The legal system is based on the Dutch legal system of civil and criminal law.

There is no income tax on an AEC (Aruba Exempt Company) or its shareholders.

Campione

In Europe. Campione d'Italia ("sample of Italy") is on the shores of Lake Lugano, a little piece of Italian soil completely surrounded by Switzerland. Located in the Swiss canton of Ticino, about 16 miles from the Italian border and 5 miles from Lake Lugano, Campione is a tiny one square mile dot on the Swiss maps. As a separate country from Switzerland, Campione is not subject to Swiss laws, taxes, or tax treaties. Campione operates no border controls, so its approximately 2,200 residents travel freely.

Although officially Italian, residency in Campione brings many of the benefits of Swiss residency; including Swiss banking, postal, and telephone services, Swiss auto registration and driver's license, and the Swiss postal code CH-6911.

The legal system is based on Italian Law. There is no income tax, capital gains tax, gift tax, or estate tax in Campione imposed on non-residents.

There is no exchange of information agreement between Campione and the U.S. or Canada. Disclosure of information under a tax treaty between the U.S. and Switzerland is unlikely.

A corporation can be formed in Campione under Italian law with as little as US$1,000. The private limited liability company is known as an SRL (Societa Responsibilita Limitada). It takes longer to form a corporation in Campione than in Switzerland, but, unlike a Swiss corporation, a corporation formed in Campione can be entirely owned by foreigners. Shareholders have complete anonymity. Corporations formed in Campione have a number of advantages over Swiss corporations. They are able to use Swiss banking facilities. They have a mailing address that appears Swiss. They are not subject to Switzerland's high income and withholding taxes providing that business is done outside of Italy. The tax rate is SFr3,000 per employee per year. If no personnel are employed, taxes can be reduced to nearly zero.

Costa Rica

In Central America. South of Nicaragua, north of Panama. Main language is Spanish, some English. Moderate tropical climate. Costa Rica has had democratic politics, and has been independent since 1836. The present constitution has been in force since 1948.

Costa Rica's secrecy law provides total confidentiality and secrecy in bank transactions. The law also applies to attorneys. Costa Rica is a stable democratic republic, independent since 1836. The presidential head of state has full executive powers. The government is divided into executive, legislative, and judicial systems. The present constitution has been in force since 1948. Costa Rica is the only Latin American country to have no army. The legal system is based on Spanish civil law.

There is an income tax in Costa Rica for individuals and companies doing business in Costa Rica. There is also a withholding tax on dividends of non-resident shareholders. Income sourced outside of Costa Rica is not liable for income tax.

There are currently no exchange controls in Costa Rica. The official currency is the Cost Rican Colon. Although there is no tax treaty between the U.S. and Costa Rica, there is an exchange of information agreement that has been signed as part of the Caribbean Basin Initiative. No tax treaty has been signed between Canada and Costa Rica.

Costa Rica Stock Exchange
PO.Box 1736-1000
San Jose, Costa Rica
tel. 506-22-8011, fax 506-22-0131

- *Services Offered:* government services

Magna Charta Society of Business Administrators Limited
Apartado 2604-1000
San Jose, Costa Rica
fax 506-233-1909

- *Services Offered:* company formation, trust formation

Cyprus

In the Eastern Mediterranean. Main language is Greek, Turkish, English. For centuries part of the Ottoman Empire, Cyprus passed to Britain as security for a loan that was never repaid. Cyprus gained independence in 1960 under a constitution designed to calm ethnic rivalries between the Greek and Turkish population. In 1974 a coup by the Greeks threatened to join Cyprus to Greece, and Turkey invaded to block the move. Today the island is divided between the Turkish northern third and the Greek southern section.

There are no exchange controls. Currency is the Cypriot Pound. Cyprus allows the formation of private insurance companies.

A.K. CosmoServe
89 Kennedy Ave., Office 201, PO.Box 6624
Nicosia, Cyprus, 1640
tel. 357-2-379210, fax 357-2-379212

- *Services Offered:* investment advisor, company formation, trust formation, accounting services, corporate services, mail forwarding

---

Agni Timothi Law Offices
16 Zenas De Tyras, Karantokis Building, 3rd Floor, PO.Box 3341
Nicosia, Cyprus
tel. 357-2-476412, fax 357-2-472011

- *Services Offered:* law office

Chr. P. Kinanis & Co.
Nicosia, Cyprus
tel. 357-2-362888, fax 357-2-362777

- *Services Offered:* company formation

Gryphon Managers & Consultants Ltd.
Suite 103, 8 Acropolis Avenue, Acropolis 139, PO.Box 8770
Nicosia, Cyprus, CY-2082
tel. 357-2-424035, fax 357-2-498824

- *Services Offered:* company formation, trust formation, accounting services, corporate services

---

Riggs Valmet International Ltd.
PO.Box 151
Paralimni, Cyprus
tel. 357-3-824508, fax 357-3-824508

- *Services Offered:* company formation

Dominica

Government of Dominca-Ministry of Finance
Roseau, Dominica
tel. 809-448-2401, fax 809-448-0054tel. 809-448-0406

- *Services Offered:* government services

Overseas Development Banking Group
42 Kennedy Avenue, PO.Box 525
Roseau, Dominica
tel. 809-448-0886, fax 809-448-0882

- *Services Offered:* company formation, trust formation, private banking, corporate services, estate planning services

---

Prevost & Williams
42 Hillsborough Street
Roseau, Dominica
tel. 809-448-2808, fax 809-449-8361

- *Services Offered:* company formation, bank formation

Greece

In Southeast Europe. Main language is Greek. English, Italian, French, and German is also spoken.

There are no exchange controls. Currency is the Drachma. Greece imposes no taxes on offices or branches of foreign companies of any type dealing with management, agents, or operation of ships.

Hungary

In Central Europe. Main language is Hungarian. German, some English, and some French is also spoken.

There are no exchange controls. Currency is the Forint. Bank deposits can be registered on a passbook system with no names recorded anywhere. This secrecy surpasses that available elsewhere, but means that if you loose the book, you've lost your money.

Ireland

Non-resident companies that do not conduct business within Ireland are exempt from corporation tax on income arising outside of Ireland.

Anglo Irish Bankcorp
Stephen Court, 18-21 St.Stephen's Green
Dublin, Ireland, 2
tel. 01-676-0141, fax 01-661-1981

- *Services Offered:* investment advisor, private banking

Baring International Fund Managers (Ireland) Limited
2nd Floor, IFSC House, Custom House Docks
Dublin, Ireland, 1
tel. 852-841-1441, fax 852-845-9050

- *Services Offered:* mutual fund manager

Custom House Asset Management Limited
31 Kildare Street
Dublin, Ireland, 2
tel. 353-1-661-3400, fax 353-1-661-3601
- *Services Offered:* company formation

Hill Samuel Bank Limited
Hill Samuel House, 25/28 Adelaide Road
Dublin, Ireland, 2
tel. 353-1-610444, fax 353-1-611413
- *Services Offered:* investment advisor, company formation, trust formation, private banking, loans and credit, safekeeping services

---

John Fitzgerald & Associates
6, Sullivan's Quay
Cork, Ireland
tel. 353-21-963877, fax 353-21-310273
- *Services Offered:* company formation

Riggs Valmet (Ireland) Ltd.
30 Lower Leeson Street
Dublin, Ireland, 2
tel. 353-1-330180, fax 353-1-334526
- *Services Offered:* company formation

Vitacom Company Services
65 Cliff Rd., Tramore
Waterford, Ireland
tel. 353-51-386054, fax 353-51-386921
- *Services Offered:* company formation

Liberia

In Africa. The only tax haven in Africa, Liberia lies on the west coast between Guinea, the Ivory Coast and Sierra Leone. Population is approximately 2.5 million, with over 300,000 in the capital city Monrovia. The official language is English. Climate is tropical.

In 1822 an American group landed a party of freed slaves on the coast in Monrovia in an attempt to establish a haven for such people. In 1847 Liberia declared itself independent and adopted a constitution similar to that of the United States. Liberian offices in New York and Zurich assist in establishing operations.

The legal system is based on U.S. law, and is proclaimed in the Liberian Code of Laws of 1956.

Official currency is the Liberian Dollar. Liberia offers a zero tax rate to firms and Trusts externally owned and receiving all income from outside sources. No taxes are imposed on Liberian corporations provided that more than 50% of the stock is held by non-residents, and that no income is derived from trading within Liberia.

Liberia maintains tax treaties with Germany and Sweden. The identity of company owners can be kept discreet through bearer shares held anonymously or by nominees. Directors, shareholders, and officers may reside anywhere in the world. Registered office may be located in any jurisdiction. Shares may be bearer form. Because shares can be held in bearer form and changes in directors and shareholders need not be recorded after incorporation means that the beneficial owner can have complete anonymity.

Macao

In the South Pacific. A Portuguese colony attached by an isthmus to China. Maximum 15% tax.

Montserrat

In the Eastern Caribbean. A 39.5 square mile island, 27 miles southwest of Antigua, population approximately 15,000. Main language is English. Climate is tropical with relatively low humidity, average temperature 76°F to 86°F.

Montserrat was discovered by Christopher Columbus in 1493 and named after that part of Spain for the similarity of the jagged mountain peaks. Colonized by the Irish in 1632, the island was long fought over by the French and British before being ceded to Britain in 1783.

During the 1980's Montserrat became plagued by money laundering activities related to illegal drug activities, theft and fraud. The U.S. Senate's report, *Crime and Secrecy: The Use of Offshore Banks and Companies* and the Coopers & Lybrand *Survey of Offshore Finance Sectors of the Caribbean Dependent Territories* prepared for the British Government (known as the

Gallagher Report) were especially damaging to Montserrat's international banking industry. Both reports expanded the "interpretation" of any activity considered a crime in Montserrat. After the release of the 1989 Gallagher Report, 259 of the 330 banks chartered in Montserrat had their bank charters revoked. Of the 259, most were organized by one company. A moratorium on new bank charters has recently been lifted.

Montserrat's secrecy laws prohibit the unauthorized disclosure of information pertaining to a clients affairs to a third party. Montserrat's secrecy law allows the disclosure of confidential information relating to drug, theft, and fraud investigations. The *Gallagher Reports* have widened the "interpretation" of any activity considered a "crime" in Montserrat, although confidential information relating strictly to taxation can not be released to foreign tax authorities.

Montserrat is a British dependency with a ministerial system of government and its own constitution. The government is headed by a resident British Governor. The legal system is based on English Common Law and is supplemented by local statutes.

There is no income tax in Montserrat for income derived outside of Montserrat. There is no capital gains tax in Montserrat for capital gains derived outside of Montserrat. There is no gift tax or estate tax in Montserrat.

There are currently no exchange controls in Montserrat. The official currency is the East Caribbean Dollar. There is no double-taxation agreement between the U.S. and Montserrat, although there is a double-taxation agreement between the UK and Montserrat. There are also double-taxation agreements with Denmark, Japan, Norway, Sweden, and Switzerland. There is no double-taxation agreement between Canada and Montserrat.

Montserrat has recently been devastated by volcanic eruptions, hence, is not really in the "tax haven" business in any sort of meaningful way. However, my prediction is that once the volcano settles down, the government of Montserrat will do virtually everything in its power to restore economic prosperity to the island. To do this, they will have to update their legislation to become more competetive than any other jurisdiction. Only time will tell.

Royal Bank of Canada
Parliament Street, PO.Box 222
Plymouth, Montserrat, W.I.
tel. 809-491-2426, fax 809-491-3991, telex 360-5713
- *Services Offered:* private banking, retail banking

Netherlands Antilles

In the Caribbean. The Leeward and Windward Islands, separated by 500 miles of Caribbean sea. The Leeward Islands (includes Curacao and Bonaire) are 35 miles north of Venezuela. The Windward Islands (includes St.Maarten, St.Eustatius, Saba) are 144 miles east of Puerto Rico. Total population approximately 200,000. Main language is Dutch, English, Papiamento, and Spanish. Climate is tropical with average humidity, average temperature 77 to 82°F.

Curacao - A Spanish navigator, Alonso de Ojeda, a Lieutenant of Christopher Columbus, discovered Curacao in 1499. The Spaniards settled in the early 1500's. In 1634 Holland captured Curacao and founded a Dutch settlement. In 1954 the Netherlands Antilles achieved self-government.

Bonaire - Bonaire, inhabited by the Arawak Indians for centuries, was discovered by Amerigo Vespucci in 1499. He called the island Bonah or "Lowland." After a century of colonization, the Spaniards were dispossessed of the island by the Dutch in 1636. In 1639, Bonaire became a Dutch colony and the Dutch West India Company was formed developing Bonaire's salt production, corn, and livestock industries. During the early 1800's Bonaire was taken over by the British and the island suffered from the activities of French and British pirates. The Dutch regained control of the island in 1816. In 1954 Bonaire became an autonomous island territory with an elected Island Council Government as part of the Netherlands Antilles.

St.Maarten - St.Maarten was discovered by Christopher Columbus on November 11, 1493. The island was named after St.Martin of Tours, as the date of its discovery coincided with the feast of St.Martin. Though

Spain originally claimed St.Maarten, it was deserted when the Dutch set up an outpost in 1631. Ousted by Spain in 1633, the Dutch returned in 1648 to establish an accord with the French, dividing the island between them. The Dutch and French have co-existed peacefully in St.Maarten since then.

In 1954 the Netherlands Antilles achieved self-government as a sovereign island territory. The Governor represents the Royal Crown of the Netherlands. The legal system is based on the Netherlands legal system.

Companies pay an income tax of less than 5% in the Netherlands Antilles. There is no capital gains tax or gift tax in the Netherlands Antilles for companies. The tax treaty between the U.S. and the Netherlands Antilles was terminated in 1980. There is no exchange of information agreement between Canada and the Netherlands Antilles.

Algemene Bank Nederland NV
Pietermaai 17
Willemstad, Curacao, Netherlands Antilles
tel. 599-9-611488

- *Services Offered:* private banking

Banco di Caribe NV
Schottegatwey Oost 205
Willemstad, Curacao, Netherlands Antilles
tel. 599-9-616588

- *Services Offered:* retail banking

Banco Industrial del Venezuela CA
Heerenstraat 19
Willemstad, Curacao, Netherlands Antilles
tel. 599-9-611621

- *Services Offered:* retail banking

ING Bank (Antilles) Trust
Kaya Flamboyan 9, PO.Box 3895
Willemstad, Curacao, Netherlands Antilles
tel. 599-9-370000, fax 599-9-370963

- *Services Offered:* trust formation, private banking

Maduro & Curiel's Bank NV
Plaza Jojo Correa 2-4, PO.Box 305
Willemstad, Curacao, Netherlands Antilles
tel. 599-9-661100, fax 599-9-661130, telex 1127-MCBNKNA

- *Services Offered:* retail banking

Touche Ross & Co.
Scharlooweg 41, PO.Box 809
Willemstad, Curacao, Netherlands Antilles
tel. 599-9-614288, fax 599-9-613626

- *Services Offered:* accounting services

New Caledonia

In the South Pacific. A French territory. No income tax for residents.

Saint-Pierre and Miquelon

In the North Atlantic. French dependencies off the south coast of Newfoundland. Zero income tax to residents.

Seychelles

Minister of Finance
Central Bank Building, Independence Avenue, PO.Box 313
Victoria, Seychelles
tel. 248-21790, fax 248-22265

- *Services Offered:* government services

Singapore

Bank of Nova Scotia
Ocean Building, #15-01, 10 Collyer Quay
Singapore, 0104
tel. 65-535-8688, fax 65-532-2440

- *Services Offered:* investment advisor, private banking, retail banking, safekeeping services

---

Barclays Private Banking
50 Raffles Place, 21-01 Shell Tower
Singapore, 0104
tel. 65-224-8555, fax 65-221-9624

- *Services Offered:* investment advisor, company formation, trust formation, private banking, retail banking, loans and credit, deposit backed MC/Visa, safekeeping services

---

Coutts & Co. AG
50 Raffles Place, No. 05-05, Shell Tower
Singapore, 0104
tel. 65-223-3132, fax 65-223-5098

- *Services Offered:* investment advisor, company formation, trust formation, private banking, safekeeping services

---

HSBC Kay Hian James Capel Pte. Ltd.
80 Raffles Place, #30-01, UOB Plaza 1
Singapore, 048624
tel. 65-533-2936

- *Services Offered:* investment advisor

Swiss Bank Corporation
6 Battery Road, #35-01
Singapore, 0104
tel. 65-224-2200, fax 65-531-3444, telex RS 24140 SINSUIS

- *Services Offered:* retail banking

TrustNet Group
Raffles City, Singapore
tel. 65-438-3363, fax 65-438-3373

- *Services Offered:* company formation, trust formation, law office, accounting services, corporate services

Tonga

In the South Pacific. A monarchy 800 km south of Samoa, 720 km southeast of Fiji. Highly developed infrastructure. New businesses receive long tax holidays. Legal system based on English common law.

Uruguay

Uruguay, sometimes called "the Switzerland of South America," is offering citizenship, residency, and a passport in qualifying cases. Uruguay is a former Province of Brazil and a Spanish colony that gained independence in 1828. There is no personal income tax or capital gains tax in Uruguay, and there are also no currency restrictions. Uruguay boasts a large banking and financial services industry, and offers basic banking and financial secrecy. The climate is warm, the scenery is beautiful, and the government is a stable democracy. Those wishing to apply for citizenship are required to purchase a government bond for approximately US$75,000, which is guaranteed by the Central Bank to pay 6.5% per annum, payable annually, with a 10-year maturity. Each additional family member is required to buy a US$10,000 bond offering the same terms. Applicants are required to provide a notarized birth certificate, marriage license, health clearance stating good health and lack of any communicable diseases, professional references from lawyer, doctor, or minister, bank references, a police statement showing no criminal record, and multiple copies of passport photos are required..

Allgemeines Treuunternehmen-Eurofiducia Management S.A.
Misiones 1372, Piso 6, Oficina 602
Montevideo, Uruguay, 11000
tel. 598-2-962689, fax 598-2-960246

- *Services Offered:* company formation, trust formation, estate planning services

---

ING Bank (Luxembourg) Trust - Uruguay Branch
11000 Montevideo, Misiones 1352/1360
Uruguay
tel. 598-2-960961, fax 598-2-958955

- *Services Offered:* trust formation, private banking

Mossack Fonesca & Co.
Wilson Ferreira Aldunate 1294, Apto. 801
Montevideo, Uruguay
tel. 598-2-903-1680, fax 598-2-903-1699

- *Services Offered:* company formation

Vanuatu

In the South Pacific. A chain of 80 small tropical islands 2,250 km northeast of Sydney, Australia. Population is approximately 150,000 people spread out over a 1,300 km arc of the ocean. Main language is Melanesian, French, and English. Climate is tropical.

Vanuatu (formerly New Hebrides) became independent in 1980. The present constitution was adopted on July 20, 1980 and the government is headed by an elected president. The government is divided into executive, legislative, and judicial bodies. The legal system is based on English Common Law and is supplemented by local statutes influenced by the British prior to independence.

The island chain's capital, Port Vila, is the home of over 1,500 tax-exempt companies and over 90 tax-exempt banks. Connections through Australia. Allows the formation of private insurance companies. No significant taxes on anything. No tax treaties, no exchange control, name-plate banks are welcome.

There is no income tax, capital gains tax, gift tax, or estate tax in Vanuatu. There are no exchange controls in Vanuatu. The official currency is the Vatu. There is no exchange of information agreement between Vanuatu and the U.S. or Canada.

Financial Centre Association of Vanuatu
Port Vila, Vanuatu
tel. 678-22166, fax 678-27272

- *Services Offered:* government services

Pacific International Trust Company Ltd
PO.Box 45
Port Vila, Vanuatu
tel. 678-22957, fax 678-23405

- *Services Offered:* private banking, Booklet: Port Vila, Vanatu - The Pacific's Premier Financial Centre.

Westpac Banking Corporation Limited
PO.Box 32
Port Vila, Vanuatu
tel. 678-22084, fax 678-24773

- *Services Offered:* loans and credit, deposit backed MC/Visa

Western Samoa

In the south Pacific. A group of Polynesian islands northeast of Australia and Fiji. Population approximately 180,000. Main language is Samoan and English.

Western Samoa has a bank secrecy law prohibiting the unauthorized disclosure of information pertaining to a clients affairs to a third party. Bank secrecy can be lifted in cases of illegal drug activities, theft, or fraud.

Western Samoa gained independence in 1962. The government is headed by a head of state, a prime minister, and a cabinet of ministers. Two major parties (both supporting offshore banking) are represented in parliament. The legal system is based on English Common Law and is supplemented by local statutes.

There is no income tax or capital gains tax in Western Samoa for companies. There is no exchange of information agreement between Western Samoa and the U.S. or Canada.

Bank of Western Samoa
Beach Road, PO.Box L-1855
Apia, Western Samoa
tel. 685-22-422, fax 685-22-595

- *Services Offered:* retail banking

Central Bank of Samoa
PO.Private Bag
Apia, Western Samoa
tel. 685-24-071, fax 685-20-880, telex 200SX 24100

- *Services Offered:* retail banking

Epati, Stevenson & Nelson
PO.Box 210
Apia, Western Samoa
tel. 685-21-751, fax 685-24-166, telex 685-247 COCENTR SX

- *Services Offered:* law office

European Pacific Trust Company Limited
PO.Box 2029
Apia, Western Samoa
tel. 685-21-758, fax 685-21-407, telex 685-265 FIRSTPAC SX

- *Services Offered:* private banking

Offshore Finance Centre
Apia, Western Samoa
tel. 685-24-071, fax 685-20-880

- *Services Offered:* corporate services

Pacific Commercial Bank
PO.Box 1860
Apia, Western Samoa
tel. 685-20-000, fax 685-22-848

- *Services Offered:* retail banking

Va'ai & Co.
PO.Private Bag
Apia, Western Samoa
tel. 685-20-545, , telex 685-202 UNITEDCO SX

- *Services Offered:* law office

CHAPTER 7

QUICK REFERENCE GUIDE

QUICK REFERENCE #1
PRIVACY AND STATUTES

	Bank Secrecy?	English Common Law?	Independent Country?	Exchange Controls?
Andorra	yes	no	yes	no
Anguilla	yes	yes	no	no
Antigua	yes	yes	yes	no
Austria	yes	no	yes	no
Bahamas	yes	yes	yes	yes
Bahrein	---	---	yes	---
Barbados	no	yes	yes	no
Belize	yes	yes	yes	no
Bermuda	no	yes	no	yes
BVI	yes	yes	no	no
Campione	---	no	---	no
Cayman Islands	yes	yes	no	no
C.I. - Guernsey	no	no	yes	no
C.I. - Jersey	no	no	yes	no
Cook Islands	yes	yes	no	no
Costa Rica	yes	no	yes	no
Cyprus	---	---	yes	no
Gibraltar	yes	yes	no	no
Greece	no	no	yes	no

	Bank Secrecy?	English Common Law?	Independent Country?	Exchange Controls?
Hong Kong	no	yes	no	no
Isle of Man	no	yes	yes	no
Liberia	---	no	yes	---
Liechtenstein	yes	no	yes	no
Luxembourg	yes	no	yes	no
Macao	---	---	---	---
Malta	yes	yes	yes	no
Monaco	---	no	yes	no
Montserrat	yes	yes	no	no
Nauru	yes	no	yes	no
Netherland Antilles	---	no	yes	no
Niue	yes	yes	yes	no
Panama	yes	no	yes	no
St.Kitts & Nevis	yes	yes	yes	no
Switzerland	yes	no	yes	no
Tonga	---	yes	---	---
Turks & Caicos	yes	yes	no	no
Vanuatu	---	yes	yes	no
Vatican	yes	no	yes	no
Western Samoa	yes	yes	yes	---

QUICK REFERENCE #2
COMPANY DISCLOSURE

	disclosure to gov't of beneficial owners?	public disclosure of registered shareholders?	financial statements to be filed?	bearer shares possible?
Andorra	yes	---	---	---
Anguilla	---	---	---	---
Antigua	no	no	no	yes
Austria	---	---	---	---
Bahamas	no	no	no	yes
Bahrein	---	---	---	---
Barbados	---	---	no	---
Belize	no	no	no	yes
Bermuda	no	no	no	no
BVI	no	no	no	yes
Campione	no	---	---	---
Cayman Islands	no	no	no	yes
C.I. - Guernsey	yes	no	yes	---
C.I. - Jersey	yes	yes	no	no
Cook Islands	no	no	no	yes
Costa Rica	---	---	---	---
Cyprus	---	---	---	---
Gibraltar	yes	yes	no	no
Greece	---	---	---	---

	disclosure to gov't of beneficial owners?	public disclosure of registered shareholders?	financial statements to be filed?	bearer shares possible?
Hong Kong	yes	---	yes	no
Isle of Man	no	yes	no	no
Liberia	no	---	---	yes
Liechtenstein	no	yes	yes	yes
Luxembourg	---	---	---	---
Macao	---	---	---	---
Malta	no	yes	no	---
Monaco	---	yes	yes	no
Montserrat	---	---	---	---
Nauru	no	yes	no	yes
Netherland Antilles	---	---	---	---
Niue	no	no	no	---
Panama	no	yes	no	yes
St.Kitts & Nevis	no	no	no	yes
Switzerland	no	---	yes	yes
Tonga	---	---	---	---
Turks & Caicos	no	no	no	yes
Vanuatu	---	---	---	---
Vatican	---	---	---	---
Western Samoa	---	---	---	---

QUICK REFERENCE #3
MINIMUM REQUIREMENTS

	minimum number of directors	minimum number of shareholders	directors may be corporate?	secretary may be corporate?
Andorra	---	---	---	---
Anguilla	1	1	---	---
Antigua	1	1	yes	yes
Austria	---	---	---	---
Bahamas	1	1 *	yes	yes
Bahrein	---	---	---	---
Barbados	---	---	---	---
Belize	1	1	yes	yes
Bermuda	2	1	yes	no
BVI	1	1	yes	yes
Campione	---	---	yes	yes
Cayman Islands	1	1	yes	yes
C.I. - Guernsey	1	2	---	yes
C.I. - Jersey	1	2	no	yes
Cook Islands	1	1	yes	no
Costa Rica	---	---	---	---
Cyprus	---	---	---	---
Gibraltar	1	1	yes	yes
Greece	---	---	---	---

* 2 shareholders required for incorporation.

	minimum number of directors	minimum number of shareholders	directors may be corporate?	secretary may be corporate?
Hong Kong	2	2	yes	yes
Isle of Man	2	1	no	no
Liberia	---	---	yes	yes
Liechtenstein	---	---	---	yes
Luxembourg	---	---	---	---
Macao	---	---	---	---
Malta	---	---	yes	yes
Monaco	2	2	no	yes
Montserrat	---	---	---	---
Nauru	1	1	yes	yes
Netherland Antilles	---	---	---	---
Niue	1	1	---	---
Panama	3	---	no	no
St.Kitts & Nevis	1	1	yes	yes
Switzerland	1	3	no	yes
Tonga	---	---	---	---
Turks & Caicos	1	1	yes	yes
Vanuatu	---	---	---	---
Western Samoa	---	---	---	---

CHAPTER 8

NORTH AMERICAN CONTACTS:

Financial contacts:

Bank of Nova Scotia
One Liberty Plaza, 26th Floor, 165 Broadway
New York, NY, USA, 10006
tel. 212-225-5000, fax 212-225-5286

- *Services Offered:* private banking, retail banking, loans and credit, safekeeping services

Blue Chip Capital Management Limited
c/o 1701 Woodward Drive, Suite 114
Ottawa, ON, Canada, K2C 0P7
toll free 888-265-6661, fax 613-226-1074

- *Services Offered:* investment advisor, mutual fund manager, private banking, global investing information, deposit backed MC/Visa

Blue Chip Capital Management Limited
c/o 1575 Military Road
Niagara Falls, NY, USA, 14304-4706
toll free 888-265-6661, fax 800-560-0645

- *Services Offered:* investment advisor, mutual fund manager, private banking, global investing information, deposit backed MC/Visa

Chemical Bank Private Banking
270 Park Avenue, 46th Floor
New York, NY, USA, 10017-2070
tel. 212-270-3359, fax 212-687-0967

- *Services Offered:* investment advisor, company formation, trust formation, private banking, retail banking, loans and credit, safekeeping services

---

InterBank Immigration Services, Inc.
13873 Park Center Road, Suite 300
Herndon, VA, USA, 20171
tel. 703-359-1000, fax 703-318-3155, net: www.greencard-interbank.com

- *Services Offered:* investment products, immigration services

---

Swiss Bank Corporation (Canada)
207 Queen's Quay West, Suite 780, PO.Box 103
Toronto, ON, Canada, M5J 1A7
tel. 416-203-2180, fax 416-203-4384

- *Services Offered:* investment advisor, private banking

Union Bank of Switzerland
299 Park Avenue
New York, NY, USA, 10171-0026
tel. 212-715-3000, fax 212-715-3946, telex MCI 620317 UBS UW

- *Services Offered:* investment advisor, private banking, retail banking, loans and credit, safekeeping services

Company formation agents and law offices:

Caribeco USA Ltd.
1200 N. Federal Highway, Suite 200
Boca Raton, FL, USA, 33432
tel. 407-391-4308, fax 305-426-6313

- *Services Offered:* company formation, trust formation, bank formation, deposit backed MC/Visa

---

CHQ Incorporated
1555 E. Flamingo Rd., Suite 240 Q
Las Vegas, NV, USA, 89119
tel. 702-796-5487, fax 702-732-0883

- *Services Offered:* company formation, mail forwarding

Corporate Service Center
1919 Central Avenue
Cheyenne, WY, USA, 82001
tel. 307-634-7920, fax 307-634-8801, toll free 800-991-2677

- *Services Offered:* company formation, corporate services

Corporate Service Center, Inc.
1280 Terminal Way, Suite 3
Reno, NV, USA, 89502
tel. 702-329-7721, fax 702-329-0852, toll free 800-638-2320

- *Services Offered:* company formation, corporate services

Czerlau & Associates Limited
1701 Woodward Drive, Suite 114
Ottawa, ON, Canada, K2C 0P7
tel. 800-226-5703, fax 613-226-1074

- *Services Offered:* company formation, trust formation, corporate services, estate planning services, deposit backed MC/Visa, safekeeping services, telephone calling cards, mail forwarding, books or newsletters, data encryption

Czerlau & Associates Limited
1575 Military Rd.
Niagara Falls, NY, USA, 14304-4706
toll free 800-226-5703

- *Services Offered:* company formation, trust formation, corporate services, deposit backed MC/Visa, safekeeping services, telephone calling cards, mail forwarding, books or newsletters, data encryption

Czerlau & Associates Limited
5516 Spring Garden Rd.
Halifax, NS, Canada, B3J 3G6
tel. 800-226-5703

- *Services Offered:* company formation, trust formation, estate planning services, deposit backed MC/Visa

Delaware Business Incorporators, Inc.
PO.Box 5722
Wilmington, DE, USA, 19808
tel. 302-996-5819, fax 800-423-0423

- *Services Offered:* company formation

Delaware Registered Agents & Incorporators, Inc.
1220 Market Building
Wilmington, DE, USA, 19801
tel. 302-571-1117, fax 302-571-8115, toll free 800-346-1117

- *Services Offered:* company formation, corporate services, mail forwarding

Estate Planning & Preservation Strategies, L.L.C.
6991 E. Camelback Rd, Suite C-230
Scottsdale, AZ, USA, 85251
tel. 602-874-1235, fax 602-874-1238, toll free 800-932-9248

- *Services Offered:* company formation, trust formation, estate planning services

---

Harris & Harris Barristers & Solicitors
190 Attwell Drive, Suite 400
Toronto, ON, Canada, M9W 6H8
tel. 416-798-2722, fax 416-798-2715

- *Services Offered:* company formation, trust formation, law office, corporate services, estate planning services, safekeeping services

---

Laughlin Associates, Inc.
2533 N. Carson Street
Carson City, NV, USA, 89706
tel. 702-883-8484, fax 702-883-4874, toll free 800-648-0966

- *Services Offered:* company formation, corporate services

Laughlin Wyoming, Inc.
1704 Westland Rd.
Cheyenne, WY, USA, 82001
toll free 800-996-2677

- *Services Offered:* company formation, corporate services

Liberty Consulting
160 Frederick Street, Suite 203
Toronto, ON, Canada, M5A 4H9
tel. 416-955-9511

- *Services Offered:* company formation

Mossack Fonseca & Co. (Canada)
3141 Westridge Blvd.
Peterborough, ON, Canada, K9K 1Z5
tel. 705-750-1965, fax 705-741-5457

- *Services Offered:* company formation, trust formation

Mossack Fonseca & Co. (Canada)
250 - 1075 West Georgia Street
Vancouver, BC, Canada, V6E 3C9
tel. 604-688-3934, fax 604-688-2921

- *Services Offered:* company formation, trust formation

Nagel & Goldstein
1100 Liberty Avenue
Pittsburgh, PA, USA, 15222
tel. 412-263-2707, fax 412-263-3424, toll free 800-944-0004

- *Services Offered:* law office

Nevis Services Limited
125 Half Mile Road, Suite 200
Red Bank, NJ, USA, 07701-6748
tel. 212-575-0818, fax 212-575-0812

- *Services Offered:* company formation, corporate services

Potter, Day & Associates
12625 High Bluff Drive, Suite 110
San Diego, CA, USA, 92130-2053
tel. 619-755-6672, fax 619-755-6673

- *Services Offered:* company formation, law office

Sabourin and Sun Inc.
2221 Yonge Street, Suite 503C
Toronto, ON, Canada, M4S 2B4
tel. 416-932-0305, fax 416-932-1879

- *Services Offered:* company formation, trust formation, corporate services

---

Skinner, Sutton & Watson
548 California Avenue
Reno, NV, USA, 89509
tel. 702-324-4100, fax 702-333-8171

- *Services Offered:* company formation, trust formation, law office

---

Steven F. Stucker, Chartered
400 W. King Street, Suite 301
Carson City, NV, USA, 89703
tel. 702-884-1979, fax 702-884-1938

- *Services Offered:* company formation, law office

The Company Corporation
Three Christina Centre, 201 N. Walnut Street
Wilmington, DE, USA, 19801
tel. 302-575-0440, fax 302-575-1346, toll free 800-542-2677

- *Services Offered:* company formation, corporate services

The Offshore Incorporators
36 Castle Frank Road, Suite 101
Toronto, ON, Canada, M4W 2Z7
tel. 416-323-1786, fax 416-323-0825

- *Services Offered:* company formation

Trident Corporate Services Inc.
3210-2 Peachtree Road N.E.
Atlanta, GA, USA, 30305
tel. 404-233-5275, fax 404-233-9629

- *Services Offered:* company formation

USA Corporate Services Inc.
170 Washington Ave.
Albany, NY, USA, 12201
tel. 518-433-1400, fax 518-433-1489, toll free 800-888-4360

- *Services Offered:* company formation

Government representative offices:

Anguilla Department of Tourism
271 Main St.
Northport, NY, USA, 11768
tel. 516-261-1234, fax 516-261-9606, toll free 800-553-4939

- *Services Offered:* travel services & information

Antigua and Barbuda Consulate
121 South East 1st Street, Suite 508/9
Miami, FL, USA, 33131

- *Services Offered:* government services

Antigua and Barbuda Consulate
60 St.Clair Avenue, Suite 205
Toronto, ON, Canada, M4T 1N5

- *Services Offered:* government services

Antigua and Barbuda Department of Trade and Tourism
610 Fifth Avenue, Suite 311
New York, NY, USA, 10020
tel. 212-541-4117, fax 212-757-1607

- *Services Offered:* government services

Antigua and Barbuda Embassy
3216 New Mexico Ave. N.W.
Washington, DC, USA, 20016
tel. 202-362-5122, fax 202-362-5225, telex 7108 221130

- *Services Offered:* government services

Antigua and Barbuda High Commission
112 Kent Street, Suite 205 Place Ville, Tower B
Ottawa, ON, Canada, R1P 5P2

- *Services Offered:* government services

Antigua and Barbuda Permanent Mission
610 - 5th Avenue, Suite 311
New York, NY, USA, 10020

- *Services Offered:* government services

Austrian Embassy
445 Wilbrod St.
Ottawa, ON, Canada, K1N 6M7
tel. 613-563-1444, fax 613-563-0038

- *Services Offered:* government services

Bahamas High Commission
50 O'Connor St., Suite 1313
Ottawa, ON, Canada, K1P 6L2
tel. 613-232-1724, fax 613-232-0097

- *Services Offered:* government services

Bahamas Tourist Offices
121 Bloor Street East, Suite 1101
Toronto, ON, Canada, M4W 3M5
tel. 416-968-2999, fax 416-968-6711

- *Services Offered:* travel services & information

Bahamas Tourist Offices
150 East 52nd Street, 28th Floor, North
New York, NY, USA, 10022
tel. 212-758-2777, fax 212-753-6531

- *Services Offered:* travel services & information

Barbados High Commission
151 Slater St., Suite 210
Ottawa, ON, Canada, K1P 5H3
tel. 613-236-9517, fax 613-230-4362
- *Services Offered:* government services

Barbados Industrial Development Corp.
800 Second Ave.
New York, NY, USA, 10017
tel. 212-867-6420
- *Services Offered:* government services

Barbados Tourism Authority
5160 Younge Street, Suite 1800
North York, ON, Canada, M2N 6L9
tel. 416-512-6569, fax 416-512-6581, toll free 800-268-9122
- *Services Offered:* travel services & information

Belize High Commission
112 Kent St., Suite 2005, Tower B
Ottawa, ON, Canada, K1P 5P2
tel. 613-232-7389, fax 613-232-5804
- *Services Offered:* government services

Bermuda - Department of Tourism
1200 Bay Street, #1004
Toronto, ON, Canada, M5R 2A5
tel. 416-923-9600, fax 416-923-4840, toll free 800-387-1304
- *Services Offered:* travel services & information

British Virgin Island Tourist Board
370 Lexington Avenue
New York, NY, USA, 10017
tel. 212-696-0400
- *Services Offered:* travel services & information

Caribbean Tourist Association
20 East 46th Street
New York, NY, USA, 10170
tel. 212-682-0435
- *Services Offered:* travel services & information

Channel Islands Tourist Board
Taurus House, 512 Duplex Ave.
Toronto, ON, Canada, M4R 2E3
tel. 416-485-8724, fax 416-267-7600

- *Services Offered:* travel services & information

Costa Rica Republic Embassy
408 Queen St., Suite 200
Ottawa, ON, Canada, K1R 5A7
tel. 613-234-5762

- *Services Offered:* government services

Cyprus Republic High Commission
2211 R. St. N. W.
Washington, DC, USA, 20008
tel. 202-462-5772, fax 202-483-6710

- *Services Offered:* government services

Department of Finance
Distribution Centre
Ottawa, ON, Canada, K1A 0G5
tel. 613-995-2855, fax 613-996-0518

- *Services Offered:* government services, booklet Where Your Tax Dollars Go

---

Embassy of The Commonwealth of The Bahamas
2220 Massachusetts Ave. N.W.
Washington, DC, USA, 20008
tel. 202-319-2660, fax 202-319-2668

- *Services Offered:* government services

Hong Kong Tourist Association
590 Fifth Avenue, 5th floor
New York, NY, USA, 10036-4706
tel. 212-869-5008, fax 212-730-2605

- *Services Offered:* travel services & information

Hungarian Tourist Board-Embassy of the Republic of Hungary
150 East 58th Street, 33rd Floor
New York, NY, USA, 10155
tel. 212-355-0240, fax 212-207-4103

- *Services Offered:* travel services & information

Hungary, Embassy of the Republic of
7 Delaware Ave.
Ottawa, ON, Canada, K2P 0Z2
tel. 613-232-1711, fax 613-232-5620

- *Services Offered:* government services

Infernal Revenue Service
Box 25,866
Richmond, VA, USA, 23289, zzz3-telephone, fax 804-228-3939

- *Services Offered:* government services (ha!)

Liberia, Embassy of the Republic
160 Elgin St., Suite 2600
Ottawa, ON, Canada, K1N 8S3
tel. 613-232-1781, fax 613-563-9869

- *Services Offered:* government services

Libya, Embassy of the Socialist Peoples
Jamahiriya to the United Nations, 309 - 315 E. 48th St.
New York, NY, USA, 10017
tel. 212-752-5775

- *Services Offered:* government services

Luxembourg National Tourist Office
17 Beekman Place
New York, NY, USA, 10022
tel. 212-935-8888

- *Services Offered:* travel services & information

Luxembourg, Embassy of
2200 Massachusetts Ave. N. W.
Washington, DC, USA, 20008
tel. 202-265-4171, fax 202-328-8270

- *Services Offered:* government services

Monaco, Consular Representatives
1800 McGill College Ave., 14 floor
Montreal, QC, Canada, H3A 3K9
tel. 514-849-0589

- *Services Offered:* government services

Montserrat Tourist Office
775 Park Ave.
Huntington, NY, USA, 11743
tel. 516-351-4922, fax 516-425-0903, toll free 800-646-2002

- *Services Offered:* travel services & information

Netherlands Foreign Investment Agency
303 East Wacker Drive
Chicago, IL, USA, 60601
tel. 312-616-8400

- *Services Offered:* government services

Netherlands, Royal Netherlands Embassy
275 Slater St., 3rd floor
Ottawa, ON, Canada, K1P 5H9
tel. 613-237-5030, fax 613-237-6471

- *Services Offered:* government services

Panama, Permanent Mission of
2862 McGill Ter N. W.
Washington, DC, USA, 20008
tel. 202-483-1407, fax 202-483-8413

- *Services Offered:* government services

Privacy Commissioner of Canada
112 Kent Street, 3rd Floor
Ottawa, ON, Canada, K1A 1H3
tel. 613-995-2410, toll free 800-267-0441

- *Services Offered:* government services

Saint Kitts and Nevis High Commission
112 Kent St., Suite 1610
Ottawa, ON, Canada, K1P 5P2
tel. 613-236-8952, fax 613-236-3042

- *Services Offered:* government services

Saint Vincent / Grenadines High Comm.
112 Kent St., Suite 1610
Ottawa, ON, Canada, K1P 5P2
tel. 613-236-8952, fax 613-236-3042

- *Services Offered:* government services

Seychelles High Commission
820 2nd Ave., Suite 900F
New York, NY, USA, 10017
tel. 212-687-9766

- *Services Offered:* government services

Singapore Republic High Commission
Two United Nations Plaza, 25th floor
New York, NY, USA, 10017
tel. 212-826-0840, fax 212-826-2964

- *Services Offered:* government services

Switzerland, Embassy of
5 Marlborough Ave.
Ottawa, ON, Canada, K1N 8E6
tel. 613-235-1837, fax 613-563-1394

- *Services Offered:* government services

EUROPEAN CONTACTS:

Financial contacts:

American Express Europe Limited
PO.Box 77, Prestamex House
Brighton, UK, BN2 1YX
tel. 44-1273-548427, fax 44-1273-563650

- *Services Offered:* retail banking, deposit backed MC/Visa

Anglo Irish Bankcorp
Moor House, 119 London Wall
London, UK, EC2Y 5ET
tel. 44-1716-284004, fax 44-1716-284458

- *Services Offered:* investment advisor, private banking

Bank Julius Baer
Bevis Marks House, Bevis Marks
London, UK, EC3A 7NE
tel. 44-1716-234211, fax 44-1712-836146, telex 887 272

- *Services Offered:* investment advisor, private banking, retail banking, safekeeping services

Bank of N.T. Butterfield & Son Ltd.
24 Chiswell Street
London, UK, EC1Y 4TY
tel. 44-1718-148800, fax 44-1718-148821, telex 8812016 BNTBLN

- *Services Offered:* retail banking

Bank of Nova Scotia
West End, 10 Berkeley Square
London, UK, W1X 6DN
tel. 44-1714-914200, fax 44-1716-299362

- *Services Offered:* private banking, retail banking, loans and credit, safekeeping services

Blue Chip Capital Management Limited
Fleet Street
London, UK, EC3R 2BR
toll free 888-265-6661, fax 800-560-0645

- *Services Offered:* investment advisor, mutual fund manager, private banking, global investing information, deposit backed MC/Visa

---

HSBC James Capel
Thames Exchange, 10 Queen Street Place
London, UK, EC4R 1BL
tel. 0171-260-9000, fax 0171-621-0496
- *Services Offered:* investment advisor

ING Bank (Netherlands) Trust
Prinses Irenestraat 61, PO.Box 2838
Amsterdam, Netherlands, 1000 CV
tel. 31-20-5405800, fax 31-20-6447011
- *Services Offered:* trust formation, private banking

Jyske Bank Private Banking (International)
Vesterbrogade 9
Copenhagen, Denmark, DK-1780
tel. 45-33-787878, fax 45-33-787833, fax 45-33-787811
- *Services Offered:* investment advisor, private banking, retail banking

---

Lloyds Bank Private Banking
Bolsa House, 80 Cheapside
London, UK, EC2V 6EE
tel. 44-1712-489822, fax 44-1714-893230
- *Services Offered:* investment advisor, private banking

Robeco UK Limited
46, Berkeley Square
London, UK, W1X 6LA
tel. 44-171-409-35-07, fax 44-171-493-54-19
- *Services Offered:* private banking

Sarasin Investment Management Limited
Sarasin House, 37-39 St. Andrews Hill
London, UK, EC4V 5DD
tel. 0171-236-3366, fax 0171-248-0173
- *Services Offered:* investment advisor, global investing information

---

Seymour Pierce Butterfield Limited
24 Chiswell Street
London, UK, EC1Y 4TY
tel. 44-1718-148700, fax 44-1718-148711, telex 8811530 SPBLTD
- *Services Offered:* private banking

Swiss Bank Corporation
66 Hanover Street
Edinburgh, UK, EH2 1HH
tel. 44-1312-259186, telex 7-2567

- *Services Offered:* retail banking

Swiss Bank Corporation Nederland N.V.
Hoogoorddreef 5, Postbus 2333, 1100 DV Amsterdam Z-O
Amsterdam, Netherlands
tel. 31-20-6-510-510, fax 31-20-6-961-671, telex 1-1386

- *Services Offered:* retail banking

Company formation agents and law offices:

FinEscort Accounting Firm
36 Leningradsky Prospect, PO.Box 29
Moscow, Russia, 125083
tel. 7-095-213-0358, fax 7-095-212-2082

- *Services Offered:* accounting services

HDVB - Hoegen Dijkhof &Van Brakel
Emmastraat 40
Amsterdam, Netherlands, NL-1075 HW
tel. 31-20-679-1801, fax 31-30-6769081

- *Services Offered:* company formation, trust formation, corporate services

---

ING Bank (Netherlands) Trust
Prinses Irenestraat 61, PO.Box 2838
Amsterdam, Netherlands, 1000 CV
tel. 31-20-5405800, fax 31-20-6447011

- *Services Offered:* trust formation, private banking

Jordan & Sons Ltd.
20-22 Bedford Row
London, UK, WC1R 4JS
tel. 44-1714-003333, fax 44-1714-003366

- *Services Offered:* company formation, corporate services

Jyske Bank (London)
10-12 Alie Street
London, UK, E1 8DE
tel. 44-171-264-7700, fax 44-171-264-7717

- *Services Offered:* investment advisor, company formation, trust formation, private banking, retail banking, loans and credit, deposit backed MC/Visa, safekeeping services

---

Proform Company Services Limited
25a Priestgate
Peterborough, UK, PE1 1JL
tel. 44-1733-893455, fax 44-1733-892512

- *Services Offered:* company formation, trust formation, bank formation

---

Riggs Valmet Trust Management B.V.
148 Westblaak
Rotterdam, Netherlands, 3012 KM
tel. 010-413-7372, fax 010-733-3178

- *Services Offered:* company formation

Shutts & Bowen
48 Mount Street
London, UK, W1Y 5RE
tel. 44-1714-934840, fax 44-1714-934299

- *Services Offered:* law office

The Company Store Limited
Harrington Chambers, 26 North John Street
Liverpool, UK, L2 9RU
toll free 0800-26-26-62

- *Services Offered:* company formation

Notes

Notes

Notes

Notes

Notes

Notes

Notes